1998 Re[...]

to accompany

Mishkin
THE ECONOMICS OF MONEY, BANKING, AND FINANCIAL MARKETS
Fifth Edition

Edited by

James W. Eaton
Bridgewater College

Frederic S. Mishkin
Columbia University

1998 Readings to accompany Miskin, *The Economics of Money, Banking, and Financial Markets, Fifth Edition*

Copyright © 1998 Addison Wesley Longman, Inc.

All rights reserved. Printed in the United States of America. No part of these materials may be used or reproduced in any manner whatsoever without written permission from the publisher, except testing materials, transparencies, and transparency masters may be copied for classroom use. For information, address Addison Wesley Educational Publishers Inc., One Jacob Way, Reading, Massachusetts 01867-3999.

ISBN: 0-321-01754-4

3 4 5 6 7 8 9 10-VG-01009998

CONTENTS

PREFACE vii

PART ONE   *INTRODUCTION* 1

     Reading 1   *The Money Market* 3
                        Timothy Q. Cook and Robert K. LaRoche

     Reading 2   *Logging on to Electronic Means of Payment* 9
                        Michelle L. Kezar

     Reading 3   *The Changing Meaning of Money* 19
                        John V. Duca

PART TWO   *FINANCIAL MARKETS* 27

     Reading 4   *Adding Duration to the Toolbox* 29
                        Michelle Clark Neely

     Reading 5   *The Name Is Bond—Indexed Bond* 34
                        Michelle Clark Neely

     Reading 6   *The Yield Curve as a Predictor of U.S. Recessions* 39
                        Arturo Estrella and Frederic S. Mishkin

     Reading 7   *Big MacCurrencies* 48

     Reading 8   *Budget Deficit Cuts and the Dollar* 52
                        Ramon Moreno

PART THREE   *FINANCIAL INSTITUTIONS* 57

     Reading 9   *A Look At America's Corporate Finance Markets* 61
                        Stephen D. Prowse

Reading 10	*For Better and For Worse: Three Lending Relationships* 71 Mitchell Berlin	
Reading 11	*Financial Fragility and the Lender of Last Resort* 83 Desiree Schaan & Timothy Cogley	
Reading 12	*Bad Debt Rising* 88 Donald P. Morgan and Ian Toll	
Reading 13	*Loan Lending Magic* 96 Laura Fortunato	
Reading 14	*Efficiency of U.S. Banking Firms—An Overview* 101 Simon Kwan	
Reading 15	*Small Business Lending and Bank Consolidation: Is There Cause for Concern?* 106 Philip E. Strahan and James Weston	
Reading 16	*Bank Branches in Supermarkets* 117 Lawrence J. Radecki, John Wenninger, and Daniel K. Orlow	
Reading 17	*Cracking the Glass-Steagall Barriers* 126 Simon Kwan	
PART FOUR	*CENTRAL BANKING AND THE CONDUCT OF MONETARY POLICY* 131	
Reading 18	*Central Banking in a Democracy* 135 Alan S. Blinder	
Reading 19	*Why Central Bank Independence Helps to Mitigate Inflationary Bias* 148 Timothy Cogley	
Reading 20	*Fed's Huge Empire, Set Up Years Ago, Is Costly and Inefficient* 154 John R. Wilke	
Reading 21	*Where Is All the U.S. Currency Hiding?* 160 John B. Carlson and Benjamin D. Keen	

Reading 22	*Falling Reserve Balances and the Federal Funds Rate* 167 Paul Bennett and Spence Hilton	
Reading 23	*Never Mind Those Ms* 177	
Reading 24	*Inflation Targeting: A New Framework for Monetary Policy?* 180 Ben S. Bernanke and Frederic S. Mishkin	
Reading 25	*A Predictable and Avoidable Mexican Meltdown* 200 Joseph A. Whitt, Jr.	
Reading 26	*Mexico's Liquidity-Driven Financial Panic* 206 Marco Espinosa and Steven Russell	
Reading 27	*The EMU: A Groundbreaking Monetary Experiment* 211 Fiona Sigalla and David Gould	

PART FIVE   MONETARY THEORY 215

Reading 28	*Nobel Views on Inflation and Unemployment* 217 Carl E. Walsh	
Reading 29	*Monetary Policy and Real Economic Growth* 222 Owen F. Humpage	
Reading 30	*What Causes Inflation?* 229 Laurence Ball	
Reading 31	*Stock Market Fundamentals* 242 Joseph G. Haubrich	
Reading 32	*Activist Monetary Policy for Good or Evil? The New Keynesians vs. the New Classicals* 249 Tom Stark and Herb Taylor	

PREFACE

This *Reader* helps make *The Economics of Money, Banking, and Financial Markets, Fifth Edition* a unique teaching package to meet the needs of both professors and students. A basic problem of textbooks in the Money and Banking or Financial Markets and Institutions fields is that current events and financial innovation make many of the facts in the textbooks obsolete soon after they are published. To minimize this problem, *The Economics of Money, Banking, and Financial Markets* stresses a few basic economic principles that never go out of date, rather than a set of facts that quickly do so, to understand the role of money in the economy and the structure of financial markets and institutions. To make this economic approach to teaching Money and Banking or Financial Markets and Institutions even more effective, it is important to keep the textbook analysis up to date by supplementing it with current articles on money, financial markets and institutions. This is what this *Reader* does.

UNIQUE FEATURES OF THIS READER

Up-to-date

In contrast to other readers in the Money and Banking or Financial Markets and Institutions field, this *Reader* is updated annually, with half or more of the articles new each year. In this latest edition of the *Reader*, nineteen of the thirty-two articles are new; twelve of them were published in 1997 and another seven during the second half of 1996. These include articles on inflation-indexed bonds, Big Mac prices and purchasing power parity, the influence of competition and firm size on lending relationships, automatic lending machines, efficiency of U.S. banking firms, in-store bank branches, the Fed's place in a democratic society, inflation targeting, the Mexican financial crisis, European Monetary Union, the Nobel Lectures of Milton Friedman and Robert Lucas, monetary policy and economic growth, and the determinants of stock prices. No other reader in the field is as current, and this will continue to be the case with the appearance of a new edition of the *Reader* every year.

A New Way to Teach Financial Markets and Institutions

The Economics of Money, Banking, and Financial Markets develops a unifying economic framework to organize students' thinking about financial markets and institutions so that they can make sense of, rather than be confused by, all the facts about our financial system. The strength of this approach, in contrast to the approach used in other textbooks which focus on a set of facts about financial institutions, is that it will not go out of date. Because this approach stresses lasting economic concepts, it allows instructors to discuss the latest developments in financial markets and institutions. As part of this approach to teaching financial markets and institutions, instructors will want to use current articles in class to illustrate the economic forces that are driving changes in financial markets. This *Reader* is designed to make it easier for instructors to do this and keep their teaching current. Nearly half of the readings are devoted to financial markets and institutions. Because the need for current discussion of financial markets and institutions is so important to teaching Money and Banking or Financial Markets and Institutions, future annual editions of the *Reader* will have a similarly high proportion of current articles that focus on financial markets and institutions.

The numerous, current readings on financial markets and institutions that will appear annually in this and future editions of the *Reader* and the stress on economic analysis in the textbook provide a whole new way of teaching financial markets and institutions. This new approach makes it less likely that students will memorize a mass of facts that will be forgotten after the final exam and that soon become obsolete because of the rapid pace of financial innovation. Instead, they will have an understanding of the dynamism of our financial markets and institutions and will see that what they have learned applies to current developments in financial markets, illustrating the relevance of their course work.

Pedagogical Aids

Each of the *Reader*'s five parts begins with an introduction (written by James Eaton) which provides the student with a brief summary of each article. In addition, the introduction suggests the chapter(s) with which the reading might be assigned, thus helping instructors decide how to organize their courses. We suggest that instructors read through all the part introductions as they plan their courses to become aware of the various options for matching readings with the text chapters they assign.

James Eaton has also written several discussion questions which follow each reading in order to encourage students to think about how the reading relates to material in the text. Instructors may find these questions useful for class discussions of the reading or as written assignments in problem sets.

Low Price

Because we believe that this *Reader* is such an important supplement to courses in Money and Banking or Financial Markets and Institutions, it will be sold with the text at a particularly low price. This should give students the benefit of the *Reader* without making its cost prohibitive.

SUGGESTIONS AND ACKNOWLEDGMENTS

It is hoped that students and instructors who use this *Reader* will find it an effective pedagogical tool. We welcome any comments or suggestions concerning the articles in this edition of the *Reader* or articles which would be appropriate for future editions. Please send your comments and suggestions to:

James W. Eaton
Department of Economics and Business
Bridgewater College
Bridgewater, Virginia 22812
jeaton@bridgewater.edu

We owe sincere thanks to several people for their assistance in the preparation of this edition of the *Reader*. Special thanks go to Elizabeth Middleton, whose skillful typing continues to give the *Reader* its uniform, polished appearance; and to Joan Twining, business and economics supplements editor at Addison Wesley Longman. Above all, we would like to thank our wives Mary and Sally, and our children Amanda, Elizabeth and Matthew (for Eaton) and Matthew and Laura (for Mishkin), who put up with us while projects like this claim a large share of our time. We hope they know that they are infinitely more important to us than a book.

James W. Eaton
Frederic S. Mishkin

1998 Readings

to accompany

Mishkin
THE ECONOMICS OF MONEY, BANKING, AND FINANCIAL MARKETS
Fifth Edition

PART ONE

INTRODUCTION

The three readings for Part One introduce some of the institutions and issues critical to the successful operation of the financial system—the money market, money itself and the forms in which it is evolving, and the difficulties of defining a monetary aggregate that will be an accurate guide for monetary policy.

In Reading 1, **"The Money Market,"** Timothy Q. Cook and Robert K. LaRoche provide an overview of money market participants and financial instruments. This reading supplements Chapter 2's introduction to the financial system.

Reading 2, **"Logging on to Electronic Means of Payment"** by Michelle L. Kezar, surveys electronic alternatives to cash and checks and obstacles impeding their rapid adoption by businesses and consumers. This reading can be used early in the course with Chapter 3's discussion of the evolution of the payments system and electronic money or reserved for use when financial innovation is discussed in Chapter 10.

John V. Duca in Reading 3, **"The Changing Meaning of Money,"** explains how changes in technology, demographics, and preferences have weakened monetary aggregates' usefulness as economic indicators. The reading shows the difficulty of formulating an empirical definition of money and can supplement Chapter 3's distinction between theoretical and empirical definitions of money or Chapter 19's discussion of monetary policy targets.

READING 1

The Money Market

Timothy Q. Cook and Robert K. LaRoche

The major purpose of financial markets is to transfer funds from lenders to borrowers. Financial market participants commonly distinguish between the "capital market" and the "money market," with the latter term generally referring to borrowing and lending for periods of a year or less. The United States money market is very efficient in that it enables large sums of money to be transferred quickly and at a low cost from one economic unit (business, government, bank, etc.) to another for relatively short periods of time.

The need for a money market arises because receipts of economic units do not coincide with their expenditures. These units can hold money balances—that is, transactions balances in the form of currency, demand deposits, or NOW accounts—to insure that planned expenditures can be maintained independently of cash receipts. Holding these balances, however, involves a cost in the form of foregone interest. To minimize this cost, economic units usually seek to hold the minimum money balances required for day-to-day transactions. They supplement these balances with holdings of money market instruments that can be converted to cash quickly and at a relatively low cost and that have low price risk due to their short maturities. Economic units can also meet their short-term cash demands by maintaining access to the money market and raising funds there when required.

Money market instruments are generally characterized by a high degree of safety of principal and are most commonly issued in units of $1 million or more. Maturities range from one day to one year; the most common are three months or less. Active secondary markets for most of the instruments allow them to be sold prior to maturity. Unlike organized securities or commodities exchanges, the money market has no specific location. It is centered in New York, but since it is primarily a telephone market it is easily accessible from all parts of the nation as well as from foreign financial centers.

The money market encompasses a group of short-term credit market instruments, futures market instruments, and the Federal Reserve's discount window. The table summarizes the instruments of the money market. The major participants in the money market are commercial banks, governments, corporations, government-sponsored enterprises, money market mutual funds,

Reprinted from *Instruments of the Money Market* edited by Timothy Q. Cook and Robert K. LaRoche, Federal Reserve Bank of Richmond, 1993, 1-5.

PART I Introduction

The Money Market

Instrument	Principal Borrowers
Federal Funds	Banks
Discount Window	Banks
Negotiable Certificates of Deposit (CDs)	Banks
Eurodollar Time Deposits and CDs	Banks
Repurchase Agreements	Securities dealers, banks, nonfinancial corporations, governments (principal participants)
Treasury Bills	U.S. government
Municipal Notes	State and local governments
Commercial Paper	Nonfinancial and financial businesses
Bankers Acceptances	Nonfinancial and financial businesses
Government-Sponsored Enterprise Securities	Farm Credit System, Federal Home Loan Bank System, Federal National Mortgage Association
Shares in Money Market Instruments	Money market funds, local government investment pools, short-term investment funds
Futures Contracts	Dealers, banks (principal users)
Futures Options	Dealers, banks (principal users)
Swaps	Banks (principal dealers)

futures market exchanges, brokers and dealers, and the Federal Reserve.

COMMERCIAL BANKS

Banks play three important roles in the money market. First, they borrow in the money market to fund their loan portfolios and to acquire funds to satisfy noninterest-bearing reserve requirements at Federal Reserve Banks. Banks are the major participants in the market for federal funds, which are very short-term—chiefly overnight—loans of immediately available money; that is, funds that can be transferred between banks within a single business day. The funds market efficiently distributes reserves throughout the banking system. The borrowing and lending of reserves takes place at a competitively determined interest rate known as the federal funds rate.

Banks and other depository institutions can also borrow on a short-term basis at the Federal Reserve discount window and pay a rate of interest set by the Federal Reserve called the discount rate. A bank's decision to borrow at the discount window depends on the relation of the discount rate to the federal funds rate, as well as on the administrative arrangements surrounding the use of the window.

Banks also borrow funds in the money market for longer periods by issuing large negotiable certificates of deposit (CDs) and by acquiring funds in the Eurodollar market. A large denomination CD is a certificate issued by a bank as evidence that a certain amount of money has been deposited for a period of time—usually ranging from one to six months—and will be redeemed with interest at maturity. Eurodollars are dollar-denominated deposit liabilities of banks located outside the United States (or of International Banking Facilities in the United States). They can be either large CDs or nonnegotiable time deposits. U.S. banks raise funds in the Eurodollar market through their overseas branches and subsidiaries.

A final way banks raise funds in the money market is through repurchase agreements (RPs). An RP is a sale of securities with a simultaneous agreement by the seller to repurchase them at a later date. (For the lender—that is, the buyer of the securities in such a transaction—the agreement is often called a reverse RP.) In effect this agreement (when properly executed) is a short-term collateralized loan. Most RPs involve U.S. government securities or securities issued by government-sponsored enterprises. Banks are active participants on the borrowing side of the RP market.

A second important role of banks in the money market is as dealers in the market for over-the-counter interest rate derivatives, which has grown rapidly in recent years. Over-the-counter interest rate derivatives set terms for the exchange of cash payments based on subsequent changes in market interest rates. For example, in an interest rate swap, the parties to the agreement exchange cash payments to one another based on movements in specified market interest rates. Banks frequently act as middleman in swap transactions by serving as a counterparty to both sides of the transaction.

A third role of banks in the money market is to provide, in exchange for fees, commitments that help insure that investors in money market securities will be paid on a timely basis. One type of commitment is a backup line of credit to issuers of money market securities, which is typically dependent on the financial condition of the issuer and can be withdrawn if that condition deteriorates.

PART I Introduction

Another type of commitment is a credit enhancement—generally in the form of a letter of credit—that guarantees that the bank will redeem a security upon maturity if the issuer does not. Backup lines of credit and letters of credit are widely used by commercial paper issuers and by issuers of municipal securities.

GOVERNMENTS

The U.S. Treasury and state and local governments raise large sums in the money market. The Treasury raises funds in the money market by selling short-term obligations of the U.S. government called Treasury bills. Bills have the largest volume outstanding and the most active secondary market of any money market instrument. Because bills are generally considered to be free of default risk, while other money market instruments have some default risk, bills typically have the lowest interest rate at a given maturity. State and local governments raise funds in the money market through the sale of both fixed-and variable-rate securities. A key feature of state and local securities is that their interest income is generally exempt from federal income taxes, which makes them particularly attractive to investors in high income tax brackets.

CORPORATIONS

Nonfinancial and nonbank financial businesses raise funds in the money market primarily by issuing commercial paper, which is a short-term unsecured promissory note. In recent years an increasing number of firms have gained access to this market, and commercial paper has grown at a rapid pace. Business enterprises—generally those involved in international trade—also raise funds in the money market through bankers acceptances. A bankers acceptance is a time draft drawn on and accepted by a bank (after which the draft becomes an unconditional liability of the bank). In a typical bankers acceptance a bank accepts a time draft from an importer and then discounts it (gives the importer slightly less than the face value of the draft). The importer then uses the proceeds to pay the exporter. The bank may hold the acceptance itself or rediscount (sell) it in the secondary market.

GOVERNMENT-SPONSORED ENTERPRISES

Government-sponsored enterprises are a group of privately owned financial intermediaries with certain unique ties to the federal government. These agencies borrow funds in the financial markets and channel these funds primarily to the farming and housing sectors of the economy. They raise a substantial part of their funds in the money market.

MONEY MARKET MUTUAL FUNDS AND OTHER SHORT-TERM INVESTMENT POOLS

Short-term investment pools are a highly specialized group of money market intermediaries that includes money market mutual funds, local government investment pools, and short-term investment funds of bank trust departments. These intermediaries purchase large pools of money market instruments and sell shares in these instruments to investors. In doing so they enable individuals and other small investors to earn the yields available on money market instruments. These pools, which were virtually nonexistent before the mid-1970s, have grown to be one of the largest financial intermediaries in the United States.

FUTURES EXCHANGES

Money market futures contracts and futures options are traded on organized exchanges which set and enforce trading rules. A money market futures contract is a standardized agreement to buy or sell a money market security at a particular price on a specified future date. There are actively traded contracts for 13-week Treasury bills, three-month Eurodollar time deposits, and one-month Eurodollar time deposits. There is also a futures contract based on a 30-day average of the daily federal funds rate.

A money market futures option gives the holder the right, but not the obligation, to buy or sell a money market futures contract at a set price on or before a specified date. Options are currently traded on three-month Treasury bill futures, three-month Eurodollar futures, and one-month Eurodollar futures.

DEALERS AND BROKERS

The smooth functioning of the money market depends critically on brokers and dealers, who play a key role in marketing new issues of money market instruments and in providing secondary markets where outstanding issues can be sole prior to maturity. Dealers use RPs to finance their inventories of securities. Dealers also act as intermediaries between other participants in the RP market by making loans to those wishing to borrow in the market and borrowing from those wishing to lend in the market.

Brokers match buyers and sellers of money market instruments on a commission basis. Brokers play a major role in linking borrowers and lenders in the federal funds market and are also active in a number of other markets as intermediaries in trade between dealers.

FEDERAL RESERVE

The Federal Reserve is a key participant in the money market. The Federal Reserve controls the supply of reserves available to banks and other depository institutions primarily through the purchase and sale of Treasury bills, either outright in the bill

PART I Introduction

market or on a temporary basis in the market for repurchase agreements. By controlling the supply of reserves, the Federal Reserve is able to influence the federal funds rate. Movements in this rate, in turn, can have pervasive effects on other money market rates. The Federal Reserve's purchases and sales of Treasury bills—called "open market operations"—are carried out by the Open Market Trading Desk at the Federal Reserve Bank of New York. The Trading Desk frequently engages in billions of dollars of open market operations in a single day.

The Federal Reserve can also influence reserves and money market rates through its administration of the discount window and the discount rate. Under certain Federal Reserve operating procedures, changes in the discount rate have a strong direct effect on the funds rate and other money market rates. Because of their roles in the implementation of monetary policy, the discount window and the discount rate are of widespread interest in the financial markets.

QUESTIONS

1. What is the money market? Why does it exist? What are the basic characteristics of money market instruments?

2. Who are the principal borrowers in the money market? Through what instruments do they borrow?

3. Describe banks' various roles in the money market.

READING 2

Logging on to Electronic Means of Payment

Michelle L. Kezar

Stretched out on the couch, you flip on the TV. You skip past the nature channel to the banking channel and select your checking account. As you scan the register, you realize that you forgot to buy a birthday present for your mother.

Not to worry. You go upstairs and flick on your personal computer. You log onto the Internet and look for a present at the virtual mall. Within an hour, you find the perfect gift: a recipe book. You run your debit card through the card reader built into your computer. You know that the bank will automatically deduct the cost of the purchase from your checking account, and that the present will be mailed to your mother in time.

As you leave the mall, though, you hear a digitized voice coming from your computer: "Your rental payment is overdue." Quickly, you tell your PC to pay the rent. As you log off, the phone on your other line rings. It is your landlord asking for your late rent payment. "It's in the e-mail," you say smugly.

Some day soon this scenario could be a reality. Debit cards, smart cards, electronic cash, electronic checks—all of these electronic means of payment (EMOP) are now coming into use. Slowly, they are beginning to replace paper checks and paper cash.

Electronic means of payment are a big step beyond credit cards, the first and now widespread alternative to payment by cash or check. A credit card issuer acts as an intermediary between the merchant and the consumer. For the merchant, it takes on, for a fee, the burden of verification and debt collection. For the consumer, it consolidates transactions, puts off the due date, and acts as a buffer in disputes.

EMOP often eliminate the intermediary. When a customer makes a purchase, his bank account is debited. For the merchant, payment is guaranteed and almost immediate. For the consumer, EMOP offer convenience, instant proof that the "money" is good, and automated bookkeeping.

Not surprisingly, EMOP are widely touted as the wave of the future. But the hype was there 20 years ago, too. *Business Week* in 1975 predicted that EMOP soon "will revolutionize the very concept of money itself." Less than two years later, though, the same magazine noted, "Suddenly it appears

---

Reprinted from Federal Reserve Bank of Richmond *Cross Sections*, 12, 4 (Winter 1995/96), 10-18. The views expressed in *Cross Sections* are those of the contributors and not necessarily those of the Federal Reserve Bank of Richmond or the Federal Reserve System.

PART I Introduction

that the great electronic ... revolution that has been 'just around the corner' for a decade may never arrive at all."

What happened was that revolutions take time. People were unlikely to give up writing checks overnight. They were going to require other reasons to invest in the home PCs needed for some EMOP transactions. Merchants also were hesitant to embrace EMOP because they faced start-up costs. Another problem was that the communication networks and supporting tools were not established. Software programmers had hardly begun the work needed to address the prickly issue of privacy or the major threats of theft and fraud. And the standardization of equipment and networks that would be needed to minimize cost and complexity for both consumers and merchants was far from complete.

In the last few years there has been enormous progress in making electronic means of payment a reality. Many consumers, for example, can use their ATM cards as debit cards to pay retailers. And today some 44 percent of American households surveyed now contain at least one PC, according to an *American Banker*/Gallup report. A consumer now can navigate the Internet, likely to be the major communications link for electronic payments, with user-friendly software. Entrepreneurs, banks, and other financial institutions are working vigorously on the details of various EMOP transactions. And a growing number of these transactions are now being tested in marketplace trials.

Still, the obstacles to EMOP remain immense. So the transition to a cashless society is certain to be a bumpy one—unlikely to be concluded within the next decade or two. Changes in the payment system, notes Thomas Hoenig, president of the Federal Reserve Bank of Kansas City, "tend to be evolutionary, not revolutionary."

EMOP TRANSACTIONS

Whatever the timetable for the arrival of a cashless society, experts agree that someday everyone will be EMOP users. Use of debit cards and smart cards will grow most rapidly. The use of electronic cash and checks, which require computer access, will increase more slowly.

Debit Cards. Like a credit card, a debit card has a magnetic strip from which a card reader can extract data. When consumers use a debit card issued by a bank to make purchases, they authorize deductions from their checking accounts at that bank. If the merchant processes the card on-line, which is usually the case, the deduction is immediate. For the consumer's protection, the user must furnish a separate personal identification number (PIN) when the card is used.

The Bank of Delaware launched the first debit card program in 1966. Several other banks ran pilot programs through the mid-1970s, but major efforts to launch debit cards did not develop until the early 1980s. Currently, most banks and many nonbank companies such as Visa and Mastercard issue debit cards or ATM cards that also can function as debit cards. A consumer can use debit cards in many of the places that accept credit cards, such as gas stations, supermarkets, and other retail stores.

READING 2 Logging on to Electronic Means of Payment

Smart Cards. Unlike a debit card, which deducts money from a bank account after a purchase, a smart card requires an outlay from the user's account prior to a purchase. A smart card, as the name implies, can do much more than a simple debit card can do. That's because it has an embedded microprocessor chip, which makes it possible to store, retrieve, and in some cases to manipulate data.

There are two basic types of smart cards. The simpler type, known as "stored value," is one a consumer buys with a preset dollar amount and then spends down. It is, in effect, disposable. The more versatile type, commonly termed "intelligent," is loaded with value from a user's bank account whenever needed. The user can do this at an ATM. Instead of "spitting out money," the ATM adds value to the card representing a specific amount, such as $100, according to Bob Gilson, executive director of the Smart Card Forum, a multi-industry group that is promoting the smart card. Some banks offer cards that can have value added to them using a PC or a specially equipped telephone.

Potentially, the intelligent smart card would be able to store not only cash balances, but also data on shopping patterns, store coupons, citizenship status, and medical history. Card users eventually may be able to pay for a night on the town, including money for the babysitter with nothing more than a smart card. Consumers already are seeing the benefit of the cards—more than 30 million cards are being used worldwide.

Smart card technology was first developed by a French journalist, Roland Moreno, in 1974. France has been driving the technology ever since, running the first trial of smart cards in 1982. Several U.S. banks and other financial organizations recently have announced smart-card trials. The list includes Citibank, Chemical Bank, and Electronic Payment Services.

A major test in connection with the 1996 Olympics in Atlanta is planned by three banks—First Union Bank, Wachovia, and NationsBank—that are teaming up with Visa. As part of the team project, First Union, headquartered in Charlotte, N.C., expects to issue about a million cards in the Atlanta area. About 70 percent of the cards will be disposable, stored-value cards. The remaining 30 percent will be rechargeable cards.

One company that has added a twist to the smart card is the London-based Mondex. It developed a smart card that enables individuals to transfer value electronically—not just between buyers and sellers, but between any individuals. To transfer value from one card to another, a cardholder uses a handheld wireless device that has been dubbed an electronic wallet. The wallet stores five currencies simultaneously and displays the stored value on a screen.

The electronic wallet moniker is not an idle overstatement, according to Benjamin Miller, publisher and editor of *Personal Identification Newsletter*. In the future, he says, such a device will store everything that is currently kept in a conventional wallet—money, identification, allergy warnings, licenses, credit cards, phone numbers, and, yes, other smart cards. Predicts Miller: "Someday everyone will carry an electronic wallet."

PART I Introduction

Mondex started testing the card in Swindon, England, in July 1995. In August, Wells Fargo Bank in San Francisco announced that it will distribute 90 cards to employees—the first U.S. test for Mondex.

Electronic Cash. The Internet offers plenty of opportunities to shop on-line. Already, the estimated 30 million Internet users loom as an enticing new market waiting to be reached by marketers worldwide. According to *Internet World*, the Internet "represents the cheapest new business opportunity in history .... Many businesses will use the Internet as an alternative form of distribution because of its large reach and relatively low cost."

Technology companies have attempted to stimulate the growth of the on-line marketplace by developing electronic cash, also known as e-cash. E-cash is nothing more than a digital representation of money. To get e-cash, a consumer funds an account with a bank connected to the Internet. The bank converts funds from the user's account to e-cash. The bank then transfers the e-cash to the consumer's PC.

A consumer who wants to buy something using e-cash, for example, "travels" to an Internet store. After selecting an item, the consumer selects the "buy" option, which automatically transfers e-cash from the consumer's computer to the merchant's computer. The merchant's computer automatically contacts the Internet bank to verify that the e-cash is valid; if so, the bank approves the transaction and credits the merchant's account. The Internet store then ships the items to the user.

DigiCash, based in Amsterdam, appears to be taking the lead in developing e-cash systems for the Internet. In a year-old trial still underway, it is giving 10,000 volunteers $100 of Cyberbucks, DigiCash's version of e-cash. The recipients cannot exchange Cyberbucks for any existing currency, but they can use them to purchase goods at any of the 75 participating Internet shops, which include such disparate businesses as Encyclopedia Britannica and the Road Runner Shop. The $100 may not seem like much for a shopping expedition these days, but it's a useful amount for Internet shopping. Many shops in DigiCash's trial program are selling wares for less than a dollar.

Merchants worldwide who want to tap more deeply into the market for small cash transactions, ones for less than $10, are helping to fuel the work on EMOP. An estimate by *The Economist* puts this global market at $2 trillion. According to Smart Card Forum, 88 percent of U.S. commercial transactions are made with cash or checks and 83 percent of those transactions are for less than $10.

Glenn Edelman, assistant to the vice president of e-cash business development for DigiCash, believes that a majority of payments on the Internet will be small. One reason for this, notes Edelman, is that there is a need to be able to sell parts of products, such as an article from a magazine instead of the entire issue. Although credit card transactions for small amounts are costly for merchants, with e-cash, Edelman believes, many merchants are more likely to offer low-priced products and services.

READING 2 Logging on to Electronic Means of Payment

KEY TERMS

Debit card. A debit card is a plastic card issued by a bank or other financial institution by which purchases are deducted directly from the cardholder's checking account.

E-cash. E-cash is a digital representation of money that consists of binary code. Consumers will be able to use e-cash to buy goods and services from stores on the Internet. To get e-cash, consumers fund an account with a bank connected to the Internet. The bank converts funds from the user's account to e-cash. The bank then transfers the e-cash to the consumer's PC.

E-check. An e-check is the electronic equivalent of a paper check that can be used when the parties and banks involved are connected to an electronic network, such as the Internet. A consumer writes an e-check using a PC and sends the "check" over the network to the other party. The recipient forwards the e-check to his bank for deposit. The bank then forwards the e-check to the consumer's bank for collection.

Internet. This is a collection of international computer networks that links schools and universities, businesses, government agencies, libraries, nonprofit organizations and individuals. It is an outgrowth of a government research project called Arpanet, created to link government agencies and universities. When it was developed in 1969, electronic commerce was nowhere in the plan. Now businesses run over 60 percent of the networks that comprise the Internet. CommerceNet estimates that more than 20 million people in 140 countries have access.

Smart card. A smart card is a plastic card, issued by a bank or other financial institution, that has cash value. The card has an embedded microprocessor chip that can store, retrieve, and in some cases manipulate data to transfer value and track a person's cash balance. An intelligent type can be reloaded with cash value and can store much more data, such as a person's medical history, shopping patterns, or citizenship status.

The current DigiCash project is intended in part to "gauge popularity and to deal with any glitches" in its e-cash system, says Edelman. The system moved another step toward reality this past October when Mark Twain Bancshares, a regional bank holding company based in St. Louis, agreed to set up e-cash accounts on the Internet. Using technology developed by DigiCash, Mark Twain Bancshares will be the first issuer of e-cash for payments by personal computer. The bank initially is limiting the trial to 10,000 accounts and keeping transactions among its account holders.

PART I Introduction

Electronic Checks. As more people sign onto the Internet, interest in electronic checks also is growing. With such a system, a purchaser uses a PC to write the equivalent of a check and then sends the "check" to the seller who, in turn, forwards it to his bank. The seller's bank verifies that the e-check is valid, then transfers money from the purchaser's bank account to the seller's bank account. E-checks also can be used for transactions with other individuals, provided all users are connected to the same network.

For purchasers, there is a downside to using e-checks instead of paper checks: Purchasers lose much of their float—the time between when a transaction is charged to an account and when money is taken out of an account. That's because the receiving bank need not wait for the couriers required to transport paper checks.

For sellers, though, there is an enormous upside in greatly reduced costs of check processing. Some compelling numbers come from the Financial Services Technology Consortium (FSTC), a group of banks, technology companies, and government research and development projects. FSTC says that the cost of an average paper-check transaction, including paper, printing, postage, and processing, is 84 cents. In comparison, the cost of an e-check is only 29 cents.

One organization already using e-checks is the Commonwealth of Virginia. In May 1994, its Department of Accounts started paying some of the state's bills with e-checks. Richard Davis, the department's assistant fiscal manager, estimates that in general the cost of making electronic payments is 30 percent below the cost of printing and mailing paper checks.

REVOLUTIONS TAKE TIME

Considering the development of EMOP and their supporting technology, it's hard to see why electronic payments have not made more rapid inroads in the financial system. but developers had to overcome major obstacles before EMOP could become commonplace. And while present real-world tests seem to promise rapid advances for EMOP, some major issues remain.

Technical Standardization. One big reason that EMOP progress has been slow to date is that businesses lacked a common set of technical standards for collecting and processing payments data. When businesses use a multitude of systems and there are a large number of people involved, "it may be extremely difficult to achieve the coordination necessary to obtain a common set of standards," noted the Federal Reserve's Hoenig in a speech.

Success in standardization to date differs widely among EMOP transactions. For example, both the information on the magnetic strip of a debit card and the characteristics of the machine that reads it must be standardized to gain wide acceptance by merchants. That task has been largely achieved. One reason is that debit-card standards have advanced with ATM standards. By 1993, as a result of bank mergers, a handful of ATM networks controlled more than half the market, making technical coordination much easier than before.

READING 2 Logging on to Electronic Means of Payment

Compared with debit cards, much standardization is still needed with smart cards. A major player in the standardization effort is the Smart Card Forum whose mission, says Executive Director Gilson, is finding "a way for all the networks to learn to talk to one another."

As for the Internet, until recently it was a network used to connect universities and government agencies. Now that transactions over the Internet are developing, says Cathy Medich, executive director of CommerceNet, "procedures that are consistent are important for [electronic means of payment] to go forward."

CommerceNet, a consortium of companies that includes Bank of America, Intel, Netscape, and Hewlett Packard, was founded in 1993 to "look at the issues of [creating] an electronic [marketplace] on the Internet," Medich says. The companies involved hope that they will be able to develop standards that will make e-cash almost as common as real cash.

Start-up Costs. For merchants, all EMOP transactions involve significant up-front costs for infrastructure. A merchant who accepts debit cards, for example, would have to lay out between $100 and $600 for each on-line card reader. For smart cards, that figure might be as much as $1,000. "The issue of infrastructure," says Edgar Brown, senior vice president at First Union, "is the biggest stumbling block to the growth of any kind of transaction product."

For consumers, debit cards and smart cards have no up-front costs beyond the cash needed to fund them. But for those without a PC at home—an estimated 56 percent today—getting onto the Internet to use e-cash or e-checks will require an outlay of about $1,500 to $2,000, which for some could be significant. And even for those who already own PCs, Internet access adds another monthly bill to pay.

Consumer Resistance. Start-up costs aside, many consumers have balked at the idea of abandoning paper checks for their transactions. One reason is that consumers are largely comfortable with the recordkeeping that canceled paper checks provide. Another is the time and effort required to learn to use the new technologies.

Perhaps just as important is the loss of float with EMOP. The use of a paper check typically gives purchasers several days of float. As noted earlier, an e-check eliminates most of that float. When a person uses a debit card online, he gets zero float. And with a smart card or e-cash, he gets what might be called negative float: The stored value may sit for days or weeks before being used and earns no interest the entire time.

Even so, consumer acceptance of debit-card transactions has been growing at a healthy clip. According to *Bank Network News*, the number of debit-card transactions grew 30 percent between 1990 and 1993, to more than 700 million transactions. And in 1994 the number of on-line installed terminals doubled to 344,000 units.

At the same time, consumers are showing undeniable signs of interest in e-cash and e-checks. A 1995 *American Banker*/Gallup Consumer Survey found that 12 percent of respondents who own PCs have used them for electronic means of payment transactions. People still are "exploring," says

PART I Introduction

CommerceNet's Medich, "but they are much more used to the on-line world now."

Privacy and Security. As consumers become more knowledgeable about smart cards and the Internet, they are likely to become more concerned about potential loss of privacy. A smart card, for example, can store a vast amount of personal data. Privacy advocates worry that employers, insurers, and government officials, not to mention marketers, may obtain that data. Some worry that a smart card may be the precursor to a national ID card—complete with such personal details as prior criminal record or a person's medical history.

For many, the Internet is even more scary. Its inherently open structure gives users access to any transaction that occurs on the Internet. Such accessibility does not merely threaten privacy. It makes all too easy the theft and wrongful use of account numbers, which may lead to financial loss for Internet users. The current inability to provide confidentiality is why credit card information for Internet transactions is sent separately by phone or fax.

Finding a solution to this problem is critical to the future of e-cash and e-checks. "A lot of digital cash approaches are basically begging people to try to break them," says Kawika Daguio, federal representative for regulatory and trust affairs at the American Bankers Association (ABA).

The solution for on-line credit card purchases, e-cash, and e-checks may lie in encryption. Encryption uses complex mathematical formulas to garble messages. Companies such as CyberCash Inc., based in Reston, Va., are working on codes intended to prevent snoopers from reading, and criminals from stealing, confidential information on the Internet.

CyberCash signed an agreement with First National Bank of Omaha under which merchants honoring the bank's credit card will use CyberCash software to process credit card payments on the Internet while maintaining confidentiality. According to *American Banker*, more than 44,000 merchants will have access to the system.

Some e-cash developers maintain that the key to privacy is anonymity—a feature that DigiCash and Mondex are building into their systems. Dan Eldridge, vice president of e-cash business development for DigiCash, believes that the ability to make anonymous transactions with e-cash will prove to be an important plus for e-cash compared to other EMOP transactions.

Other EMOP experts, however, believe that it will be necessary to compromise on privacy to achieve the best protection against fraud. ABA's Daguio notes that the data that a credit card issuer now has on a user's spending habits allows it to identify atypical transactions and alert the user to the possibility of illegal card use. "The real battle," says Daguio, "is between anonymity and accountability."

DigiCash is certain that, given a choice, consumers will opt for anonymity. One reason for this is the perils of loss from Internet transactions are invisible and somewhat abstract. With smart cards, though, the possibilities for physical loss or theft are easier to visualize. Carrying a smart card is just like carrying cash: If the card is lost, the money stored on it, as well as any stored information, is gone.

If that happens, a person's maximum loss may or may not be limited under current law. Under the Electronic Fund Transfer Act (EFTA), a loss resulting from illegal use of an ATM or debit card is limited to $50. Under debate is whether smart cards fall under EFTA. A reload of a rechargeable type of smart card resembles an ATM withdrawal, but a disposable stored-value card has little in common with either an ATM or a debit card.

If, in fact, losses resulting from a misplaced or stolen smart card are covered to any degree, there remains the problem of proving how much value was stored on the card. With anonymous transactions, there is little chance of making a case.

EMOP raise two other security issues as well—not so much for individual users as for the public as a whole. Some EMOP transactions may make it easier to launder money. Transactions with a smart card such as Mondex's leave no audit trail. So criminals who need to move large amounts of money could easily do so with on plastic card instead of suitcases. The same problem applies to unrecorded transfers via e-cash.

The other concern is counterfeiting. By reproducing the binary code of e-cash, for example, a forger could reproduce e-cash. "All you have to do is break into the system once ... and you can do whatever you want," says ABA's Daguio. He believes that the counterfeiting threat has received too little attention. He noted that precautions are taken with paper currency and the same should hold true for e-cash. "We don't put five billion dollars in cash in trucks and send them out on the highway because we look at the risks," he says. Some of the developers of e-cash who are out there, he claims, don't look at the possible risks.

Reproducing binary code might not be any easier than counterfeiting paper money, however, especially with the advent of high-quality photocopying and laser printing. Smart card developers expect to rely in part on encryption techniques and in part on operating procedures. And DigiCash and its competitors hope to protect e-cash by building an electronic signature or "watermark" into it.

All of the privacy and security issues of EMOP represent not just technical and marketing challenges, but also, at least potentially, public policy concerns. Outside of EFTA, these concerns have yet to be reflected in legislation or regulation. If EMOP make inroads into the nation's payments system, which now seems likely to happen over the next decade or so, there will almost certainly be a perceived need for regulation that addresses the potential hazards of the new environment.

For now, many technical and marketing issues still await resolution. But resolution appears a lot closer than it was when EMOP were first hyped 20 years ago.

PART I Introduction

> **QUESTIONS**
>
> 1. Is the electronic means of payment revolution more likely to occur now than when it was first anticipated 20 years ago? Why?
>
> 2. What electronic alternatives exist for cash and checks—the most common means of payment today? How do these EMOP work?
>
> 3. What are the main obstacles to widespread use of EMOP? Can they be easily overcome? Explain.
>
> 4. What costs do consumers incur in using EMOP?

READING 3

The Changing Meaning of Money

John V. Duca

Because inflation can quickly disrupt an economy, central banks have tried to develop policies to keep inflation in check. One approach assumes that there is a stable relationship between economic activity and the measured money supply. Recently, this relationship has been changing because people have been changing how they handle their finances and how they pay for goods and services. As a result, what the measured money supply means, in terms of what it reveals about economic activity, has also changed.

DOES M2 STILL MEASURE UP?

Money and economic activity are linked by the famous equation of exchange:

money x money's velocity = the price level x real GDP,

or

$$M \times V = P \times Y.$$

In other words, changing hands V times during a year, the money stock, M, facilitates the transaction of Y goods, which each cost P dollars. Converting this equation into growth rates yields two important relationships:

$$\text{inflation} = \text{money supply growth} + \text{velocity growth} - \text{real output growth}$$

and

$$\text{nominal GDP growth} = \text{money supply growth} + \text{velocity growth}$$

where *nominal GDP growth* equals growth in the dollar volume of gross domestic production (output growth plus inflation). U.S. output typically grows at about 2.5 percent annually. Thus, the equation of exchange strongly suggests that over the long run, inflation can be kept at zero by limiting money supply growth to equal 2.5 percent minus growth in velocity.

Money holdings typically fall and velocity rises as the spread between a riskless short-term market interest rate and the average yield on monetary assets rises. The stability of the relationship between interest rates and velocity

Reprinted from Federal Reserve Bank of Dallas *The Southwest Economy*, Issue 6, 1995, 6-9.

PART I   Introduction

is what makes it possible for money to be a useful indicator of not only inflation, but also of nominal GDP *(P x Y)*, since GDP data are available after a long lag, unlike data on money and interest rates. If velocity is predictable, then by controlling money supply growth, the Federal Reserve can control long-run inflation. While this sounds easy, shifts in how people conduct their finances and how they pay for goods can undermine the stability of the money—GDP relationship, thus making the Fed's inflation-fighting job more difficult in practice.

History bears this out. The M1 monetary aggregate that measures the money supply as checking deposits plus currency was once touted as the "holy grail" by monetarists. But M1 began to fall from grace in the mid-1970s when its velocity was unusually high, and M1 growth underpredicted real GDP, based on prior velocity behavior. Then in the early 1980s, the interest-rate sensitivity of M1 jumped as financial innovations and deregulation created new deposits that combined savings and transactions features and helped firms avoid holding non-interest-bearing demand deposits. As a result, attention turned to M2, a broader and less interest-rate-sensitive aggregate that was created in 1980.

M2 was redefined to include not only conventional M1, passbook savings accounts and small time deposits, but also new types of money market mutual funds, overnight instruments and, in 1982, money market deposit accounts. M2 had a stable relationship with nominal GDP during the 1980s (Small and Porter 1989). However, this relationship broke down in the 1990s as M2 became more sensitive to bond yields and as households shifted toward bond and stock mutual funds and toward Treasury securities (see Duca 1995b for references).

Such breakdowns in the link between money and nominal output have spurred efforts to either redefine money to include new types of "money" or revise money models to account for changing relationships between money and nominal output.[1] Understanding why the money—income relationship can shift is critical to finding new ways of deriving information from money.

WHY THE MONEY—NOMINAL GDP RELATIONSHIP CAN SHIFT

A stable link between M2 and nominal GDP will hold as long as people handle their finances in the same way.[2] However, a market economy will continuously create new financial products and markets will react to fundamental changes in the tastes of households (*Table 1*).

Since the early 1980s, the attractiveness to households of owning non-M2 assets has increased because of two types of technological change: lower costs of transferring funds from nonmonetary assets to transactions deposits (from bond mutual funds to money market funds, for instance) and greater use of financial services from nonasset products (such as credit cards). Nonmonetary assets are any assets not included in the definition of the monetary aggregates, while nonasset products are instruments or ways of conducting transactions that do not directly

Table 1
How Market Forces Can Cause Unusual Weakness in Money

Fundamental type of factor	Examples
Technological innovations	
Lower transfer costs	Lower mutual fund commission (load) fees
	Easier purchase of Treasury securities
	Electronic banking
	Easier banking and investing by phone
Financial services from nonassets	More widespread credit cards and lines
	Automatic teller machines
	Electronic wires and transfers
Demographics, preferences and learning	
Demographic shifts	Rising population share of middle-aged people preparing for retirement
Preferences and financial sophistication	Rising share of households sophistication with portable pensions due to IRA/Keogh laws and increased job uncertainty
	Greater tolerance of investment risk

and immediately involve holding an asset (for example, using a credit card to pay for something) until final settlement is made. As the cost of shifting between non-M2 assets and checkable deposits falls, the incentive to hold checking deposits to avoid transfer costs declines. Since households balance the transfer cost savings from holding money against the higher yields on alternative assets, lower transfer costs have induced lower money holdings. For example, over the past 10 years, the costs of shifting from a bond mutual fund to a checkable money market fund have fallen as transfer fees have fallen and as transfers have become easier. As a result, when longer term interest rates (on bond funds) are high relative to short-term rates (on money market funds), people are more likely to hold bond funds today than 10 years ago when transfers involved higher fees and greater headaches.

Thanks to improvements in financial products, households and firms can now better coordinate cash inflow with cash outflow. As a result, they can reduce check usage by consolidating many purchases into fewer check payments. They also have less need to hold checking balances for unexpected expenses.

Aside from technological changes, a rise in households' awareness of assets outside of M2 and their tolerance for risk can lead to unusual weakness in M2. For example, if households needed less extra return on stocks to compensate them for the extra investment risk, then at a given gap between the yields on M2 and stocks, they will hold less M2 and more stocks.

TECHNOLOGY AND NEW PRODUCTS

Lower Asset Transfer Costs

The costs of shifting between non-M2 and checkable M2 assets have fallen in several ways. First, load (commission) fees on mutual funds have fallen sharply over the past two decades.[3] Furthermore, many mutual funds now also allow a greater number of free transfers among funds in asset management accounts. These accounts offer a host of investments, including bonds and equities, and allow no-cost shifts among investments within mutual fund families that typically include a checkable money market fund. So, a person who unexpectedly gets hit with a big car repair bill can use the phone to shift funds from an equity fund to a money market fund (without incurring a fee) and then write a money market fund check. Furthermore, many banks now offer mutual funds and allow customers to jointly manage their mutual fund and deposit balances. Additionally, the Federal Reserve has made it easier for people to buy Treasury securities, a change that, coupled with interest rates, encouraged people to take money out of M2 deposits and buy Treasury securities.[4]

More generally, the spread of better information technology is lowering transfer costs. In particular, the rise of electronic banking (especially via personal computer) poses potentially large reductions in the pecuniary and convenience costs of making such transfers.[5] Unfortunately, continuous data on asset transfer costs over long periods are lacking. Nevertheless, the limited evidence implies that lower transfer costs have led people to reduce M2 balances. In particular, lower transfer costs of using bond and equity funds likely explains why most of the unusual weakness in M2 during the 1990s has been in small time deposits (which compete with stocks and bonds) and money market mutual funds (which were unusually weak when relative yields on stocks and bonds yields were high).

Financial Services from Nonassets

In the 1970s and 1980s, technological advances and high interest rates induced firms to avoid using non-interest-bearing demand deposits to conduct transactions. Cash management techniques, coupled with the increased use of electronic transfers, allowed firms to more easily and cheaply tap nonmonetary assets to meet cash shortfalls. Breaking with the tradition of holding a lot of non-interest-bearing demand deposits, firms adopted cash management techniques that enabled them to better predict their cash needs. Also, firms increasingly used wire transfers when they needed to shift funds. The result was a decline in demand deposits held by firms.

Financial innovations later spread to households after improvements in computer software made such innovations cost-effective for people. By providing liquidity and by enabling households to weather temporary changes in asset prices (such as stock prices), credit cards and credit lines likely induced many households to hold less money and more nonmoney assets.

For example, using 1983 data, Duca and Whitesell (1995) find that each 10-percentage-point rise in the probability of owning a credit card lowers checking accounts by 9 percent and checkable money market mutual funds and money market deposit accounts by 11 percent. The impact of credit cards on checkable balances is likely larger today because credit cards are more widely accepted, credit card purchases are more quickly processed, and consumers are now offered greater incentives to use credit cards. Another important innovation is the spread of automatic teller machines (ATMs). ATMs have reduced the need for people to carry extra cash by allowing them to easily withdraw cash from their checking or savings accounts.[6]

Evidence shows that because people gained a greater choice in how to pay for goods, the composition of M2 had shifted away from transactions and toward nontransactions accounts. Coupled with lower transfer costs, greater use of nonmoney ways of making payments could now be lowering M2, in addition to altering its composition.

ARE DEMOGRAPHICS, PREFERENCES AND LEARNING PLAYING A ROLE?

Greater tolerance of investment risk can stem from changes in employment patterns, demographics and in other factors that boost financial awareness.

Demographics

According to the life-cycle theory of consumption, people borrow when they are young because their income is below that of later years, save in middle age when their income is highest and then draw down their savings in retirement. An implication of this theory is that savings rates and the share of wealth invested in higher earning non-M2 assets should rise in the peak earning years before retirement. By increasing the average need to fund retirement, demographic trends may be inducing an overall shift toward risky assets with higher expected long-term yields and away from lowering earning M2 deposits. Alternatively, as people reach their peak earning years, their ratio of income to spending falls. As this ratio falls, so too will the public's demand for low-transactions cost M2 deposits.

Consistent with these implications, Duca and Whitesell (1995) find that small time and savings deposits are higher for older age groups, after controlling for income and wealth. Furthermore, Morgan (1994) finds that the average share of household assets held in stocks and bonds rises with the population share of 35- to 54-year-old people.

PART I   Introduction

Changing Preferences and Learning

Two factors that could be depressing M2 holdings are households' increased awareness of investments outside of M2 and an associated rise in households' willingness to tolerate risk in the assets they control. Aside from new technology and financial products, increased job uncertainty and the liberalization of IRA/401K accounts have induced a shift toward portable (defined contribution) retirement plans that have given households a greater role in managing their retirement assets. This shift, in turn, has induced households to incur large, one-time costs to learn more about bond and equity investments for retirement. In addition, with many mutual funds, people can count their IRA/Keogh mutual fund balances along with other mutual fund holdings toward meeting the minimum balances requirements for opening asset management accounts. As a result, IRA and Keogh assets effectively reduce the minimum balance requirement on non-IRA/Keogh mutual fund assets. Consistent with this, both IRA/Keogh and non-IRA/Keogh bond and equity fund assets rose in the mid-1980s after tax laws were eased and in the early 1990s.[7] Cross-section data confirm a big shift in household portfolios toward bond and equity funds and away from bank CDs since the late 1980s.[8]

CONCLUSION

The recent breakdown in the link between nominal GDP and conventionally defined M2 reflects how technological changes have enabled households to hold less money and more nonmonetary assets. Such innovations have reduced the costs of transferring funds from other assets to checking accounts, or, as in the case of credit cards and lines, have reduced the need to hold money that arises from mismatches of cash inflow and outflow. Changes in tastes and the age composition of the U.S. population may also be heightening the extent to which people can substitute other financial assets for money.

The information revolution will likely further reduce the benefits from holding traditional forms of money by fostering the spread of new electronic types of money, banking through personal computer, credit lines and financial management software. Together with these advances, a likely continuing shift toward portable (defined contribution) retirement plans and tax incentives will likely increase peoples' role in managing their retirement assets. These factors will likely lead people to further reduce their holdings of conventionally defined "money" and increase their investments in higher earning alternative assets. As a result, what growth in conventionally measured money means for inflation will continue to change.

ENDNOTES

I thank the late Stephen Goldfeld and my many colleagues throughout the Federal Reserve System for sharing their insights on money with me over the years.

1. For example, see Collins and Edwards (1994), Duca (1995a and 1994) and Koenig (1995).
2. For a more technical discussion, see Duca's (1995b) modified version of Milbourne's (1986) model of money.
3. For evidence, see Orphanides, Reid and Small (1994).
4. See Feinman and Porter (1992).
5. For more details, see Holland and Cortese (1995) and Lewis (1995).
6. Daniels and Murphy (1994a) find that a 100-percentage-point rise in the probability of ATM use increased the velocity of currency (transactions/currency) by 40 to 45 percent for transactions account holders, while Daniels and Murphy (1994b) estimate that a 5-percent rise in the proportion of ATM users would boost average transactions account balances by 4.5 percent. Together, these studies imply that ATMs induced households to shift from holding cash to holding transactions balances in the mid-1980s.
7. See Duca (1995a) for evidence.
8. See Kennickell and Starr-McCluer (1994) for cross-section evidence. These factors are consistent with a study by Blanchard (1993), who found that the extra return that investors demand from equities over bonds has trended downward since the 1940s and abruptly fell in the early 1980s.

REFERENCES

Blanchard, Olivier J. (1993), "Movements in the Equity Premium," *Brookings Papers on Economic Activity*, no. 2: 75-138.

Collins, Sean, and Cheryl L. Edwards (1994), "Redefining M2 to Include Bond and Equity Mutual Funds," Federal Reserve Bank of St. Louis *Review*, November/December, 7-30.

Daniels, Kenneth N. and Neil B. Murphy (1994a), "The Impact of Technological Change on the Currency Behavior of Households: An Empirical Cross-Section Study," *Journal of Money, Credit, and Banking* 26 (November): 867-74.

_____, and _____ (1994b), "The Impact of Technological Change on Transactions Account Balances: An Empirical Cross-Section Study," *Journal of Financial Services Research* 17 (January): 113-19.

Duca, John V. (1995a), "Should Bond Funds Be Included in M2?" *Journal of Banking and Finance* 19 (April): 131-52.

_____ (1995b), "Sources of Money Instability," Federal Reserve Bank of Dallas *Economic Review*, Fourth Quarter.

_____ (1994), "Would the Addition of Bond or Equity Funds Make M2 a Better Indicator of Nominal GDP?" Federal Reserve Bank of Dallas *Economic Review*, Fourth Quarter, 1-14.

_____, and William C. Whitesell (1995), "Credit Cards and Money Demand: A Cross-Sectional Study," *Journal of Money, Credit, and Banking* 27 (May): 604-23.

Feinman, Joshua, and Richard D. Porter (1992), "The Continued Weakness in M2," FEDS Working Paper no. 209, Board of Governors of the Federal Reserve System (Washington, September).

Holland, Kelley, and Amy Cortese (1995), "The Future of Money," *Business Week*, June 12, 66-78.

Kennickell, Arthur B., and Martha Starr-McCluer (1994), "Changes in Family Finances from 1989 to 1992: Evidence from the Survey of Consumer Finances," *Federal Reserve Bulletin*, October, 861-82.

Koenig, Evan F. (1995), "Long-Term Interest Rates and the Recent Weakness in M2," manuscript, Federal Reserve Bank of Dallas, June.

Lewis, Peter H. (1995), "Chemical Aims to Expand Electronic Banking," *New York Times*, July 7, D5.

PART I Introduction

Milbourne, Ross (1986), "Financial Innovation and the Demand for Liquid Assets," *Journal of Money, Credit, and Banking* 18 (November): 506-11.

Morgan, Donald P. (1994), "Will the Shift to Stocks and Bonds by Households Be Destabilizing?" Federal Reserve Bank of Kansas City *Economic Review*, Second Quarter, 31-44.

Orphanides, Athanasios, Brian Reid, and David H. Small (1994), "Empirical Properties of a Monetary Aggregate that Adds Bond and Stock Funds to M2," Federal Reserve Bank of St. Louis *Review*, November/December, 31-52.

Small, David H., and Richard D. Porter (1989), "Understanding the Behavior of M2 and V2," *Federal Reserve Bulletin*, April 244-54.

QUESTIONS

1. What is the equation of exchange? What insights does it provide into the causes of inflation?

2. How has the use of ATMs and credit cards affected money's velocity? Why?

3. What is the life-cycle theory of consumption? According to this theory, what should happen to velocity as the population ages? Why?

4. What is an *empirical* definition of money? Do the factors Duca discusses make M2 a better or a poorer empirical definition of money? Explain.

PART TWO

FINANCIAL MARKETS

Interest rates and foreign exchange rates are among the most important variables in the economy and explaining how they are determined in the bond market and the foreign exchange market is an essential part of courses on money, banking, and financial markets. The readings for Part Two provide examples for discussing interest rate determination, indexed bonds, the term structure of interest rates, the theory of purchasing power parity and long-run exchange rate determination, and the possible effects that cuts in the government budget deficit might have on exchange rates.

Reading 4, **"Investment Improvement: Adding Duration to the Toolbox"** by Michelle Clark Neely, discusses several types of risks bond investors face and the use of duration for assessing risk and measuring a bond's price sensitivity to interest rate changes. This reading augments Chapter 4's coverage of the inverse relation between bond prices and interest rates and the distinction between yield and rate of return on a bond.

In Reading 5, **"The Name is Bond—Indexed Bond,"** Michelle Clark Neely describes what an indexed bond is and the benefits indexed bonds can provide investors, issuers, and policymakers. This reading can be used with the discussion of the relation between inflation and interest rates in Chapter 6, monetary policy indicators in Chapter 19, and policy credibility in Chapters 26 and 28.

"The Yield Curve as a Predictor of U.S. Recessions" by Arturo Estrella and Frederic S. Mishkin, Reading 6, advocates using the spread between interest rates on ten-year Treasury notes and three-month Treasury bills for forecasting economic activity and recessions. This reading gives students a practical application of the yield curve presented in Chapter 7.

Reading 7, **"Big MacCurrencies,"** compares Big Mac prices from several countries to estimate the purchasing power parity value of the dollar. For use with Chapter 8, this reading gives students a palatable introduction to the theory of purchasing power parity and long-run exchange rate determination.

In Reading 8, **"Budget Deficit Cuts and the Dollar,"** Ramon Moreno attempts to reconcile opposing views regarding how cutting the government budget deficit will affect the U.S. dollar. He considers the short- and long-run impacts on the balance of payments, capital flows, expected inflation, productivity, and the composition of demand. This reading supplements Chapter 8's treatment of exchange rate determination.

READING 4

Adding Duration to the Toolbox

Michelle Clark Neely

An increasing number of Americans are taking control of personal investment decisions—whether to meet retirement, children's college education or other financial goals. To do this, they're seeking useful, understandable tools that will guide them in making profitable choices. One tool that investors in fixed-income securities—individual bonds or bond mutual funds—have for assessing risk versus reward is an economic formula known as *duration*. Although it is far from a perfect measure of risk, duration is a useful supplement to more common, traditionally used measures, like a bond's credit rating and maturity.

BOND RISK BASICS

Bond investors face several types of risk. One is credit or default risk; that is, the risk that the bond issuer will not repay the principal invested. Since very few debt issuers default on their obligations, however, it is less of a worry for most investors than another major risk, interest rate risk. This is the risk that the market value of an investment—the price an investor would receive if an asset were sold today—will change because of changing market interest rates.

The degree of interest rate risk associated with a given fixed-income security (or bond) depends on the size and timing of the cash flows—interest and principal—from that bond. To see this, consider a zero coupon bond, a bond that pays no interest until maturity.[1] Because no interest is received until maturity, an investor in a zero coupon bond loses out on any opportunity to reinvest potential earnings at higher market interest rates. In addition, if the investor were forced to sell prior to maturity, he could face a substantial loss if current interest rates on a comparable bond were higher than the interest rate on his zero coupon bond.

However, if the same investor were to purchase a coupon-paying bond—like a U.S. Treasury bond—instead, his interest rate risk in a rising interest rate environment would be reduced since interest or coupon payments received at six-month or year intervals could be reinvested at higher interest rates. This would offset some of the loss that might occur if the investor needed to sell the bond prior to maturity.

Reprinted from Federal Reserve Bank of St. Louis *The Regional Economist*, April 1996, 10-11.

Interest rate risk, then, comprises two distinct types of risks, which frequently counteract each other: price or *market risk* and *reinvestment risk*. Market risk is the risk that an already-issued bond's market price will fluctuate because of changes in market interest rates. It arises because of the inverse relationship between market interest rates and a bond's price. The longer the maturity of the bond, the greater the market risk since the purchaser of an existing bond with a below-market yield will be stuck with it for as long as he holds the bond. Of course, market risk is not an issue for investors who hold bonds to maturity because the face value, not the market value, of the bond is received at maturity.

Reinvestment risk encompasses the risk that cash flows received from an existing investment, like semiannual coupon payments, could be reinvested at different interest rates than those paid on the existing security. When the market interest rates rise, reinvestment risk works in the investor's favor because the cash flows received can be reinvested in higher-yielding securities. When rates fall, however, reinvestment risk works against the investor.

An investor faces market risk whenever his planned holding period for a fixed-income security is less than its maturity. These risks tend to work in opposite directions, however: Rising market interest rates increase market risk but decrease reinvestment risk, while declining interest rates decrease market risk but increase reinvestment risk. In other words, an initial capital loss (from rising market interest rates) may, in time, be more than offset by greater returns from reinvested earnings and vice versa.

DURATION: THE NET EFFECT

So how does an investor know how much interest rate risk—the net effect of market and reinvestment risk—he's assuming when purchasing a bond or shares in a bond mutual fund? That's where duration comes in. Basically, duration measures the average life of a fixed-income security or a portfolio of securities. It is a more precise measure of the life of a bond than maturity because it takes into consideration any cash flows that are received prior to maturity. In general, the sooner cash flows are received and the larger the amount, the lower the duration, or interest rate risk, of the bond.

More specifically, duration is calculated as the weighted average time to maturity of a bond, using the relative present values of the cash flows from the bond as weights. The calculation yields a single number called *Macaulay's duration* that is expressed in units of time, which correspond to the receipt of cash flows.[2] Macaulay's duration depends on the number of cash flow payment periods and the interval between them, the size of the cash flows and the current yield to maturity of the instrument.[3]

To see how duration can be used to judge the riskiness of a fixed-income security, consider two bonds, A and B, which on the surface, at least, appear to be very similar. Bond A is a coupon bond with a face value of $1,000 and a maturity of 20 years; its coupon rate is 8 percent, and it pays interest annually.

Bond B is a zero coupon U.S. Treasury bond that pays principal and interest of $2,600 at maturity. The current yield to maturity on 20-year bonds is 10 percent. Both bonds yield combined principal and interest of $2,600 over 20 years. Which bond, then, has the most interest rate risk?

Although the total cash flows from bonds A and B are equal at maturity, their risk profiles for the intervening years are very different. Bond A has a duration of 9.75 years while Bond B, the zero coupon bond, has a duration of 20 years, equal to its maturity. Bond A has the lower duration and is, therefore the least risky of the two because the investor will start receiving cash flows much sooner than the holder of Bond B. If an investor were in a position where he would need to sell a bond—all else equal—his capital loss would be lowest with Bond A. The duration of Bond B is twice as large as the duration of Bond A because all of the interest is deferred until maturity.

DURATION DYNAMICS

The example above illustrates how differences in the timing of cash flows change the duration of a bond. Listed below are several other properties of duration that an investor can use either to differentiate the risk characteristics of similar bonds or to anticipate how changes in bond characteristics alter its duration.

- *The duration of a bond is always less than its maturity, except for a zero coupon bond, whose duration is always equal to its maturity.*

- *Duration declines as the coupon rate rises, holding maturity and yield to maturity constant.*

- *Duration declines as the yield to maturity rises, holding the coupon rate and maturity constant.*

- *Duration increases as maturity increases, holding the coupon rate and yield to maturity constant.*[4]

Another useful feature of duration is that, by rearranging the duration equation, it can be used to predict the sensitivity of a bond's price to very small increases in interest rates. This rearranged calculation is called *modified duration.*[5] The percentage change in the price of a bond can be approximated by multiplying the percentage point change in the yield to maturity by negative one and the bond's modified duration. The modified duration for Bond A, the 20-year coupon bond with a duration of 9.75 years, is 8.86 years. If market interest rates rise one percentage point to 11 percent, the price of this bond will decline about 8.9 percent to $911.40. For Bond B, the zero coupon bond, a one percentage point increase in market interest rates would lead to a whopping 18.2 percent *decline* in price. Of course, if interest rates decline one percentage point, Bondholder A would enjoy about a 9 percent capital gain, and Bondholder B would reap an 18 percent gain.

This simple relationship between duration, interest rates and bond prices can help an investor determine an optimal investment strategy based on his expectations about future interest rates.[6] For example, if an investor expects interest rates to rise in the near future, he would likely want to keep the duration of his bonds or bond mutual fund short to minimize any potential losses, should a sale become necessary.[7] Conversely, in a falling interest rate environment, an investor may want to lengthen the duration of his fixed-income securities, for two reasons; first, he may be able to sell them for a nice gain and second, a longer duration positions an investor to take advantage of a rebound in interest rates, which could lead to profitable reinvestment opportunities. An investor may also wish to use duration to partially hedge or immunize interest rate risk: Market risk and reinvestment risk almost completely offset each other when the duration of a security is equal to the investor's planned holding period.

Duration has been used to measure and hedge interest rate risk to varying degrees by financial institutions and other institutional investors for decades. With an increasing number of brokers and bond mutual fund managers calculating and keeping an eye on duration, individual investors would be wise to add it to their investment toolbox, too.

ENDNOTES

1. Zero coupon bonds, like T-bills and certain other instruments, are frequently sold at a discount from their face value and do not pay periodic interest or a coupon. The return, or compounded interest, on these investments is the difference between the discounted purchase price and the face value of the instrument.

2. The mathematical formula for Macaulay's duration (D) is:

$$D = \frac{\sum_{t=1}^{N} \frac{t \cdot C_t}{(1+r)^t}}{\sum_{t=1}^{N} \frac{C_t}{(1+r)^t}}$$

where N = number of cash flows, t = time to receipt of the cash flow, C_t = cash flow amount in period t, and r = yield to maturity. The expression $C_t/(1+r)^t$ is the present discounted value of the cash flow received in each period t. The sum of all these cash flows is equal to the market value or price of the bond.

3. The yield to maturity is the expected rate of return, or interest rate, on a given debt security held until maturity. Because the yield to maturity can be difficult to calculate, the current market interest rate on comparable securities is usually used in the duration calculation.

4. This last property only holds true for par and premium bonds. For deep-discount bonds, duration increases with maturity to a distant point and then declines. That's because bonds with really long maturities behave like *perpetuities*, bonds that pay coupons forever. See Bierwag (1987) or Kritzman (1992) for details.

5. The modified duration calculation is: $D_m = D/(1+r)$ where D_m is modified duration, D is Macaulay's duration and r is the yield to maturity or current market interest rate.

6. Duration has its limitations, mostly because it is based on some unrealistic assumptions. For example, duration and modified duration calculations implicitly assume that short-term and long-term interest rates are equal, i.e., the yield curve is flat. See Bierwag (1987).

7. The duration of a bond mutual fund is the weighted average of the durations of the individual bonds in the fund.

FOR FURTHER READING

Bierwag, Gerald O. *Duration Analysis: Managing Interest Rate Risk* (Ballinger Publishing Co., 1987).

Kritzman, Mark. "What Practitioners Need to Know About Duration and Convexity," *Financial Analysts Journal* (November/December 1992), pp. 17-20.

Saunders, Anthony. *Financial Institutions Management: A Modern Perspective* (Irwin, 1994), Chapter 6.

Williams, Gordon. "Deciphering Duration," *Financial World* (October 12, 1993), pp. 80-82.

QUESTIONS

1. Define and compare default risk, interest rate risk, market risk, and reinvestment risk.

2. How do market risk and reinvestment risk affdect an investor when interest rates fall?

3. During a period of falling interest rates, would you prefer to be holding a 15-year coupon bond or a 15-year zero-coupon bond? Explain why using the duration concept.

READING 5

The Name Is Bond—Indexed Bond

Michelle Clark Neely

Taking a cue from Canada, the United Kingdom and other countries, the U.S. Treasury decided last year to begin offering inflation-indexed bonds to investors looking to protect their savings from unexpected increases in inflation. With the first auction scheduled for early 1997, economists, finance professionals and policymakers are cheering the change. But will indexed bonds shake the market, or merely cause a stir?

WHAT'S AN INDEXED BOND?

Unlike a conventional, or nominal bond, an inflation-indexed, or real, bond promises to pay its holder a fixed real rate of return—a return that is unaffected by *unexpected* changes in the inflation rate. While a conventional bond repays an investor principal plus some stated interest, an indexed bond repays principal adjusted for inflation and a fixed interest rate applied to the adjusted principal. Investors value such protection because large increases in unanticipated inflation can eat away at an investment's real return.

Expected inflation, real returns and nominal returns are linked by a simple relationship called the *Fisher equation*, which states that the real return on a bond is roughly equivalent to the nominal interest rate minus the expected inflation rate.[1] For example, if an investor purchases a Treasury security with a 6 percent nominal interest rate, and inflation is expected to be zero during the investment period, the real expected return would be 6 percent. In the real world, however, inflation is usually positive, so in most cases the real rate of return will be less than the nominal return.

Because investors understand this relationship between inflation and real returns and want, therefore, to be compensated for any decline in purchasing power, nominal interest rates tend to rise when investors expect the inflation rate to worsen, and vice versa. But what happens if actual inflation is higher than expected inflation? An investor purchasing a conventional bond at 7 percent expects a real return of 5 percent if inflation is expected to be 2 percent during the investment period. If actual inflation turns out to be 4 percent, however, the bond's real return drops to 3 percent. If the actual

Reprinted from Federal Reserve Bank of St. Louis *The Regional Economist*, January 1997, 10-11.

inflation rate is high enough, the real return can even turn negative, causing the investor to pay the borrower for the privilege of using his money, rather than the other way around.

An *inflation risk premium* is built into nominal bond yields to compensate investors for the risk that inflation will be higher than expected. Of course, inflation risk can work the other way: If actual inflation is less than expected inflation, the investor gains while the issuer loses. Because investors are thought to be risk averse—they dislike surprise losses more than they like surprise gains of equal magnitude—the inflation risk premium in nominal interest rates is positive.

Indexed bonds eliminate inflation uncertainty. A holder of an indexed bond is assured that the real cash flow of the bond (principal plus interest) will not be affected by inflation. On the surface, at least, indexing appears to be a win-win proposition. Investors gain because their capital is protected, while issuers gain because they do not have to pay the inflation risk premium. Moreover, this joint gain increases with the term of the bond, for two reasons. First, there is a higher risk that expected inflation will differ from actual inflation the further out into the future you go, and second, any inflation forecast error is magnified with longer-term bonds because of interest compounding.

THE TREASURY EXPERIMENT

Although the Treasury's initial auction of inflation-indexed bonds is to be for 10-year notes starting at $1,000 denominations, by early 1998, the Department plans to offer indexed securities of other maturities, as well as indexed savings bonds.[2] The 10-year indexed notes will be auctioned quarterly in a uniform price auction similar to that used for other marketable Treasury securities.

The Treasury's indexed bond is structured like the Canadian real return bond. The Department will calculate semi-annual interest payments by adjusting the principal for inflation and applying the auction-determined, fixed real interest rate to the adjusted principal. The inflation adjustment will be based on the Consumer Price index for all Urban Consumers (CPI-U), a widely used, though flawed, measure of U.S. inflation.[3] To ensure that investors will not come up short from any deflation occurring during the investment period, the Treasury has promised that the final principal payment will be at least equal to the original par amount of the security at issuance.[4]

INDEXED BOND BENEFITS

Investors, issuers and policymakers—especially monetary policymakers—all stand to gain from indexed bonds. For investors, the major benefit is the guarantee of a real yield.[5] In the past, government bond investors have been burned when inflation exceeded nominal interest rates, resulting in negative real returns. Although the inflation rate has been relatively low for the past several years—hovering around 3 percent—there is always a chance that poor economic policy or an external shock could drive it higher. Consequently, the Treasury

PART II Financial Markets

Around the World with Indexed Bonds

Country of Issuance	Year of Adoption	Inflation Rate Before Introduction	Indexed Bonds as a % of Total Marketable Debt
Israel	1955	12.3%	86.0%
United Kingdom	1981	14.0	15.3
Australia	1985	4.5	3.8
Canada	1991	4.8	1.2
Sweden	1994	4.4	3.2
New Zealand	1995	2.8	<1.0

Source: Adopted from Campbell and Shiller (1996)

Department is promoting the securities to conservative investors who can ill-afford capital losses, like those saving for impending retirement or college costs and those living on fixed incomes.

The potential benefits for the Treasury are many. Indexed bonds could substantially reduce inflation risk and—depending on their share of total government debt—stabilize the Treasury's real funding costs. While unexpectedly high inflation benefits the Treasury by lowering the real return it has to pay investors, unexpectedly low inflation increases the government's funding costs. For example, the Treasury is currently paying a 15.75 percent coupon on a 20-year bond it issued in 1981 when CPI-U inflation was 10.4 percent; the real cost to the Treasury for that bond at issuance was 5.35 percent. Today, however, with inflation averaging about 3 percent, the real cost of the bond is close to 13 percent. Many analysts believe the Treasury will pay real rates of 3 percent to 4 percent on long-term indexed bonds.

The more certain benefit for the Treasury is the money it will save by eliminating the inflation risk premium on some portion of its debt. Although the size of the premium is debatable, most economists estimate it to be at least 50 basis points for short-term bonds and even more for longer-term bonds.[6] Because the Treasury borrows about $200 billion a year, the potential savings could be substantial, even if just a small portion of new debt were indexed.

One of the subtler, yet equally important, benefits brought about by indexing government debt is the information the process would provide policymakers about inflation expectations and real interest rates. For their part, monetary policymakers could ascertain a market-based estimate of inflation expectations by observing the difference in interest rates on conventional and indexed bonds of the same maturities. They could then use these estimates to assess how well the central bank is doing its job.

DEMAND DOWNSIDE

Despite these wide-reaching benefits, the success of indexed bonds is by no means certain. Demand for them will be dampened by several factors, not the least of which is the tax treatment they are subject to. The tax consequences are twofold. First, because the current U.S. tax code does not distinguish between increases in real income and increases in nominal income due to inflation, the indexed bond holder's tax liabilities will increase, lowering the after-tax real yields on these securities. Second, the Treasury has determined that investors will pay taxes on the inflation-adjusted increase in principal accrued each year (as well as the interest received), even though it is not paid out to maturity. A surge in inflation, therefore, could result in a tax liability that would swamp the current cash income from the bond. Because of this unfavorable tax treatment, many analysts think the demand for these securities will be limited to tax-deferred financial assets, like IRAs and 401(k) plans.

Another factor working against the success of indexed bonds is that, even after adjusting for inflation and risk, they still will be outperformed by stocks and many corporate bonds, especially over the long term. That's why they're likely to make up only a small portion of most investors' portfolios. But even if inflation-indexed bonds fail to dazzle the securities world, they're still likely to quench the thirst of conservative investors—without leaving them on the rocks.

ENDNOTES

1. This relationship assumes there is no default or interest rate risk premiums.
2. Treasury securities with original maturities ranging from one to 10 years are notes; securities with original maturities of greater than 10 years are bonds. The term "bond" will be used hereafter to refer to either or both.
3. See Berry and Pianin (1996) for information about biases in the CPI.
4. See the Federal Register (1996) for more detail on the structure of these bonds.
5. Indexed bond holders are not, however, immune from market risk (the risk that the price of an already-issued security will decline in response to increases in market interest rates) if they sell before maturity. That said, most analysts believe that inflation protection will reduce market risk.
6. See Campbell and Shiller (1996) for a discussion of estimates of the size of the inflation risk premium.

REFERENCES

Berry, John M., and Eric Pianin. "Hill Panel Says Inflation Overstated," *Washington Post* (December 5, 1996).
Campbell, John Y., and Robert J. Shiller. "A Scorecard for Indexed Government Debt," *National Bureau of Economic Research Working Paper No. 5587* (April 1996).
Federal Register, U.S. Department of the Treasury. 31 CFR Part 356. "Sale and Issue of Marketable Book-Entry Treasury Bills, Notes, and Bonds (Department of the Treasury Circular, Public Dept Series No. 1-93); Proposed Rule (September 27, 1996).

PART II Financial Markets

Hetzel, Robert L. "Indexed Bonds as an Aid to Monetary Policy," *Economic Review*, Federal Reserve Bank of Richmond (January/February 1992), pp. 13-23.

Shen, Pu. "Benefits and Limitations of Inflation Indexed Treasury Bonds," *Economic Review*, Federal Reserve Bank of Kansas City (Third Quarter 1995), pp. 41-56.

QUESTIONS

1. How does an inflation-indexed bond differ from a nominal bond? How will the Treasury's new bond be indexed?

2. Using the *Fisher equation*, explain the benefits inflation-indexed bonds provide investors.

3. What is an *inflation risk premium*?

4. What benefits will inflation-indexed bonds have for the Treasury and for policymakers?

READING 6

The Yield Curve as a Predictor of U.S. Recessions

Arturo Estrella and Frederic S. Mishkin

Economists often use complex mathematical models to forecast the path of the U.S. economy and the likelihood of recession. But simpler indicators such as interest rates, stock price indexes, and monetary aggregates also contain information about future economic activity. In this edition of *Current Issues*, we examine the usefulness of one such indicator—the yield curve or, more specifically, the spread between the interest rates on the ten-year Treasury note and the three-month Treasury bill. To get a sense of the relative power of this variable, we compare it with other financial and macroeconomic variables used to predict economic events.

Our analysis differs in two important respects from earlier studies of the predictive power of financial variables[1] First, we focus simply on the ability of these variables to forecast recessions rather than on their success in producing quantitative measures of future economic activity. We believe this is a useful approach because evidence of an oncoming recession is of clear interest to policymakers and market participants. Second, we choose to examine out-of-sample, rather than in-sample, performance—that is, we look at accuracy in predictions for quarters beyond the period over which the model is estimated. This feature of our study is particularly important because out-of-sample performance provides a much truer test of an indicator's real-world forecasting ability.

WHY CONSIDER THE YIELD CURVE?

The steepness of the yield should be an excellent indicator of a possible future recession for several reasons. Current monetary policy has a significant influence on the yield curve spread and hence on real activity over the next several quarters. A rise in the short rate tends to flatten the yield curve as well as to slow real growth in the near term. This relationship, however, is only one part of the explanation for the yield curve's usefulness as a forecasting tool.[2] Expectations of future inflation and real interest rates contained in the yield curve spread also seem to play an important role in the prediction of economic activity. The yield curve spread variable examined here corresponds to a forward interest rate

---

Reprinted from Federal Reserve Bank of New York *Current Issues in Economics and Finance*, June 1996.

applicable from three months to ten years into the future. As explained in Mishkin (1990a, 1990b), this rate can be decomposed into expected real interest rate and expected inflation components, each of which may be helpful in forecasting. The expected real rate may be associated with expectations of future monetary policy and hence of future real growth. Moreover, because inflation tends to be positively related to activity, the expected inflation component may also be informative about future growth.

Although the yield curve has clear advantages as a predictor of future economic events, several other variables have been widely used to forecast the path of the economy. Among financial variables, stock prices have received much attention. Finance theory suggests that stock prices are determined by expectations about future dividend streams, which in turn are related to the future state of the economy. Among macroeconomic variables, the Commerce Department's (now the conference Board's) index of leading economic indicators appears to have an established performance record in predicting real economic activity. Nevertheless, its record has not always been subjected to careful comparison tests. In addition, because this index has often been revised after the fact to improve its performance, its success could be overstated. An alternative index of leading indicators, developed in Stock and Watson (1989), appears to perform better than the Commerce Department's index of leading economic indicators. In the discussion below, we compare the predictive power of all three of these variables with that of the yield curve.[3]

ESTIMATING THE PROBABILITY OF RECESSION

To assess how well each indicator variable predicts recessions, we use the so-called probit model, which, in our application, directly relates the probability of being in a recession to a specific explanatory variable such as the yield curve spread.[4] For example, one of the most successful models in our study estimates the probability of recession four quarters in the future as a function of the current value of the yield curve spread between the ten-year Treasury note and the three-month Treasury bill. The results of the model, based on data from the first quarter of 1960 to the first quarter of 1995, are presented in a table showing the values of the yield curve spread that correspond to estimated probabilities of a recession four quarters in the future. As the table indicates, the estimated probability of a recession four quarters ahead estimated from this model is 10 percent when the spread averages 0.76 percentage points over the quarter, 50 percent when the spread averages -0.82 percentage points, and 90 percent when the spread averages -2.40 percentage points.

The usefulness of the model can be illustrated through the following examples. Consider that in the third quarter of 1994, the spread averaged 2.74 percentage points. The corresponding predicted probability of recession in the third quarter of 1995 was only 0.2 percent, and indeed, a recession did not materialize. In contrast, the yield curve spread averaged -2.18 percentage points in the first quarter of 1981, implying a probability of recession of 86.5 percent four quarters later.

Estimated Recession Probabilities for Probit Model Using the Yield Curve Spread

Four Quarters Ahead

Recession Probability (Percent)	Value of Spread (Percentage Points)
5	1.21
10	0.76
15	0.46
20	0.22
25	0.02
30	-0.17
40	-0.50
50	-0.82
60	-1.13
70	-1.46
80	-1.85
90	-2.40

Note: The yield curve spread is defined as the spread between the interest rate on the ten-year Treasury note and the three-month Treasury bill.

As predicted, the first quarter of 1982 was in fact designated a recession quarter by the National Bureau of Economic Research.

TRACKING THE PERFORMANCE OF THE VARIABLES

Using the results of our model, we can compare the forecasting performance of the yield curve spread with that of the New York Stock Exchange (NYSE) stock price index, the Commerce Department's index of leading economic indicators, and the Stock-Watson index. For each of these four variables, the chart plots the forecasted probabilities of a recession in the United States for one, two, four, and six quarters in the future together with the actual periods of recession (the shaded areas).[5]

To understand how to read the chart, consider the forecast for the fourth quarter of 1990, which is the first quarter after the peak of the business cycle and is thus at the start of the last shaded recession region in each panel. In Panel 1, which shows the forecast one quarter ahead, the probability of recession from the probit model using the yield curve spread variable (Spread) forecasted in the third quarter of 1990 for the fourth quarter of 1990 is 13 percent. Similarly, in Panel 7, which shows forecasts six quarters ahead, the forecasted probability of recession for the fourth quarter of 1990—22 percent—is generated from a model using the yield curve spread as of the second quarter of 1989.

In assessing these panels, note that even a probability of recession that is considerably less than one can be a strong signal of recession. Because in any given quarter the probability of recession is quite low, a forecasted probability of, say, 50 percent is going to be quite unusual. Indeed, the successful forecasting model described in the table yields probabilities of recession that are typically below 10 percent in nonrecession (unshaded) periods (as shown in Panel 5). Thus, even a probability of recession of 25 percent—the figure forecast for the fourth quarter of 1990 from data on the yield curve spread one year earlier—was a relatively strong signal in the fourth quarter of 1989 that a recession might come one year in the future.

PART II Financial Markets

Forecasted Probability of Recession: A Comparison of Four Indicators

Panel 1: One Quarter Ahead — NYSE, Spread

Panel 2: One Quarter Ahead — Stock-Watson, Leading indicators

Panel 3: Two Quarters Ahead — NYSE, Spread

Panel 4: Two Quarters Ahead — Stock-Watson, Leading indicators

READING 6 The Yield Curve as a Predictor of U.S. Recessions

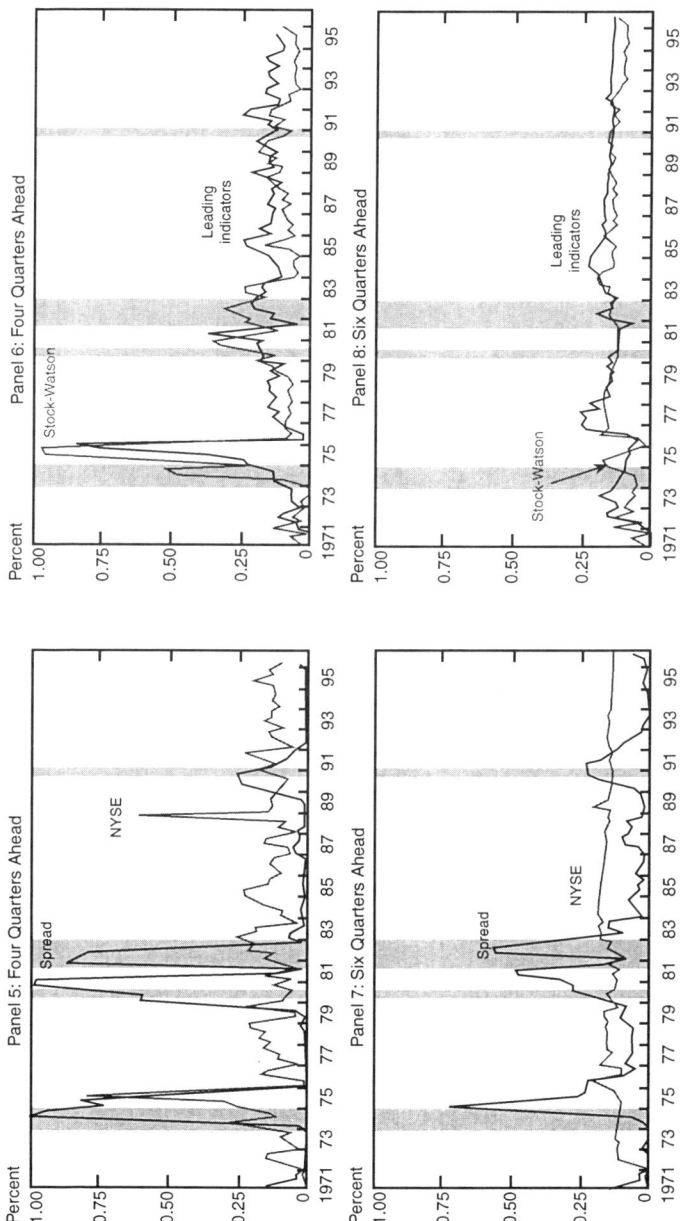

Source: Authors' calculations.

Notes: The probabilities in this chart are derived from out-of-sample forecasts one, two, four, and six quarters ahead. For example, the forecasted probabilities in Panels 1 and 2 are for one quarter ahead—that is, the probability shown is a forecast for the quarter indicated, using data from one quarter earlier—while for Panels 7 and 8, the forecasted probabilities are for six quarters ahead. *Spread* denotes the forecasts from the model using the yield curve spread (the difference between the interest rates on ten-year Treasury notes and three-month Treasury bills, both on a bond-equivalent basis) as the explanatory variable. *NYSE* denotes the results from the model using the quarterly percentage change in the New York Stock Exchange stock price index as the explanatory variable. *Leading indicators* denotes the forecasts from the model using the quarterly percentage change in the Commerce Department's (now the Conference Board's) index of leading indicators as the explanatory variable. *Stock-Watson* denotes the forecasts using the quarterly percentage change in the Stock-Watson (1989) leading economic indicator index as the explanatory variable. Shaded areas designate "recessions" starting with the first quarter after a business cycle peak and continuing through the trough quarter. The peak and trough dates are the standard ones issued by the National Bureau of Economic Research.

PART II   Financial Markets

The chart invites two basic conclusions about the performance of the four variables.[6]

- Although all the variables examined have some forecasting ability one quarter ahead, the leading economic indicator indexes, particularly the Stock-Watson index, produce the best forecasts over this horizon.

- In predicting recessions two or more quarters in the future, the yield curve dominates the other variables, and this dominance increases as the forecast horizon grows.

Let's look in more detail at the probability forecasts in Panels 1-8. Panels 1 and 2 show that the indexes of leading economic indicators typically outperform the yield curve spread and the NYSE stock price index for forecasts one quarter ahead. For the 1973-75, 1980, and 1981-82 recessions, both indexes of leading economic indicators, and particularly the Stock-Watson index, are quite accurate, outperforming the yield curve spread and the NYSE stock price index with a high predicted probability during the recession periods. However, despite excellent performance in these earlier recessions, the Commerce Department indicator provides several incorrect signals in the 1982-90 boom period, and the Stock-Watson index completely misses the most recent recession in 1990-91.[7] Although the financial variables—the yield curve spread and the NYSE stock price index—are not quite as accurate as the leading economic indicators in predicting the 1973-75, 1980, and 1981-82 recessions one quarter ahead, they do provide a somewhat clearer signal of an imminent recession in 1990.

As the forecasting horizon lengthens to two quarters ahead and beyond, the performance of the NYSE stock price index and the leading economic indicator indexes deteriorates substantially (Panels 3-8). Indeed, at a six-quarter horizon, the probabilities estimated using the three indexes are essentially flat, indicating that these variables have no ability to forecast recessions. In contrast, the performance of the yield curve spread improves considerably as the forecast horizon lengthens to two and four quarters. The estimated probabilities of recession for 1973-75, 1980, and 1981-82 based on the yield curve spread are substantially higher than at the one-quarter horizon, and the signal for the 1981-82 recession no longer comes too early (compare Panel 5 with Panel 1).

Furthermore, in contrast to other variables, the yield curve spread gives a relatively strong signal in forecasting the 1990-91 recession four quarters ahead. Although the forecasted probability is lower than in previous recessions, it does reach 25 percent (Panel 5).

There are two reasons why the signal for this recession may have been weaker than for the earlier recessions. First, restrictive monetary policy probably induced the 1973-75, 1980, and 1981-82 recessions, but it played a much smaller role in the 1990-91 recession. Because the tightening of monetary policy also affects the yield curve, we would expect the signal to be more pronounced at such times. Second, the amount of variation in the yield curve spread has changed over time and was much less in the 1990s than in the early 1980s, making a strong signal for the 1990-91 recession difficult to obtain.[8]

When we look at how well the yield curve spread forecasts recessions six quarters in the future (Panel 7), we see that the performance deteriorates from the four-quarter-ahead predictions. Nonetheless, unlike the other variables considered, the yield curve spread continues to have some ability to forecast recessions six quarters ahead.

CONCLUSION

This article has examined the performance of the yield curve spread and several other financial and macroeconomic variables in predicting U.S. recessions. The results obtained from a model using the yield curve spread are encouraging and suggest that the yield curve spread can have a useful role in macroeconomic prediction, particularly with longer lead times. Policymakers value longer term forecasts because policy actions typically take effect on the economy with long time lags. Thus, the fact that the yield curve strongly outperforms other variables at longer horizons makes its use as a forecasting tool even more compelling.

With the existence of large-scale macroeconomic models and the judgmental assessments of knowledgeable market observers, why should we care about the predictive ability of the yield curve? There is no question that judgmental and macroeconometric forecasts are quite helpful. Nevertheless, the yield curve can usefully supplement large econometric models and other forecasts for three reasons. First, forecasting with the yield curve has the distinct advantage of being quick and simple. With a glance at the ten-year note and three-month bill rates on the computer screen, anyone can compute a probability forecast of recession almost instantaneously by using a table such as ours.

Second, a simple financial indicator such as the yield curve can be used to double-check both econometric and judgmental predictions by flagging a problem that might otherwise have gone unidentified. For example, if forecasts from an econometric model and the yield curve agree, confidence in the model's results can be enhanced. In contrast, if the yield curve indicator gives a different signal, it may be worthwhile to review the assumptions and relationships that led to the prediction. Third, using the yield curve to forecast within the framework outlined here produces a probability of future recession, a probability that is of interest in its own right.

ENDNOTES

1. A list of references on this literature can be found in Estrella and Mishkin (1996).
2. The analyses in Estrella and Hardouvelis (1990, 1991) and Estrella and Mishkin (1995) suggest why the yield curve contains information beyond that related to monetary policy.

3. In Estrella and Mishkin (1996), we have examined in detail the predictive ability of these and other variables, including interest rates by themselves, other stock market indexes, interest rate spreads, monetary aggregates (both nominal and real), the component series of the index of leading economic indicators, and an additional experimental index of leading indicators developed in Stock and Watson (1992). Of all the variables, the four singled out in this article have the best ability to predict recessions.

4. For a technical discussion of this model and how it is estimated, see Estrella and Mishkin (1996). The economy is designated as "in recession" starting with the first quarter after a business cycle peak and continuing through the trough quarter. The peak and trough dates are the standard ones issued by the National Bureau of Economic Research (NBER) and used in most business cycle analysis. These dates are not without controversy, however, because the NBER methodology makes implicit assumptions in arriving at these dates.

5. Note that the forecasts in these panels are true out-of-sample results, obtained in the following way: First, a given model is estimated using past data up to a particular date, say the first quarter of 1970. Then these estimates are used to form the forecasts, say four quarters ahead. In this case, the projection would apply to the first quarter of 1971. After adding one more quarter to the estimation period, the procedure is repeated. That is, data up to the second quarter of 1970 are used to make a forecast for the second quarter of 1971. In this way, the procedure mimics what a forecaster would have predicted with the information available at any point in the past.

6. Note that all conclusions drawn from looking at the charts are confirmed by more precise statistical measures of out-of-sample fit in Estrella and Mishkin (1996).

7. these results have already been noted in very useful postmortem analyses by Watson (1991) and Stock and Watson (1992).

8. Another potential explanation is that the 1990-91 recession was relatively mild and so a weaker signal might be expected. However, as shown in Estrella and Hardouvelis (1991), the yield curve spread also provides much weaker signals for recessions in the 1950s, even though they were not mild. Furthermore, the signal for the 1969-70 recession is strong, although the recession itself was mild. Thus, the severity of the recessions does not seem to be associated with the strength of the signal from the yield curve.

REFERENCES

Estrella, Arturo, and Gikas Hardouvelis. 1990. "Possible Roles of the Yield Curve in Monetary analysis." In *Intermediate Targets and Indicators for Monetary Policy*, Federal Reserve Bank of New York.

———. 1991. "The term Structure as a Predictor of Real Economic Activity." *Journal of Finance* 46, no. 2 (June).

Estrella, Arturo, and Frederic S. Mishkin. 1995. "The Term Structure of Interest Rates and Its Role in Monetary Policy for the European Central Bank." National Bureau of Economic Research Working Paper no. 5279, September.

———. 1996. "Predicting U.S. Recessions: Financial Variables as Leading Indicators." Federal Reserve Bank of New York Research Paper no. 9609, May.

Mishkin, Frederic S. 1990a. "What Does the Term Structure Tell Us About Future Inflation?" *Journal of Monetary Economics* 25 (January): 77-95.

———. 1990b. "The Information in the Longer-Maturity Term Structure About Future Inflation." *Quarterly Journal of Economics* 55 (August): 815-28.

Stock, James and Mark Watson, 1989. "New Indexes of Coincident and Leading Indicators." In Olivier Blanchard and Stanley Fischer, eds., *NBER Macroeconomic Annual* 4.

———. 1992. "A Procedure for Predicting Recessions with Leading Indicators: Econometric Issues and Recent Performance." Federal Reserve Bank of Chicago Working Paper WP-92-7, April.

Watson, Mark. 1991. "Using Econometric Models to Predict Recessions." Federal Reserve Bank of Chicago *Economic Perspectives* 15, no. 6 (November-December).

READING 6 The Yield Curve as a Predictor of U.S. Recessions

QUESTIONS

1. How do Estrella and Mishkin define the yield curve spread? Do you expect this spread to be positive or negative most of the time? Why?

2. What relationship do Estrella and Mishkin find between the yield curve spread and the probability of recession? Is this relationship plausible? Explain.

3. How do Estrella and Mishkin attempt to ascertain the value of the yield curve spread relative to other possible predictors of recession? What do they conclude about its predictive ability?

READING 7

Big MacCurrencies

Is the world's exchange-rate system on the brink of collapse? Just like the old gold standard and the fixed rates of the Bretton Woods system, another international currency benchmark could be doomed: the hamburger standard. For more than a decade, *The Economist's* Big Mac index has provided a delectable guide to whether currencies are at their "correct" level. But news in February that McDonald's was about to slash the American price of its Big Mac by 65% sent shivers through financial markets. Would this blatant competitive devaluation reduce the hamburger standard to ashes?

It certainly threatened to leave us in a pickle. The Big Mac index is based upon the theory of purchasing-power parity (PPP)—the notion that a dollar should buy the same amount in all countries. In the long run, argue PPP fans, currencies should move towards the rate which equalises the prices of an identical basket of goods in each country. Our "basket" is a McDonald's Big Mac, which is now produced in over 100 countries. The Big Mac PPP is the exchange rate that would leave hamburgers costing the same in America as abroad. Comparing actual exchange rates with PPP provides one indication of whether a currency is under- or over-valued.

Massive discounting in America by McDonald's would distort our PPP calculations. But financial markets have been given a reprieve: the discounts do not yet affect the Big Mac. So our annual burgernomics-fest can be served.

The first column in the table shows local-currency prices of a Big Mac; the second converts them into dollars. The average American price (including tax) is $2.42. China is the place for bargain hunters: a Beijing Big Mac costs only $1.16. At the other extreme, Big Mac fans pay a beefy $4.02 in Switzerland. In other words, the yuan is the most undervalued currency (by 52%), the Swiss franc the most overvalued (by 66%).

The third column calculates Big Mac PPPs. For example, dividing the German price by the American one gives a dollar PPP of DM2.02. The actual rate on April 7th was DM1.71, implying that the D-mark is 18% overvalued against the dollar. But over the past two years the dollar has risen nearer to its PPP against most currencies.

The yen is now close to its PPP of ¥121. Two years ago the Big Mac index suggested that it was 100% overvalued against the dollar.

The Economist, April 12, 1997, 71. © 1997 The Economist Newspaper Group, Inc. Reprinted with permission. Further reproduction prohibited.

READING 7 Big MacCurrencies

The hamburger standard

	Big Mac Prices		Implied PPP* of the dollar	Actual $ exchange rate 7/4/97	Local currency under(-)/over(+) valuation,† %
	In local Currency	In dollars			
United States‡	**$2.42**	2.42	-	-	-
Argentina	Peso2.50	2.50	1.03	1.00	+3
Australia	A$2.50	1.94	1.03	1.29	-20
Austria	Sch34.00	2.82	14.0	12.0	+17
Belgium	BFr109	3.09	45.0	35.3	+28
Brazil	Real2.97	2.81	1.23	1.06	+16
Britain	£1.81	2.95	1.34††	1.63††	+22
Canada	C$2.88	2.07	1.19	1.39	-14
Chile	Peso1,200	2.88	496	417	+19
China	Yuan9.70	1.16	4.01	8.33	-52
Czech Republic	CKr53.0	1.81	21.9	29.2	-25
Denmark	DKr25.75	3.95	10.6	6.52	+63
France	FFr17.5	3.04	7.23	5.76	+26
Germany	DM4.90	2.86	2.02	1.71	+18
Hong Kong	HK$9.90	1.28	4.09	7.75	-47
Hungary	Forint271	1.52	112	178	-37
Israel	Shekel11.5	3.40	4.75	3.38	+40
Italy	Lire4,600	2.73	1,901	1,683	+13
Japan	¥294	2.34	121	126	-3
Malaysia	M$3.87	1.55	1.60	2.50	-36
Mexico	Peso14.9	1.89	6.16	7.90	-22
Netherlands	Fl5.45	2.83	2.25	1.92	+17
New Zealand	NZ$3.25	2.24	1.34	1.45	-7
Poland	Zloty4.30	1.39	1.78	3.10	-43
Russia	Rouble11,000	1.92	4,545	5,739	-21
Singapore	S$3.00	2.08	1.24	1.44	-14
South Africa	Rand7.80	1.76	3.22	4.43	-27
South Korea	Won2,300	2.57	950	894	+6
Spain	Pta375	2.60	155	144	+7
Sweden	SKr26.0	3.37	10.7	7.72	+39
Switzerland	SFr5.90	4.02	2.44	1.47	+66

PART II Financial Markets

The hamburger standard

	Big Mac Prices		Implied PPP* of the dollar	Actual $ exchange rate 7/4/97	Local currency under(-)/over(+) valuation,† %
	In local Currency	In dollars			
Taiwan	NT$68.0	2.47	28.1	27.6	+2
Thailand	Baht46.7	1.79	19.3	26.1	-26

*Purchasing-power-parity; local price divided by price in the United States †Against dollar
‡Average of New York, Chicago, San Francisco and Atlanta ††Dollars per pound
Source: McDonald's

Some critics find these conclusions hard to swallow. Yes, we admit it, the Big Mac is not a perfect measure. Price differences may be distorted by trade barriers on beef, sales taxes, or large variations in the cost of non-traded inputs such as rents. All the same, the index tends to come up with PPP estimates that are similar to those based on more sophisticated methods.

Moreover, research by Robert Cumby, an economist at Georgetown University, suggests that a currency's deviation from Big Mac PPP can be a useful predictor of exchange rates. Over the past year, the Big Mac index has correctly predicted the direction of exchange-rate movements for eight of 12 currencies of large industrial economies. Of the seven currencies which changed by more than 10%, the Big Mac standard got the direction right in six cases. Better than some highly-paid currency forecasters. Investors who turned up their noses at the Big Mac index should now be feeling cheesed off.

READING 7 Big MacCurrencies

QUESTIONS

1. What is the core insight of the theory of purchasing-power parity? How are Big Mac prices used to calculate an implied purchasing-power parity of the dollar? How is the dollar's PPP value interpreted?

2. How accurate are the Big Mac estimates of the dollar's PPP value?

3. According to the Big Mac index, the Swiss franc is overvalued 66 percent relative to the dollar, while the Chinese yuan is undervalued 52 percent. How are these figures derived from the Big Mac index, and what predictions for future exchange rate movements do they support? Explain.

4. Which three currencies were closest to their implied purchasing-power parity exchange rates (as determined by the Big Mac index) on April 7, 1997? What are the pair-wise exchange rates between these three currencies?

READING 8

Budget Deficit Cuts and the Dollar

Ramon Moreno

Since the spring of this year, policymakers and academics have disagreed on how expected reductions in the U.S. budget deficit will affect the U.S. dollar. Prominent policymakers, including the Federal Reserve Board Chairman, the Bundesbank President, and the Japanese Finance Minister have state publicly that such reductions may lead to a strengthening of the U.S. dollar. Well-known U.S. academics have criticized this view, arguing that budget deficit cuts will lead to a dollar depreciation.

This *Weekly Letter* assesses these conflicting views in the context of standard explanations of the determinants of the exchange rate. A review of these explanations suggests that U.S. academics are focusing on the short-run impact of lower budget deficits on the dollar, whereas policymakers are focusing on medium- and long-run effects.

BUDGET DEFICIT CUTS IN THE SHORT RUN

The simplest way to think of how budget deficits affect the dollar is to use a Keynesian framework where the dollar adjusts to restore equilibrium in the balance of payments. The dollar depreciates if the balance of payments is in deficit, and it appreciates if it is in surplus. So the key to predicting what happens to the dollar when the budget deficit is cut is to see what happens to the balance of payments.

Roughly speaking, the balance of payments is the sum of the trade balance and net capital flows. And part of the ambiguity in the debate is because a cut in the budget deficit affects these two components of the balance of payments differently. It tends to *increase* the trade balance, because it cuts today's income, which reduces the demand for imports; in other words, it can create a balance of payments *surplus*. At the same time, it tends to encourage capital *outflows*, because it tends to lower U.S. interest rates relative to foreign rates—that creates a balance of payments *deficit*.

Reprinted from Federal Reserve Bank of San Francisco *Weekly Letter*, No. 95-42, December 15, 1995. The opinions expressed in this article do not necessarily reflect the views of the management of the Federal Reserve Bank of San Francisco, or of the Board of Governors of the Federal Reserve System.

Which effect is likely to dominate? In the case of a small open economy the answer is clear: A budget deficit cut will push the balance of payments toward a deficit and hence will produce a depreciation of the currency. The reason is that the fall in the domestic interest rate will produce a large incremental capital outflow, because from the point of view of a small economy, the supply of international capital is unlimited.

For a large economy like the U.S., the effects of a budget deficit cut are ambiguous. The supply of international capital is no longer unlimited, so that as domestic income declines, the trade balance increase may exceed the capital outflow associated with the fall in interest rates, causing a balance of payments surplus and dollar *appreciation*. This ambiguity is resolved by (plausibly) assuming that the tendency for budget deficit cuts to result in capital outflows outweighs the effects on the trade balance. Thus, the academics' insistence that a budget deficit cut will tend to lead to a weaker dollar may be motivated by focusing on short-run effects.

BUDGET DEFICIT CUTS AND LONG-RUN EFFECTS

Shifting the focus to the longer-run impacts of budget deficit cuts, we can explore two reasons why such cuts can lead to dollar appreciation.

First, *a budget deficit cut may lead to capital inflows and a balance of payments surplus if the risk premium on domestic interest rates falls by enough.* Suppose investors are worried that the continued accumulation of U.S. government debt may make investors reluctant to hold U.S. treasury securities some time in the future, exposing them to sudden capital losses. In order to bear this risk, investors require a premium, which is reflected in the spread between domestic and foreign interest rates. A budget deficit cut may reassure investors that the future stock of U.S. government debt will not be so large, which would reduce the risk premium. If the reduction is large enough, there may be incipient capital inflows even if the budget deficit cut causes the domestic interest rate to fall. The dollar would then appreciate to restore balance of payments equilibrium.

Second, *a budget deficit reduction may reduce inflationary pressures.* Many international economists believe that in the long run, when prices can adjust, the value of the dollar depends on the relative price of representative baskets of U.S. and foreign goods and therefore on relative money supplies and money demands. This is an implication of the theory of purchasing power parity, and it is known as the monetary approach to the exchange rate. A decline in the budget deficit today may reduce the expected rate of long-run money creation and inflation required to finance current and prospective deficits. The decline in long-run inflationary expectations causes the long-run nominal interest to fall and money demand to rise and the dollar to appreciate in the long-run. Such an expected future appreciation in the dollar from its current expected long-run level will lead to an appreciation in the dollar today, which will offset the tendency towards depreciation in the short-run highlighted earlier.

It is not clear how big a role these reasons are likely to play. For example, Allan Meltzer has point out that historically risk premium effects have been small in the U.S.; however, he notes that they may be rising because private financing of U.S. net debt has been replaced by financing by foreign central banks. In addition, several observers have questioned whether the effect of budget deficit cuts on inflationary expectations is empirically relevant, since the U.S., like other industrial countries, has not monetized its deficits in recent years. However, evidence from other countries suggests that in the absence of credible measures to reduce the budget deficit, the pressure on the central bank to resort to inflationary finance tends to grow.

EFFECTS ON PRODUCTIVITY OR THE COMPOSITION OF DEMAND

While much of the discussion in the financial press focuses on the effects of *deficit reduction* on the dollar, the effect of specific tax and government expenditure policies on sectoral productivity or the composition of demand may have implications for the exchange rate in the long run that are separate from those associated with deficit financing. These policies affect the real, or inflation-adjusted, dollar exchange rate, which, holding monetary factors constant, will affect the nominal exchange rate as well. Some insights into these effects can be gained by assessing how the long-run (real) exchange rate is determined and the possible effects of tax and spending policies.

In what follows, it is useful to think of an economy with two goods, traded and non-traded, and of the real exchange rates as the relative price of traded to non-traded goods. This relative price is widely taken to represent the real exchange rate, because it reflects the relative profitability, or competitiveness of production, in the traded goods sector. A fall in the price of traded goods relative to non-traded U.S. goods means the traded goods sector is relatively less profitable, and represents an appreciation of the dollar.

International economists believe that an important long-run determinant of the real exchange rate is productivity growth. Bela Balassa and Paul Samuelson concluded three decades ago that if productivity grows faster in the traded goods sector than in the non-traded goods sector, then in the long run, the relative price of traded to non-traded goods will fall, which means that the real exchange rate will tend to appreciate. The reason is that an increase in traded goods productivity drives up the demand for workers and their wages. The price of non-traded goods rises in response to the increase in cost, but the price of traded goods does not adjust because it is set in world markets. Richard Marston (1987) provides empirical support for this theory, finding that rising labor productivity differentials between traded and non-traded goods in Japan, in excess of those observed in the U.S., provide a good explanation of the long-run trend real appreciation of the yen against the dollar.

These findings suggest that if the budget deficit is cut by reducing spending or altering taxes in a way that increases relative productivity growth in the U.S. traded goods sector, the dollar may appreciate. Unfortunately, the quantitative effects of specific spending or tax policies on aggregate long-run productivity growth are not well understood. For example, it is tempting to argue that past Japanese subsidies to the traded goods sector enhanced that sector's productivity growth and contributed to the trend yen appreciation apparent since the 1960s. However, subsidies to specific sectors in other countries have not necessarily enhanced productivity. Further research on this question would be instructive.

Another factor believed to affect the real value of the dollar is the composition of demand. For example, a budget cut achieved by cutting government spending will cause a dollar depreciation (a fall in the price of U.S. domestic non-traded goods) if government spending is more biased towards domestic non-traded goods. There is some empirical evidence of a connection between government spending and the real exchange rate. In this context, it can be argued that the fiscal factors behind the real appreciation of the dollar in the early 1980s was not so much the result of budget deficits rising as of the increase in government spending that favored domestic goods.

Apart from the composition of government spending, the wealth of consumers is often believed to influence the demand for domestic non-traded goods and therefore the real value of the dollar. In this view, a country incurring a current account surplus accumulates wealth, thus increasing the demand for its own goods and its own money, which results in a real and nominal appreciation of the exchange rate. Thus, fiscal policies that increase the long-run stock of capital or national saving will increase national wealth and the demand for domestic goods, thus causing the dollar to appreciate in the long run. In particular, tax policies that encourage consumers to invest rather than to consume may lead to dollar appreciation.

CONCLUSIONS

The disagreement between policymakers and some academics on the effects of budget deficit reductions on the dollar appears to reflect the former's emphasis on long-run effects and the latter's emphasis on the short-run effects. It is difficult to tell which viewpoint is more credible empirically. As discussed by Kasa (1995), there is no close empirical relationship between macroeconomic fundamentals, such as budget deficits, and short-run exchange rate behavior. Furthermore, while there is some evidence that certain variables (including inflation and productivity growth) affect the exchange rate in the long run, it is difficult to isolate the impact of such long run factors on the behavior of exchange rates in the short run.

It can be argued that if the short-run reduction in the budget deficit is large relative to the planned reductions in the future, short-run effects may dominate and, under plausible conditions, the dollar will depreciate, as argued by academics. If deficit reductions will take place largely in the future, and

PART II Financial Markets

consumers and investors are mainly worried about the accumulation of government debt, long-run considerations may be dominant. In this case the dollar may appreciate, as suggested by policymakers. In either case, the types of tax or government spending policies that are used to achieve deficit reduction are likely to affect the path of the dollar as well.

REFERENCES

Kasa, Kenneth. 1995. "Understanding Trends in Foreign Exchange Rates." *FRBSF Weekly Letter* (June 9).

Marston, Richard. 1987. "Real Exchange Rates and Productivity Growth in the United States and Japan." In *Real Financial Linkages among Open Economies*, S.W. Arndt and J.D. Richardson, eds., pp. 71-96. Cambridge: MIT Press.

Meltzer, Allan H. 1995. "Comment on 'What Do Budget Deficits Do?' by L. Ball and N.G. Mankiw." Delivered at *Budget Deficits and Debt: Issues and Options*, FRB Kansas City Symposium, Jackson Hole, Wyoming.

QUESTIONS

1. How might a cut in the budget deficit affect the dollar in the short run? Can the effect on the dollar be predicted with certainty? Why?

2. Explain the reasoning behind the proposition that a budget deficit cut which reduces inflationary expectations will cause the dollar to appreciate in the long run. Illustrate this proposition using an exchange rate diagram.

3. According to Moreno, what accounts for the disagreement between academic economists and government policymakers regarding the effect of budget deficit cuts on the dollar? Under what circumstances might each side be correct?

PART THREE

FINANCIAL INSTITUTIONS

Much of the dynamism of the field of money, banking, and financial markets is related to changes in the structure and operations of financial institutions and to the innovation of new financial instruments in response to changes in the economic environment. Part Three of the text develops an economic framework for analyzing financial structure and institutions and uses it to examine such topics as the importance of financial intermediaries as sources of finance for businesses, financial innovation, bank management, banking industry structure, and bank regulatory issues. Several of these concerns are treated in the readings for Part Three. Because this area of the subject changes so rapidly, these readings play an important role in keeping course content up to date.

Reading 9, "A Look at America's Corporate Finance Markets" by Stephen D. Prowse, surveys the range of financing options available to U.S. firms and provides an explanation for the differences in financing among small, medium, and large firms. This reading supplements Chapter 9's discussion of asymmetric information and financial structure.

Reading 10 is "For Better or Worse: Three Lending Relationships" by Mitchell Berlin. Berlin discusses the significance of long-term relationships between business borrowers and lenders. He examines how long-term lender-borrower relationships are influenced by competitive conditions in lending markets and by access to alternative sources of financing, such as securities markets, that become available to business borrowers as their size increases. Instructors will find this reading an enlightening extension of Chapter 9's material on financial structure and lending or Chapter 10's discussion of customer relationships as a tool for managing credit risk.

Reading 11, **"Financial Fragility and the Lender of Last Resort"** by Desiree Schaan and Timothy Cogley, also relates to Chapter 9, specifically to the discussion of financial crises. Schaan and Cogley address asymmetric information problems in the context of financial crises and the advantages and disadvantages of intervention by monetary policymakers when a crisis is at hand.

"Bad Debt Rising," by Donald P. Morgan and Ian Toll, is Reading 12. Morgan and Toll examine trends in charge-offs on credit card loans and investigate the roles of supply and demand factors in the recent sharp increase in charge-off rates. They find rising wealth and an increase in the share of the U.S. population aged 25-54 to produce a rising debt burden accounting for the increased charge-off rate. This reading can be used with Chapter 10's discussion of bank lending and credit risk.

Reading 13, **"Loan Lending Magic"** by Laura Fortunato, describes new technology for applying for and receiving loans and considers the benefits and concerns that accompany its innovation. It gives students insight into forces that drive innovation in banking, providing a useful supplement for Chapter 10's discussion of innovation.

Simon Kwan surveys research findings on scale efficiency and X-efficiency in Reading 14, **"Efficiency of U.S. Banking Firms—An Overview."** He discusses economies of scale in banking and suggests that efforts to improve operating efficiency promise larger gains than efforts to become the optimal size. This reading augments Chapter 11's discussion of banking industry structure.

Reading 15, **"Small Business Lending and Bank Consolidation: Is There Cause for Concern"** by Philip E. Strahan and James Weston, investigates the separate roles of small and large banks in lending to small businesses and concludes that consolidation in the banking industry need not hurt small businesses. This reading can be used with Chapter 10's treatment of the bank balance sheet and bank lending or used to augment the material on banking industry structure in Chapter 11.

Reading 16 is **"Bank Branches in Supermarkets"** by Lawrence J Radecki, John Wenninger, and Daniel K. Orlow. This reading identifies competitive pressures leading banks to open in-store branches as alternatives to traditional branch offices. The authors outline the benefits of supermarket branches and consider the policy issues raised by their proliferation. This reading goes with Chapter 11's discussion of branch banking.

In Reading 17, **"Cracking the Glass-Steagall Barriers,"** Simon Kwan relates that although efforts to repeal the Glass-Steagall Act have yet to succeed, banks nonetheless are expanding their investment banking activities. Federal Reserve rulings have allowed them to underwrite heretofore ineligible securities and to derive greater shares of their revenues from securities activities. Kwan argues that these rulings have increased securities industry competition but that Glass-Steagall reform is still needed. This reading can be used with Chapter 10's discussion of financial innovation or with Chapter 12's discussion of proposed bank regulatory reforms.

READING 9

A Look At America's Corporate Finance Markets

Stephen D. Prowse

How an economy channels finance from savers—typically individuals—to those with ideas about how to invest productively—the business sector—has always been recognized as important for economic growth. Some recent academic work has emphasized this point. Historians are now attributing a greater role to the development of corporate finance markets in spurring the emergence of the railroads and other heavy industries that were key engines of growth in the industrial revolution. And some recent empirical work suggests that the level of a country's financial development helps predict its future rate of economic growth.[1] Such work has reignited economists' interest in how firms get financed in both the United States and abroad.

This article describes and analyzes the spectrum of finance markets available to U.S. corporations and examines how firms as large as General Motors and as small as the tiniest start-up get financed, with particular attention to the recent dramatic expansion in finance markets for small and medium-sized firms. It explores some reasons for this dramatic expansion. It then examines why U.S. finance markets are structured as they are. Finally, it compares other countries with the United States in terms of how their firms obtain financing and explains why some countries are now trying to emulate the U.S. structure.

HOW FIRMS IN THE U.S. GET FINANCED TODAY

As shown in Chart 1, even after adjusting for inflation, corporate finance markets have grown extremely rapidly over the past 15 years. This expansion has largely been fueled by the rapid growth of nonbank financial institutions, such as pension funds, life insurance companies and mutual funds. In comparison, commercial banks have shown steady though less rapid growth, reflecting in part the regulatory constraints on their activities and the rise of competitors such as finance companies and money market mutual funds. Nonbank financial institutions are now the major suppliers of funds to corporations, and they have helped fashion for the United States the most diverse and rich set of corporate finance markets in the world.

Firms use short-term finance markets for working capital purposes, such as financing inventories or receivables. As shown in Chart

Reprinted from Federal Reserve Bank of Dallas *The Southwest Economy*, Issue 2, 1996.

PART III   Financial Institutions

Chart 1
The Growth of Corporate Finance Markets in the United States

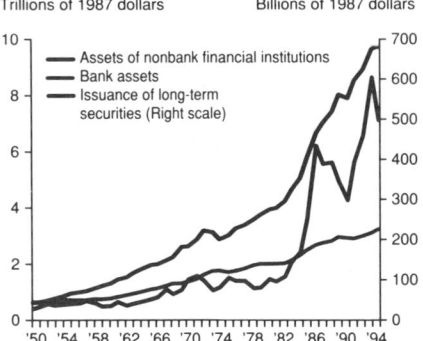

**Chart 2
Short-Term Liabilities of Nonfinancial Business, 1994**

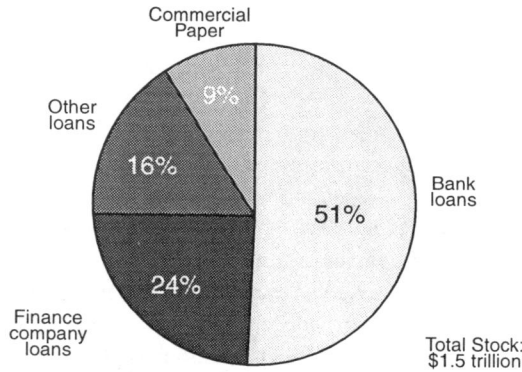

2, in 1994 short-term business liabilities totaled $1.5 trillion, and they came from a number of sources, the most important being loans from banks. Banks are somewhat unique among financial institutions in that they are important lenders to firms of all sizes. Overall, banks supply over half of all short-term business finance. Finance companies are also important lenders to business, while other intermediaries also make business loans, such as savings institutions and mortgage companies. Issuing commercial paper is typically an option only for larger, more highly rated firms.

Long-term finance markets are used to finance capital expenditures that pay back returns over a long period of time. As shown in Chart 3, issuance of long-term securities so far in the 1990s totaled almost $1.2 trillion. Five markets have contributed to this financing. The most well-known are the public markets for bonds and equity. The public bond market is the largest source of long-term finance because it caters to the biggest firms that have the largest capital needs.

**Chart 3
Issuance of Long-Term Securities In the 1990s**

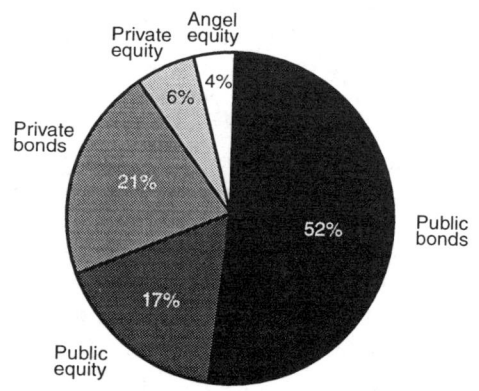

READING 9 A Look at America's Corporate Finance Markets

This article will focus on the three private markets—the private bond, private equity and angel equity markets—because they are the only realistic sources of long-term finance for small and middle-market companies and because they have grown extremely fast in recent years. Despite their importance, relatively little is known about how these markets operate.

The largest of these private markets is the private placement, or private bond, market. It offers long-term debt at fixed interest rates. Primary lenders are life insurance companies. Primary borrowers are middle-market companies with annual revenues between $100 million and $500 million that are generally not large enough to issue public bonds. Although this market receives little attention, it has grown rapidly over the past 15 years and is now quite large. Average annual issuance in recent years is almost five times greater than in the early 1980s, and in some recent years, issuance has actually exceeded that of public bonds, even though individual issue sizes are much smaller than those in the public market. In short, the private placement market is a major source of funds for middle-market firms.[2]

The private equity market consists of equity investments professionally managed by specialized intermediaries, mostly limited partnerships. These limited partnerships are funded by institutional investors such as pension funds, banks, endowments and insurance companies. Although this market is small compared with others, its growth since 1980 has been astronomic, almost 10 times faster than other long-term finance markets. I estimate that the private equity capital stock in 1994 was about $100 billion, almost 25 times larger than in 1980.[3]

One reason for this explosive growth since 1980 has been regulatory and tax changes that encouraged pension fund investment through limited partnerships (LPs). Partnerships have proved to be the most efficient vehicle for investing funds from institutional investors in firms seeking private equity. As shown on the left of Chart 4, most of the growth in the private equity market since 1980 has been through partnerships. Prior to 1980, private equity investments were undertaken mainly by wealthy families, industrial corporations or banks directly investing their own capital. This practice was inefficient because it required all individual investors to bear the costs of managing their own investments. The pooling of funds into one entity—the LP—that does all the management has proved to be a more efficient way of organizing private equity investments.

The right half of Chart 4 shows that in 1980 this market was focused almost exclusively on traditional venture capital targets—small firms, often in high-tech lines of business that have a chance of growing into highly successful large firms. Today, the market has a much wider range of activity, including nonventure investments such as expansion capital for middle-market firms, turnaround capital for firms in financial distress and buyout investments.

Finally, there is the market for angel capital. Angel capital refers to equity investments in small firms by wealthy individuals, often with entrepreneurial backgrounds. Unlike the private equity market, this is a very localized, informal

PART III   Financial Institutions

Chart 4
Stock of Private Equity

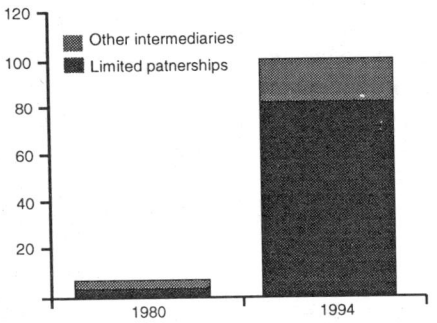
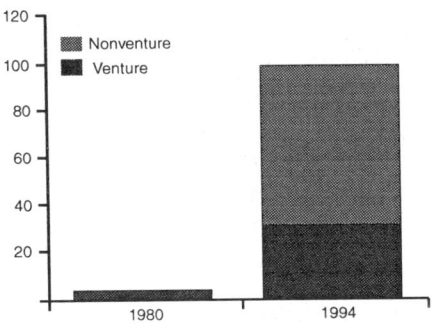

market. Angel capital is targeted at start-up or infant stage firms that cannot attract venture capital because they don't have exciting enough growth prospects. Although it's hard to estimate the size of this market, it is very important for small firms, not least because it's often the only realistic source of capital available to such firms. The most conservative estimates suggest that angels invest about $10 billion in more than 30,000 small firms each year. This market has also likely grown very fast in recent years, in part because the number of wealthy individuals in the economy has grown so fast. For example, after adjusting for inflation, there are roughly six times as many people making $1 million or more a year in the U.S. today than there were in 1980.

Why have the finance markets for small and medium-sized firms expanded so rapidly? First, these firms have become increasingly important in the economy, as illustrated in Chart 5. Per capita new business incorporations have almost doubled since the late '60s, while the share of total employment in small firms has increased sharply since the mid-'70s. The evolution to an information-based economy has probably contributed to small firm growth, since many service and technology-based firms tend to be small or medium-sized. The tendency for large firms to outsource many of their administrative functions to smaller firms (such as payroll, accounting and personnel) may also be a factor. As small and medium-sized firms have increased in importance, so has their demand for capital. Second, there has been an increased interest and ability of institutional investors to supply capital to smaller firms, as illustrated by the previously discussed pension fund involvement in the private equity market.

Chart 5
Small Business Has Been Increasing in Importance

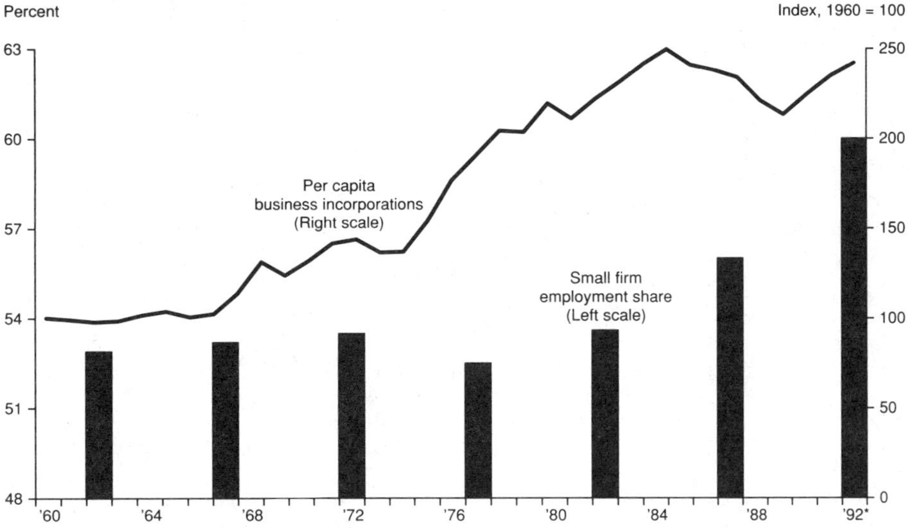

WHY CORPORATE FINANCE MARKETS ARE STRUCTURED AS THEY ARE

Why are corporate finance markets structured as they are in the United States? A partial answer lies in how the finance market has addressed two generic information problems faced by all firms trying to raise capital.

First is the selection problem, which investors face in choosing where to invest. Out of the hundreds of investment proposals investors receive from firms, how do they select the ones most likely to succeed or least likely to fail? A second problem is one of monitoring or governance: how do investors ensure that, after funding, the firm puts funds to the proper uses? These are essentially information problems: they stem from the fact that potential outside investors typically know much less about the firm than the firm's managers. This limitation impairs investors' ability both to assess which firms are the best investments and to know exactly what the firm is doing with the money made available to it.

Information problems tend to be worse for small firms, which do not produce very detailed information about themselves and are often too young to have a track record about which they can boast. Medium-sized firms, being typically somewhat more mature than small firms, have a more solid track record

PART III Financial Institutions

Table 1
Capital Sources for Firms

	Firm Size		
	Small	Medium	Large
Information Availability:	Low	More	High
Selection/monitoring problems:	High	Less	Low
Capital sources:	Angel capital		
	Private equity	Private equity	
	Bank loans	Bank loans	Bank loans
		Private bonds	
		Public equity	Public equity
			Public bonds
			Commercial paper

and tend to produce more information about their activities. They consequently suffer somewhat less from the handicap of the unknown. Large public firms make available detailed information about their activities and usually have long track records. They suffer least from such problems.

However, just as firms differ in the extent of the information problems they pose to outside investors, corporate finance markets differ in the extent to which they can deal with these shortcomings. As shown in Table 1, small firms are forced to raise funds in markets for angel capital, private equity and bank loans. Medium-sized firms may be able to tap the private bond market, while some of the larger or more promising middle-market firms may also be able to issue public equity. Large firms that suffer least from information problems gravitate toward the markets that have the fewest such safeguards and where, in general, capital is the cheapest, such as the public bond and commercial paper markets.

What type of safeguards have markets developed? Two phenomena are common in the bank loan, private placement, private equity and angel capital markets. First, as a general practice, investors in these markets have the expertise and resources to obtain information about the firms who solicit them for money. These investors report selecting about 1 percent of the hundreds of investment proposals they receive per year. Proposals are usually from firms about which there is little or no publicly available information. Thus, banks, life insurance companies and limited partnerships have staff capable of producing information about the firm from scratch and analyzing that information intelligently. These resources help mitigate the selection problem.

READING 9 A Look at America's Corporate Finance Markets

Second, investors use their direct influence or other control mechanisms to ensure that the firm makes proper use of invested funds. Such influence helps mitigate the monitoring problem. Tight covenants in bank loans and private placements, for example, give the firm little leeway to stray from the straight and narrow path.

Private equity investors and angels also use a number of mechanisms to gain management influence. Representation on the firm's board and a majority voting right position are common examples. In addition, investors typically hold the purse strings for subsequent capital. Fast-growing firms depend crucially on the initial investors to either provide subsequent capital themselves or find other investors to do so. Initial investors will be unwilling to do either task if they believe the management team has not performed up to par. And management almost always has a significant level of stock ownership in the firm, so that management's incentives are more aligned with those of the outside investors.

Chart 6 shows how this structure of financial markets works in reality, using the financing history of Dell Computer as an illustration. Dell, based in Austin, is currently the world's fifth largest personal computer maker, with annual revenues of almost $3.5 billion. Twelve years ago, Dell was merely an idea in its founder's head. In 1984, Michael Dell started making and selling IBM PC clones through the mail from his college dorm. As with almost every start-up, his first source of financing was his own personal savings. Since the company had some inventory and sales to which it could point, for the next three years Dell tapped bank lines of credit secured by inventories and receivables.

By 1987, the company had grown so fast that it had exhausted its debt capacity. Given the company's size and youth, the only realistic source of funds was private equity venture capital. That year Dell convinced a group of venture capitalists to invest $20 million in the company. As is typical in venture financings, the investors wanted some control over the company in return for their money—in this case the lead venture capitalist took the positions of president and chief operating officer. The infusion of equity proved crucial to subsequent expansion, and by 1988 Dell had become large enough to raise $28 million from the public equity markets through an initial public offering (IPO).

Dell continued to grow fast, and in 1991 returned to the public equity market for $120 million. Although Dell was a successful, fast-growing company, its relatively small size, youth and potentially volatile line of business meant that it still could not tap the public bond market. After obtaining a $200 million bank line of credit in early 1993, Dell had enough of a track record to be acceptable to public bond investors and issued $100 million of public bonds in August 1993. Thus, in 12 years, and with the aid of a variety of corporate finance markets, Dell Computer went from a one-man operation housed in a college dormitory to a multinational company that employs over 7,500 people.

PART III   Financial Institutions

Chart 6
From an Idea to a $3.5 Billion Company in 12 Years...
Dell Computer's Financing History

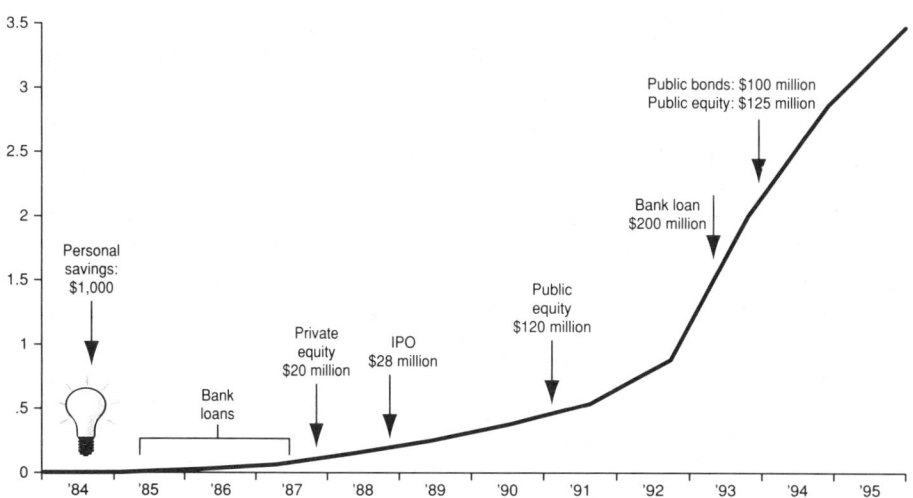

INTERNATIONAL COMPARISONS

In Japan and Germany, the corporate finance system is very different from that of the United States. Firms in these countries, large and small, typically have relied much more on bank financing than have U.S. firms. The primary reason for this reliance lies in the heavily regulated nature of German and Japanese securities markets, which has severely stunted their growth. Their public securities markets are extremely small compared with those of the United States, and their small firm finance markets are even more undeveloped. For example, many medium-sized European firms are now finding it easier to do IPOs on the U.S. NASDAQ exchange rather than raise capital domestically.

Although the bank-centered systems may have had some advantages in the past, there is an increasing feeling that such systems may not provide adequately for the credit needs of small and medium-sized firms that are the engine of future economic growth and innovation. This may be one reason many of the success stories in the past 15 years have come predominantly from the United States, while there have been few Dell's or Microsoft's in Japan or Germany. Recognizing this, policy-makers in these countries recently have deregulated their securities markets in an effort to emulate the U.S. system of corporate finance.

CONCLUSION

A recent *Business Week* cover article celebrated America's access to the public equity markets and the positive effect the recent boom in IPOs had for innovation and growth. The magazine called this phenomenon "IPO capitalism."[4] This article argues that the story is really a much bigger and broader one. Dell is a success story about the capacity of U.S. capital markets to provide funds to firms at *all* stages in their life, not just the IPO stage.

This is not to say that all deserving firms get the type of access that Dell enjoyed, nor that our capital markets could not be improved. Nor is it meant to imply that it is now easy for small firms to raise capital. Raising capital for small firms is not easy and probably never will be because of the severe information problems that small firms pose to outside investors. But the rapid expansion of markets devoted to solving these problems has made raising capital easier than it was in the past. And today there are thousands of firms of all sizes in America that are benefiting from the unique scope and breadth of U.S. corporate finance markets. Such access to capital deserves a somewhat more encompassing term than just "IPO capitalism."

As Joseph Schumpeter once put it, "Credit creation is the monetary complement to innovation." For every underlying type of "real" economy—agricultural, industrial and so forth—there are a unique set of financing problems for firms and an optimal way of addressing those problems. As American innovation moves us beyond the agrarian and manufacturing eras and into the service and information age, our capital markets must evolve also, else economic growth will surely slow. The rapid expansion of the corporate finance markets for small and medium-sized firms documented in this article is one sign that this evolution is already taking place. Indeed, U.S. corporate finance markets today appear to have become the best in the world at funding "entrepreneurial capitalism," whatever the source of that entrepreneurial spirit.

ENDNOTES

1. See R.G. King and R. Levine, "Finance and Growth: Schumpeter Might Be Right," *Quarterly Journal of Economics* 108 (August 1993): 717-37.
2. See M. Carey, S. Prowse, J. Rea and G. Udell, "The Economics of the Private Placement Market," Federal Reserve Board Staff Study, no. 166, 1993.
3. See G. Fenn, N. Liang and S. Prowse, "The Economics of the Private Equity Market," Federal Reserve Board Staff Study, no. 168, 1995.
4. See *Business Week*, December 18, 1995.

PART III Financial Institutions

QUESTIONS

1. How is the growth of corporate finance markets in the U.S. adjusted for inflation in Chart 1?

2. Describe the participants (lenders and borrowers) in the private bond, private equity, and angel equity markets.

3. Why have finance markets for small businesses experienced rapid growth?

4. What types of asymmetric information problems does the reading identify? How do these problems vary with firm size? How are they overcome in the private bond and equity and angel equity markets?

READING 10

For Better and For Worse: Three Lending Relationships

Mitchell Berlin

When bankers speak of building a relationship with a business customer these days, they usually mean selling the customer a whole range of financial products such as lock-boxes, letters of credit, and swaps, in addition to loans. When financial economists speak of *relationship lending* between banks and firms, they usually have a different, more old-fashioned idea in mind. They mean a close relationship between a firm and its banker, in which a single banker has intimate knowledge about the firm's affairs, built up over years of lending. Economists distinguish this type of lending from the more anonymous *arm's-length lending*, in which institutions and individuals provide funds to firms by purchasing their public securities (stocks and bonds).

Over the last 10 years, financial economists have accumulated a significant body of empirical knowledge about the advantages and disadvantages of relationship lending. Their empirical studies have provided insights into some basic questions: Are close, long-term relationships between borrowers and lenders feasible in an increasingly competitive financial marketplace? How do relationships that have developed between banks and firms change when firms gain access to alternative funding sources, especially public securities markets? Can firms gain the best of both worlds by a judicious mixture of bank and public borrowing?

For firms making financial decisions or banks gauging their markets, these are clearly important questions. These questions are also important ones for policymakers. In developing countries and formerly communist countries—where financial systems are being created from scratch—these are precisely the types of questions that policymakers must confront when they weigh the relative merits of a bank-oriented financial system, like that of Japan, and a securities-oriented financial system, like that of the United States. Even in the sophisticated and highly competitive financial markets of countries like the United States, public policy affects the types of banking relationships that firms and banks form. For example, recent legislative proposals to provide subsidies to promote a secondary market for small business loans—much like the secondary market for mortgages—may increase smaller firms' access to securities markets and loosen their relationships with banks. Understanding the

Reprinted from Federal Reserve Bank of Philadelphia *Business Review*, November/December 1996, 3-12.

economics of lending relationships between banks and firms can illuminate such policy debates.[1]

EXCLUSIVE RELATIONSHIPS CAN EASE CREDIT FOR SMALL FIRMS

Long-Term Exclusive Relationships Are Beneficial... Midget Widget is a small Midwestern firm with sales of $10 million and a simple financial structure.[2] Midget has only two sources of external funds. Many of the firm's input suppliers offer trade credit; for example, Midget's supplier of elbow sockets accepts payment 30 days after delivery. Midget also borrows on a continuing basis from Little Bank on the Prairie. Although Midget was started with a prayer and a loan from the owner's brother-in-law nearly 14 years ago, the firm has been taking out—and repaying—business loans from Little Bank for 10 years.

Over this 10-year period, Midget's borrowing terms have gotten better and better. At the outset, Midget was still struggling to establish its niche in the widget market and was barely profitable. But Midget has yet to miss a payment to its trade creditors or its owner's brother-in-law. When the firm first applied to Little Bank for a loan, a loan officer from the bank performed an especially careful analysis of Midget's books, made phone calls to the firm's trade creditors to ask about the firm's repayment history, and visited the widget plant to inspect the firm's inventories. In fact, this visit was only the first of many regular visits to the plant by the loan officer in charge of Midget's account.

After some careful discussions by the bank's lending committee, Little Bank decided that Midget was a good credit risk, in part because of its exemplary repayment history, but primarily because it was a promising business that had strong future prospects. The lending committee also decided that, rather than burden Midget with very high loan payments at the outset—which might backfire and push the firm into early default—the bank would charge a loan rate of only prime plus 3 percent. This rate was not high enough to cover Little Bank's initial costs of investigating the firm plus its own funding costs (mainly the costs of paying depositors), but the loan committee reasoned that these costs would be made up over time. Midget was a rapidly growing business, and Little Bank's lending committee agreed that even though the loan was risky, it was likely to be just the first in a series of future, more profitable loans.

But the initial nonprice contract terms were *very* stringent, designed to give Little Bank lots of leeway to intervene to protect its money. The loan was structured as a one-year commitment—so after only one year the bank could freely re-evaluate the firm's creditworthiness—and Midget was required to post its accounts receivable as collateral. In fact, payments by those firms receiving trade credit from Midget were made straight to the bank, rather than to Midget. In addition, the loan agreement included numerous restrictive covenants, including the bank's right to veto asset sales by the firm and strict requirements

READING 10 For Better and For Worse: Three Lending Relationships

that Midget limit borrowings from other sources.

Now, in the 10th year of their borrowing relationship, Midget's loan terms are much more attractive than at the outset. The firm now borrows at prime plus 1 percent, instead of the prime plus 3 percent that it paid initially. Instead of a one-year loan commitment, Midget now has a three-year commitment. Although the contract still has restrictive covenants, Midget's loan commitment is no longer collateralized, and the firm now receives all payments directly from its customers.

Midget can now borrow both more cheaply and without such intrusive bank controls because its default risk has dropped over time. Firms that fail are most likely to fail in their first few years of operation. After 14 years, it's clear that Midget is not a fly-by-night firm with a high risk of default. Also, it's now *cheaper* for Little Bank to lend to Midget. Over the last 10 years, the bank has developed expertise in understanding Midget's financial needs and problems, so new loan agreements and adjustments to old ones do not trigger the same intensive evaluation as they did at the outset. Moreover, keeping close tabs on collateral is time-consuming, so a bank's lending costs fall when it feels secure enough to lend without collateral.

More attractive contract terms are not the only benefit of the firm's long-term relationship with the bank. Midget's owner feels fortunate to have received a loan commitment at all this year. The regional economy is weak, and as the regional market goes, so goes the market for widgets. Other area firms that have been in business at least as long as Midget have simply been unable to get a loan on *any* terms from a bank. But, unlike Midget, many of these firms have not had a long-term, exclusive relationship with a single bank. Little Bank's knowledge of the ins and outs of Midget's financial condition—through good times and bad—allows the bank to see Midget's fundamental strengths despite the local economic problems. Little Bank also feels a commitment to help Midget through difficult times.

...But Relationships Are Harder to Form in Highly Competitive Loan Markets. From Little Bank's viewpoint the relationship has developed much as the lending committee had hoped initially. The low initial loan rates (relative to the firm's risk of default) and high costs of monitoring Midget at the outset of the relationship—which initially yielded low profit margins—have been replaced by years of handsomely profitable loans. These continuing profits are rooted partly in the knowledge and expertise that Little Bank has built up over its 10-year relationship with Midget. Little Bank's greater experience in lending to Midget gives it an advantage over potential competitors for Midget's business, all of whom would find it expensive to reproduce Little Bank's knowledge in a reasonable amount of time. As its own costs of lending to Midget have fallen, Little Bank has passed on some of the cost reduction to Midget through a lower loan rate (and more relaxed contractual controls) and kept some of the cost reduction for itself as higher profit. Even as Little Bank makes profits, it is hard for any competitor to offer Midget a better deal.[3]

PART III Financial Institutions

Just how much profit Little Bank can keep as its lending costs fall—and how Midget's loan rate evolves over time—depends mainly on the number and behavior of Little Bank's competitors, including both banks and nonbank lenders (such as finance companies). When competition in the loan market is weak and the bank doesn't have to worry so much about a competitor stealing its customer, the bank can take the entire future customer relationship into account when making a loan-pricing decision in a given period. As in Midget's case, a bank can profitably charge loan rates *below* (risk-adjusted) lending costs at the outset of the relationship—to keep the risk of early default by their risky borrowers low—knowing that it will be able to charge rates *above* lending costs as the relationship continues. In markets where competition is weak, the loan rate charged to a customer typically starts low and falls relatively slowly as lending costs fall over the life of the lending relationship. In more competitive loan markets, each bank will be more concerned about a competitor's stealing its customer at any time, which puts strong pressure on the bank to cover its lending costs *period by period*. Banks don't have the luxury of taking temporary losses in the expectation of charging relatively high rates in the future. So, in highly competitive markets, the loan rate charged to a customer usually starts high and falls more swiftly over the life of the lending relationship.

In Midget's view, more competition would certainly be welcome, as it would put pressure on Little Bank to lower its loan rate now. While grateful for Little Bank's initial commitment of funds and resources, Midget now views itself as an established firm that deserves of low rates. But in Little Bank's view, its own current profits are merely compensation for its heavy initial expenditures on evaluating and monitoring Midget's credit risk and for the relatively low loan rates that it charged Midget when it was only four years old and a relatively high-risk firm. Moreover, Little Bank would argue that it wouldn't have been willing to make such a risky loan *in the first place* without the expectation of high profits in succeeding years. And Midget might have had to wait until it had a longer track record to get outside funding.

An important lesson of Midget's story is that greater competition in loan markets can have complicated and surprising effects. Clearly, competition limits a bank's ability to increase loan rates and profits at borrowers' expense. But it also creates difficulties in building long-term relationships. In particular, it may be difficult for banks to make risky loans—for example, when firms are young and desperately in need of credit—unless the bank expects that it will ultimately profit over the life of the lending relationship. Both the competitive advantage held by an incumbent bank, because of its prior relationship with the firm, and relatively noncompetitive loan markets increase the bank's profits over the life of a lending relationship.[4]

RELATIONSHIPS BECOME LESS EXCLUSIVE AS FIRMS BECOME LARGER

Exclusive Relationships Create Tensions. Middle Marketing (popularly known as 2M) is a closely held firm with $50 million in sales, and it has been borrowing from Regional Bank for 15 years. Regional has been 2M's sole banker and, other than trade credit from its suppliers, 2M's only source of outside funds. While the relationship with Regional has been mutually beneficial, 2M is not completely satisfied. In fact, the firm's Treasurer has become increasingly dissatisfied as he has fielded phone call after phone call from Regional's competitors, who are also seeking to expand their presence in the middle market, and from investment bankers who are trying to convince 2M to go public.[5]

Although 2M no longer has to post collateral on its loans, its three-year loan agreement still has extensive covenants and contractual controls that the firm finds increasingly intrusive. Of course, 2M can always phone its account manager at Regional to request a temporary waiver or renegotiation of a covenant. For example, last year when new equipment purchases threatened to reduce 2M's liquid assets on hand and push its working capital (cash plus accounts receivable) below the minimum level stipulated in the loan contract, 2M's owner called Regional. After a review of 2M's books and some further discussions to make sure that the fall in 2M's working capital was not due to other, more ominous causes, Regional offered a temporary waiver of the covenant.[6]

But renegotiations are not always easy. Sometimes, Regional has demanded an increase in the loan rate in exchange for a relaxation of the covenant. Sometimes, Regional has demanded an offsetting tightening of another covenant. For example, during the last negotiations, although Regional allowed 2M's working capital to fall below the level usually considered prudent in the industry, it also demanded a reduction in the firm's debt-to-equity ratio. In fact, Regional and 2M have not always seen eye to eye about the risks of 2M's operating decisions, and the bank has not always agreed to contractual changes on any terms. Had Regional viewed 2M's recent decline in working capital as too risky, negotiations could easily have turned out unsuccessfully for 2M.[7] In this case, the firm might have been forced to postpone the equipment purchase or to search for another banker willing to provide funds (after duplicating Regional's investigation of the firm's finances). Either outcome would have been costly for the firm.

To Reduce Lender Power, Larger Firms Often Seek to Diversify Their Sources of Funds... By diversifying the firm's funding sources, 2M's owner feels that she would gain more discretion over production and investment decisions and also more bargaining power in negotiations with Regional. One possibility is that 2M could simply borrow from multiple banks, including Regional. Another possibility—which entails more fundamental changes in the ways that the firm does business—is that 2M could sell securities to the public in an initial public offering

(IPO). 2M is now large enough to bear the costs of selling public securities, which include the substantial and ongoing costs of providing information both to investors and to the SEC, as well as the fees paid to the underwriting firm that brings the company's securities to market. Since 2M's owner has been looking to diversify her personal portfolio by reducing her large stock holding in the firm, 2M elects an IPO.

...But Large Firms' Public Security Holders Continue to Value Bank Relationships. Although the decision to sell public securities will ultimately weaken the intensity of 2M's relationship with Regional (indeed, this is one of the reasons for 2M's decision), the firm will continue to benefit from maintaining a lending relationship. In fact, one of these benefits will be felt immediately.

One of the enduring empirical puzzles in financial economics is that stock sold in an IPO seems to be *underpriced*, in the sense that the initial buyers can turn around and resell the stock at a higher price. There is no consensus about why IPOs are underpriced, but most economists believe that it's related to investors' uncertainty about the quality of a firm new to public markets; thus, less uncertainty about the firm's prospects would reduce the amount of underpricing.

This is just what 2M's relationship with Regional appears to do. Otherwise suspicious investors act as if they view a prior borrowing relationship with a bank as good news about the firm, a type of Good Housekeeping Seal of Approval, which reduces their uncertainty about the firm's future prospects. 2M can reasonably expect that its own stock will sell at a higher initial price than that of a similar firm that doesn't have an ongoing relationship with a bank. So, in 2M's case, the extent of underpricing is likely to be reduced, which is good for 2M, since the firm will get more funds from investors when it sells its securities.[8]

After 2M has gone public, its relationship with Regional will continue to affect the price of its public securities. This is true even though a firm with publicly traded securities must disclose a lot of information about its business affairs so that investors and analysts can form their own opinions and make their own forecasts about the firm's prospects. Investors will continue to react whenever 2M renews or renegotiates its loan commitment with Regional. As long as the new contractual terms do not indicate a worsening of 2M's financial situation—say, a higher rate than in the previous loan commitment—2M's stock price will typically rise with the public announcement of the new loan contract.

This positive stock-price reaction to announcements of bank loans and loan commitments—an effect that has been found in study after study—stands in sharp contrast to the usually insignificant or negative effect of the announcement of a new public debt issue.[9] Investors' willingness to pay more for the firm's stock suggests that they view the renewal of the loan relationship (on favorable terms) as good news about its future prospects, either because the bank's information about the firm's condition is superior to that of other investors—*bank certification*—or because the firm's stockholders believe that close supervision by the bank of the firm's affairs is likely to improve the firm's performance—*bank monitoring*.

The positive effect of such an announcement has been found to be strongest when markets are uncertain about the firm's prospects—for example, when stock analysts have substantial disagreements about the firm's future earnings—or if the firm's stock price has been low and investors have been pessimistic about the firm's earnings prospects. This effect has also been found to be strongest when the *bank's* credibility—as measured by its credit rating—is greatest. All of these findings support the idea that investors place a value on the lending relationship.[10]

The story of 2M illustrates that the nature of the lending relationship changes over a firm's life-cycle. The tensions of exclusive lending relationships create powerful pressures for firms to diversify their funding sources when they become large enough. Further, the lending relationship itself eases the transition from exclusive borrowing from a single bank to diversified funding, especially borrowing on public markets. But even when a firm secures funds from public securities markets, there is a payoff to the firm that maintains ties with its banker, because the banking relationship continues to convey information to investors.

A FIRM'S ACCESS TO PUBLIC DEBT REDUCES THE BANK'S FLEXIBILITY

While the empirical evidence says that banks play a continuing role in evaluating and monitoring firms with public securities—at least until the firm reaches a very large size—another aspect of the lending relationship seems to undergo a fundamental change when the relationship becomes less exclusive. The ease of renegotiating bank loans, often seen as one of the hallmarks of lending relationships, appears to suffer.

One piece of evidence that illustrates this loss of flexibility is that the positive stock-price effect of a loan announcement depends on there being a small number of lenders. Many firms borrow from a syndicate of banks: one bank negotiates the loan commitment agreement on behalf of a number of other banks, but all members of the syndicate must ratify any adjustments in the loan agreement. When the loan agreement involves a syndicate of more than three banks, the positive effect of the loan announcement on the firm's stock price disappears. This finding makes sense because it is more difficult to renegotiate loans with a syndicate of banks than with just one or two banks; monitoring and controlling the firm through covenants is much more valuable when contractual terms can be readily revised as new information arrives and circumstances change. In effect, syndicated loan agreements are more like public debt—which is difficult to renegotiate—than a traditional bank loan.[11]

And when the firm actually has public debt—even just a little—bank debt is no longer so easy to negotiate when a firm is in financial distress. Consider Q Continuum Castings, which has sales of $250 million.[12] Its only bank is Mostly Derivatives Bancorp (MDB), which provides Q with most of its short-term financing. In 1987 Q issued its first public debt, following many other middle market firms that had entered public debt markets for the first time. The debt was used to finance the purchase of a small HMO, a testament to Q's forward-looking management, but a business outside Q's core market. This public debt represents only about 15 percent of Q's total debt financing, and MDB holds virtually all of the rest of Q's debt.

For two years, sales of castings have been lagging while the HMO business has been booming. But since the HMO is only a small part of Q's businesses, it now appears that the firm will default on its loans to MDB unless it can somehow reduce its debt payments. Q has already entered negotiations with MDB, because its current ratio (working capital divided by total assets) has fallen below the minimum specified in its loan agreements, placing the company in *technical default*. As is common in loan contracts, a technical default must be remedied within 60 days, or MDB has the right to demand immediate repayment of the loan.

During negotiations, Q argues that the doldrums in the castings market are only temporary and also notes that its HMO subsidiary is doing very well. The firm asks MDB to transform half of its short-term loans into long-term loans with lower face value and to exchange the remainder for a substantial share of Q's stock. These changes would have the effect of reducing Q's current interest payments and postponing payments to the bank to the future, which the firm is convinced will be brighter.

MDB agrees that the long-term prospects in the castings market are reasonably favorable, but it makes a counterproposal. First, all of Q's public bondholders must exchange one-half of *their* bonds for stock. Second, the bank will allow Q to stretch out its short-term loan payments, but it will not reduce the face value of its debt. Third, MDB demands that Q sell off the HMO and use the proceeds from the sale to retire some of its bank debt. Finally, the bank demands a first lien on the machines used to produce castings, that is, Q's casting equipment will now serve as collateral for the bank's loans.

The bank explains both its refusal to accept the company's offer and its own counteroffer as follows. The pain must be shared among all claimants, and it is not the bank's responsibility to bail out Q's bondholders. If the bank writes down the face value of the debt and receives stock in exchange, Q's bondholders will be receiving substantial interest payments while the bank waits for Q's finances to improve enough to begin paying dividends. And in the worst possible case, if Q does not recover and enters bankruptcy, the bank's claim would be subordinate to those of bondholders. This means that the bondholders would be paid off, while the bank would be left with an equity share that may turn out to have little or no value. By forcing Q to sell its valuable HMO subsidiary to retire bank debt and by taking collateral in the castings business, MDB guarantees that it will recover at least some of its investment, even in this worst possible case.

Although Q's management and its public bondholders feel that MDB is taking an unreasonably harsh stance, they have little choice but to accept. As a result of these renegotiations with MDB, Q does avoid the bankruptcy courts, which usually eat up valuable resources like management time and attention, not to mention expenses such as court and lawyers' fees. Yet, the firm has lost its prized jewel (the HMO), and Q's bondholders have been forced to shoulder a disproportionate share of the concessions.

The first lesson of the story of Q is that even a small amount of public debt creates a conflict between the interests of the bank and those of the firm's bondholders. The source of this conflict is that the bondholders are the primary beneficiaries if the bank takes a conciliatory stance in debt renegotiations—for example, by taking equity in the firm or forgiving principal payments. The firm's public debt tends to *harden* its bank's bargaining position, as the bank makes sure that it does not bail out the firm's bondholders by making concessions.

However, the second lesson is that Q's primary reliance on bank loans *does* ease negotiations to avoid a costly bankruptcy. After all, it would have been much more difficult for Q to achieve an agreement with the bondholders alone. MDB is well informed about Q's finances because of its relationship with the firm, and one-on-one negotiations between two well-informed parties—Q's and MDB's managers—are likely to be better organized and less fractious than negotiations with bondholders. Even though the bondholders realize that MDB's interests and their own conflict, they also know that as Q's main creditor the bank stands to lose a lot if it permits the firm to continue operations and Q ultimately fails. MDB's willingness to renegotiate, rather than pull the plug and demand immediate repayment, signals to Q's bondholders the bank's informed belief that the firm is more valuable as an ongoing business. This makes them more likely to exchange their debt for stock.[13]

CONCLUSION

The empirical literature of the last 10 years has uncovered some interesting lessons about the advantages and disadvantages of relationship lending and about the ways that lending relationships change as competitive conditions facing a firm change. Where firms have limited financing choices—for example, small firms—relationship lending generates real benefits. Relationship lending is characterized both by close monitoring of the firm by the bank and by contractual flexibility. The possibility of long-term lending relationships may make it easier for small, risky firms to borrow outside funds, but firms inevitably seek out more diversified funding sources when these become available. Indeed, a firm's prior relationship with a bank makes it easier for the firm to gain access to public securities markets, and even when the firm can issue public securities, bank relationships continue to play a role. For all but the largest firms, banks continue to have an informational advantage that markets recognize. But diversification of funding sources severely limits the bank's willingness to be flexible when firms enter financial distress, even when firms have only small amounts of public debt. Nonetheless, a close relationship with a bank does increase the likelihood of successful renegotiation when a firm enters financial distress.

PART III Financial Institutions

ENDNOTES

1. This article focuses on the empirical literature on bank lending in the United States. I have not always referenced seminal papers when later papers contain good discussions of the preceding literature. See the article by Sudipto Bhattacharya and Anjan Thakor for an excellent critical review of the theoretical literature, and the one by Leonard Nakamura for a discussion of both the empirical and theoretical literature.

2. The story of Midget Widget is based primarily on three important articles, one by Allen Berger and Gregory Udell and two by Mitchell Petersen and Raghuram Rajan. Midget and all other firms and banks in this article are fictional, as are their stories.

3. Economists would say that Midget is *locked into* its relationship with Little Bank, because the bank has an information advantage over its competitors. Of course, other banks might learn something about Midget's creditworthiness based on Little Bank's willingness to make a loan. But as long as Little Bank's credit-granting decision does not completely reveal all relevant information about Midget, Midget will be locked in.

4. This should *not* be interpreted as an argument that greater competition is a bad thing and should be discouraged, but only that there are both benefits and costs. In addition, monopoly profits are not the only way that a bank can receive compensation for its initial commitment of resources to a firm. For example, some economists have argued that holding equity stakes in firms could serve a similar function for a bank, even in highly competitive loan markets. This would require changes in laws that separate banking and commerce, which severely restrict bank equity positions in firms that are not in financial distress. Such legal changes might have complicated and far-reaching effects. For example, see the article by Loretta Mester.

5. The middle market is a fairly nebulous place. Many commentators would say that it's populated by firms with sales between $50 million and $500 million in sales, but other numbers are often used.

6. My account of renegotiations relies heavily on the articles in "A Forum on the Effects of Violating Debt Covenants," in the *Accounting Review*.

7. Even when both the bank and the firm agree about the underlying riskiness of an operating decision, they may disagree about the desirability of the decision. As a creditor with a fixed claim, the bank has a tendency to be especially wary of risky decisions, because it does not share in the high returns when the decision turns out especially well.

8. The evidence about bank relationships and IPOs can be found in two articles, one by Christopher James and Peggy Weir and another by Myron Slovin and John Young.

9. The positive stock price effect when a loan agreement is announced is significant only when the number of banks lending to the firm is small (as discussed in the next section).

10. A thorough review of the literature on the stock price effects of loan agreement announcements can be found in the article by Matthew Billet, Jon Garfinkel, and Mark Flannery. This article also performs an especially careful reexamination of prior findings. Notably, the authors call into question two earlier findings. Initial evidence indicated that only bank loans—and not other types of private debt—have positive announcement effects. Billet, Garfinkel, and Flannery summarize and add to the mounting evidence that all types of private debt have positive announcement effects. They also cast serious doubt on the prevailing belief that announcement effects are significant only for renewals and renegotiations of loan agreements, but not for first-time agreements between firms and banks. Instead, they find that announcement effects are positive and significant for both renewals and first-time agreements.

11. The empirical evidence on the stock-price effect of loan commitments by lending syndicates can be found in the article by Diana Preece and Donald Mullineaux. Their article considers—and rejects—a number of alternative explanations for the insignificant stock price effects of large syndicated loans.

12. The story of Q is based on numerous articles, but it relies most heavily on a pair of significant papers by Christopher James. These articles contain extensive bibliographies and good discussions of the previous empirical work on banks' role in debt renegotiations for financially distressed firms.

13. In his 1995 study, James also finds that bank equity participation in a debt restructuring is associated with superior performance by the firm over the succeeding three years. This finding is tantalizing, but it is particularly difficult to disentangle the direction of causality. Did the bank take equity because of the firm's superior prospects, or did the firm prosper because the bank took equity?

REFERENCES

Berger, Allen N., and Gregory F. Udell, "Relationship Lending and Lines of Credit in Small Firm Finance," *Journal of Business*, 68, 1995, pp. 351-81.

Bhattacharya, Sudipto, and Anjan V. Thakor, "Contemporary Banking Theory," *Journal of Financial Intermediation*, 3, 1993, pp. 2-50.

Billet, Matthew T., Jon A. Garfinkel, and Mark J. Flannery, "The Effect of Lender Identity on a Borrowing Firm's Equity Return," *Journal of Finance*, 50, 1995, pp. 699-718.

"Forum on the Effects of Violating Debt Covenants," in *The Accounting Review*, 68, April 1993, pp. 219-303.

James, Christopher M., "When Do Banks Take Equity? An Analysis of Bank Loan Restructurings and the Role of Public Debt," *Review of Financial Studies*, 8, 1995, pp. 1209-34.

James, Christopher M., "Bank Debt Restructurings and the Composition of Exchange Offers in Financial Distress," *Journal of Finance*, 51, 1996, pp. 711-28.

James, Christopher M., and Peggy Weir, "Borrowing Relationships, Intermediation, and the Cost of Issuing Public Securities," *Journal of Financial Economics*, 28, 1990, pp. 149-71.

Mester, Loretta J., "Banking and Commerce: A Dangerous Liaison?" *Business Review*, Federal Reserve Bank of Philadelphia, May/June 1992, pp. 17-29.

Nakamura, Leonard I., "Recent Research in Commercial Banking: Information and Lending," *Financial Markets, Institutions, and Instruments*, 2, 1993, pp. 73-88.

Petersen, Mitchell, and Raghuram Rajan, "The Benefits of Lending Relationships: Evidence from Small Business Data," *Journal of Finance*, 49, 1994, pp. 3-37.

Petersen, Mitchell, and Raghuram Rajan, "The Effect of Credit Market Competition on Lending Relationships," *Quarterly Journal of Economics*, 1995, pp. 407-43.

Preece, Diana, and Donald J. Mullineaux, "Monitoring, Loan Renegotiability, and Firm Value: The Role of Lending Syndicates," *Journal of Banking and Finance*, 1996, pp. 577-94.

Slovin, Myron, and John E. Young, "Bank Lending and Initial Public Offerings," *Journal of Banking and Finance*, 1990, pp. 729-40.

PART III Financial Institutions

QUESTIONS

1. What is the difference between *relationship lending* and *arm's-length lending*?

2. What examples of the use of collateral and restrictive covenants in bank lending does this reading provide? What roles do these play, and how are the restrictive covenants enforced?

3. Explain the following paradox: The more competition among lenders, the more difficult it will be for young firms to obtain credit and the higher the interest rate they must pay.

4. What is meant by *bank certification* and *bank monitoring*? What phenomena do these concepts help to explain?

5. How does a firm's ability to sell debt securities affect its bank's willingness to be flexible in renegotiationg loan contracts should financial difficulties arise? Why?

READING 11

Financial Fragility and the Lender of Last Resort

Desiree Schaan & Timothy Cogley

Financial crises, such as banking panics and stock market crashes, were a common occurrence in the U.S. economy before World War II. Since then, financial crises have been less common. However, events of the past decade have led to renewed concerns about financial instability and about the proper role of monetary policy in reacting to financial turbulence.

This *Weekly Letter* provides some background on the nature of financial crises, and it discusses whether and how policymakers should intervene. Our discussion borrows heavily from papers by Frederic Mishkin (1991, 1994). Because there are costs to inappropriate intervention, Mishkin suggests that the central bank should intervene only when certain informational problems make it difficult for financial markets to efficiently channel funds to productive investment opportunities. A conceptual framework is needed in order to determine when these informational problems arise. This *Letter* discusses a framework that is based upon theories of asymmetrical information, and it describes the trade-offs that policymakers face.

THEORIES OF FINANCIAL CRISES

The traditional theory of financial crises focuses on the effects of bank runs on the money supply. Other things equal, bank runs tend to reduce the money supply by increasing the public's desire to hold currency and banks' desire to hold reserves. Unless the central bank reacts by increasing the supply of currency and reserves, the money supply would fall and interest rates would rise, thus reducing the public's spending on goods and services. For example, Milton Friedman and Anna Schwartz (1963) argue that the Federal Reserve's inaction during the banking panics of the early 1930s helped turn an ordinary recession into the Great Depression. They argue that the Federal Reserve should intervene in a banking panic in order to prevent a contraction in the money supply.

In addition to this effect, modern theories of financial crises focus on the consequences of asymmetrical information between borrowers and lenders. Borrowers generally know more about their investment projects

Reprinted from Federal Reserve Bank of San Francisco *Weekly Letter*, No. 95-21, May 26, 1995. The opinions expressed in this article do not necessarily reflect the views of the management of the Federal Reserve Bank of San Francisco, or of the Board of Governors of the Federal Reserve System.

PART III Financial Institutions

than lenders, and this can lead to problems related to adverse selection and moral hazard.

Adverse selection occurs when events cause low-risk borrowers to drop out of credit markets. Borrowers invest in projects that involve various payoffs and degrees of risk. High-risk projects also tend to have high expected returns. If lenders do not have enough information to assess the risk-return tradeoffs of particular projects, they must extend credit at an interest rate that reflects the average risk of the market. The average interest rate is too high for projects with low risk and expected return, and it is too low for high-risk, high-return projects. Thus asymmetrical information tends to push low-risk borrowers out of credit markets, leaving only the high-risk borrowers.

Asymmetrical information can also give rise to moral hazard. Once a borrower has received credit, he may have an incentive to undertake activities which raise his own expected return but which also increase the probability of default. This is especially problematic when credit takes the form of a debt contract that allows for bankruptcy and when lenders have difficulty monitoring the borrower's activities.

To mitigate adverse selection and moral hazard problems, Stiglitz and Weiss (1981) show that lenders might prefer to ration credit rather than to raise interest rates when credit demand or uncertainty increases. If lenders were to raise interest rates when credit demands or uncertainty increased, low-risk, low-return borrowers would drop out of the credit market, and high-risk, high-return borrowers would remain. Thus, if creditors were to increase interest rates, the riskiness of the pool of borrowers would increase. Therefore, lenders may choose not to raise interest rates and may instead choose to supply less credit than borrowers demand at the going interest rate. Thus, borrowers who have profitable investment opportunities may be unable to find credit.

Mishkin defines a financial crisis as a situation in which adverse selection and moral hazard problems become much worse, so that financial markets are unable to channel credit to borrowers with profitable investment opportunities. Clearly, this definition does not apply to markets in which creditors can easily evaluate the riskiness of projects and monitor the behavior of investors. But in markets where information is asymmetrical, financial crises are costly, because they reduce economic efficiency and because they may lead to a sharp reduction in investment and aggregate demand. Finally, note that a market crash does not by itself constitute a crisis. A crash could reflect a sharp, adverse turn in fundamentals, as in May 1940 when the U.S. stock market crashed after the fall of France.

SYMPTOMS OF FINANCIAL CRISIS

To identify a crisis, policymakers must determine whether adverse selection or moral hazard problems have become critical. Mishkin lists a number of symptoms. One is a sharp increase in interest rates. This tends to push low-risk borrowers out of credit markets and may lead to credit rationing.

Another symptom is a sharp, unexpected decline in stock prices or inflation. This exacerbates asymmetrical information problems because it reduces the net worth of firms that seek credit. Bernanke and Gertler (1989) show how a large decline in borrower net worth can increase adverse selection and moral hazard problems. A firm's net worth performs a role that is similar to collateral, since a lender can take title to a firm's assets in case of default. Collateral mitigates adverse selection and moral hazard problems because it reduces the lender's losses if the borrower defaults. A decline in net worth implicitly reduces the value of a firm's collateral and may tighten credit rationing.

A third symptom is a banking panic or the failure of other financial institutions. Banks specialize in processing information about borrowers and in monitoring their activities. For example, they usually engage in long-term relationships with their customers, and can monitor their customers' behavior by overseeing their checking account or credit line activity. Bank services are valuable because they reduce the degree of information asymmetry between borrowers and individual savers, who are the ultimate lenders. During a panic, bank failures increase the degree of information asymmetry. Furthermore, banks that remain in business seek to protect themselves by increasing reserves relative to deposits, and this also results in a reduction of lending.

A fourth symptom is an increase in the spread between interest rates on high- and low-quality bonds. This spread reflects the difference in default risk on well-known, high-quality borrowers (such as the U.S. Treasury) and lesser-known, lower-quality borrowers. Hence, this interest rate spread tends to widen when asymmetrical information problems become severe. Historically, this has proven to be a relatively reliable indicator.

IMPLICATIONS FOR MONETARY POLICY

The classical policy prescription in the event of a financial panic is for the central bank to act as a lender of last resort. In a narrow sense, this can be justified on monetarist principles. Bank failures are contractionary because they reduce the stock of money. Thus, during a banking panic, the central bank should lend through the discount window or engage in open-market purchases in order to prevent a contraction in the supply of money.

The asymmetrical information theory suggests a broader perspective. There may also be occasions when the central bank may need to provide lender-of-last-resort services to nonbanking firms as well. This can be done through the discount window, but other policy actions also may have a role. For example, in June 1970, when Penn Central defaulted on more than $200 million in commercial paper, the Federal Reserve became concerned that at a time when financial markets were already unsettled, the liquidity of the commercial paper market might be impaired and the pressures arising in that market might spill over to other short-term credit markets. The Federal Reserve moved to suspend the maximum interest rate ceilings on large-denomination time deposits with maturities of 30 to 89 days imposed by Regulation Q. This made it easier for private banks to serve as intermediaries. Investors reluctant to lend to the commercial paper market now provided additional funds to the private banking sector, and borrowers unable to roll over their commercial paper were provided with this new source of credit. The Fed also increased liquidity in the commercial paper market by allowing banks to borrow at its discount window (see Board of Governors, 1971).

The stock market crash of 1987 provides another example of a successful intervention and illustrates the value of lender-of-last-resort activity. On Monday, October 19th, the Dow Jones Industrial Average fell by 22 percent. The day after the crash, many securities firms and exchange specialists needed credit to finance inventories of stocks whose value had fallen sharply. Also, many investors were asked to provide more collateral for securities bought on credit. These demands, known as margin calls, occur when the value of equities in an investor's account fall below a set minimum. Since the value of collateral had fallen sharply, banks were increasingly reluctant to lend. The interest rate spread between junk bonds and Treasury bills jumped by 130 basis points during the week of the crash and rose by another 60 basis points over the following two weeks. The presence of both the stock market crash and the increase in the spread of interest rates between high- and low-quality bonds indicates that asymmetrical information may have increased in the securities sector.

The Federal Reserve became concerned about a possible systemic breakdown in the market's clearing and settlement systems, and it announced a readiness to "serve as a source of liquidity to support the economic and financial system." The Federal Reserve then proceeded to accommodate the increase in demand for liquidity in the economy by buying government securities on the open market. This provided banks with the extra reserves they needed to extend credit to the securities dealers. The Fed also tried to maintain a high level of visibility in the financial markets to help calm fears of a potential crisis. The Fed placed examiners in major banking institutions to monitor banking developments, and also closely monitored securities firms' demands for credit (Greenspan 1988).

While lender-of-last-resort activity may help protect against financial crises, there is a cost. If depositors know that the central bank will bail private banks out if their loans go bad, they may have less incentive to monitor the riskiness of the banks' portfolios. Likewise, if nonbanking institutions know that the central bank will step in during a financial crisis, they might take on more risks that are associated with an economy-wide financial crisis. Because of these costs, lender-of-last-resort activity should probably be used sparingly.

CONCLUSION

Theories based on asymmetrical information suggest that financial markets can be fragile, since lenders may opt out of the

READING 11 Financial Fragility and the Lender of Last Resort

market when credit demands increase or when uncertainty is especially great. By serving as a lender of last resort, central banks can play an important role in reducing financial panics, as they can ensure that credit markets remain liquid in the event of a crisis. However, this literature suggests that central banks should intervene sparingly, as too much involvement may cause market participants to assume more risk.

REFERENCES

Bernanke, Ben, and Mark Gertler. 1989. "Agency Costs, Net Worth, and Business Fluctuations." *American Economic Review* 79, pp. 14-31.

Board of Governors of the Federal Reserve System. 1971. *Annual Report*, 1970.

Friedman, Milton, and Anna Schwartz. 1963. *A Monetary History of the United States.* Princeton: Princeton University Press.

Greenspan, Alan. 1988. "Statement before the Committee on Banking, Housing, and Urban Affairs, February 2, 1988." Reprinted in the *Federal Reserve Bulletin* (April), pp. 217-225.

Mishkin, Frederic S. 1991. "Asymmetric Information and Financial Crises: A Historical Perspective." In *Financial Markets and Financial Crises, A National Bureau of Economic Research Project Report*, ed. R. Glenn Hubbard, pp. 69-108. Chicago: University of Chicago Press.

———. 1994. "Preventing Financial Crises: An International Perspective." NBER Working Paper No. 4636.

Stiglitz, Joseph, and Andrew Weiss. 19891. "Credit Rationing in Markets with Imperfect Information." *American Economic Review* 71, pp. 393-410.

QUESTIONS

1. Describe the traditional and modern theories of financial crises and their economic effects.

2. How are adverse selection and moral hazard problems worsened during a financial crisis? What signals that these problems are worsening can policymakers look for?

3. Why did the Fed intervene in the financial system following the 1970 Penn Central default and the 1987 stock market crash? Is there a drawback to such intervention? Explain.

READING 12

Bad Debt Rising

Donald P. Morgan and Ian Toll

Credit card charge-offs—the loans that banks write off as uncollectible—are on the rise. Although this trend has only recently made news, it has been under way for more than a decade. From 1971 to 1983, commercial banks charged off just 2.3 percent of their credit card loans on average. Since 1983 the charge-off rate has averaged 3.8 percent and is now approaching 5 percent. This increase in charge-offs parallels the trend in the household debt burden, which has climbed steeply since the early 1980s.

What is behind the rise in bad debt? Most analysts tend to blame lenders, arguing that banks are granting credit cards to riskier borrowers without raising rates to compensate. That supply-side focus is easy to understand given the aggressive marketing of credit cards in recent years, but it overlooks another possibility: perhaps rising demand for credit is driving up debt burdens and charge-offs.

This edition of *Current Issues* weighs both supply and demand explanations for the rise in bad debt. Beginning with the supply side, we ask whether continued growth in credit card balances—despite growing risk—reflects a greater willingness on the part of credit card lenders to gamble on risky borrowers. Although several developments in the credit card industry have the potential to expand the supply of credit card lending, we find no evidence that a supply shift has occurred. Interest rate spreads on credit cards have not fallen since the early 1980s, nor have charge-offs on credit cards risen faster than charge-offs on other consumer loans.

Our look at the demand side of the story is more revealing. Our analysis shows that changes in two important demand factors—wealth and the share of heavy borrowers in the population—have influenced the growth of debt burdens. Before 1983, these variables moved in offsetting directions, tending to stabilize credit demand and the debt burden. Since 1983, however, wealth and the share of heavy borrowers in the population have increased together. Using regression analysis, we show that the combined force of these two demand shifts does a good job of explaining the rise in debt burdens and bad debt.

Reprinted from Federal Reserve Bank of New York *Current Issues in Economics and Finance*, March 1997.

CHARGE-OFFS AND THE HOUSEHOLD DEBT BURDEN: PARALLEL TRENDS

The rise in charge-offs closely mirrors the trend in the overall household debt burden, defined as the ratio of total debt to income (Chart 1).[1] These parallel trends are no mere coincidence; a mounting debt burden *causes* higher charge-offs because heavily indebted borrowers are more exposed to income shocks such as layoffs, illness, and divorce. Credit card borrowers are especially sensitive to such shocks because credit cards provide revolving loans that are usually not secured. When income drops, the revolving feature of credit card loans allows cardholders to slow the repayment of their debt—or even run up their balances.[2] As their debt accumulates, borrowers are then tempted to default on their credit card debt because these loans are rarely secured by collateral.

Despite this rising risk of charge-offs, credit card balances have expanded dramatically—in real terms, by 11.5 percent per year between 1984 and 1996.[3] Why are analysts so quick to suggest that the rapid growth in credit card debt reflects expanding supply? Several developments in the credit card industry could lead one to suspect a supply shift. As we explain below, the potential for high profits, the securitization of credit card loans, and the use of credit-scoring models to assess the risk of borrowers could encourage lenders to take on more risk.

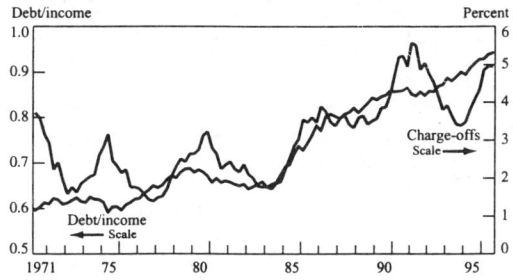

Chart 1
Credit Card Charge-offs and the Household Debt Burden

Sources: Federal Financial Institutions Examination Council, Reports of Condition and Income; Ausubel (1995); Board of Governors of the Federal Reserve System, Flow of Funds Accounts.

SUPPLY-SIDE DEVELOPMENTS

Profitability in the credit card industry has been two to three times higher than in the overall banking system since the early 1980s, when credit card rates were deregulated. Ausubel (1991) argues that profits in the industry are higher than one would expect in a competitive industry, even allowing for the higher charge-offs and the other risks associated with credit card lending. If he is correct, competition for those profits would drive up charge-offs as new lenders who were willing to gamble on riskier borrowers entered the market.[4]

A more recent development that could be expanding credit card lending is securitization. Until the late 1980s, credit card lenders had to screen potential borrowers, monitor the credit, and bear the risk. Today, lenders can package the loans made to individual borrowers into securities and sell them to investors. Securitization allows the lenders to specialize in their comparative advantage—screening and monitoring—while shifting some of the risk to investors.[5]

PART III Financial Institutions

Specialization, in turn, could lower the cost of producing credit and thus increase the supply of lending. Securitization might also expand the credit card lending of banks, in particular, by reducing the amount of capital they must hold to satisfy the requirements imposed by bank regulators.[6]

The advent of credit-scoring models could also cause a shift in the supply of credit cards. These models enable lenders to use the credit histories of millions of borrowers to predict the default risk of loan applicants. By automating the credit-screening process, these computerized models could increase the supply of credit card loans by lowering the costs of producing credit. The models may also allow more accurate screening, so lenders can target narrower risk classes and price their cards accordingly. This ability to slice and price the market more precisely could expand credit card lending.

A LOOK AT THE EVIDENCE

But have these factors created a supply shift? If so, we would expect to see interest rates on credit card loans falling relatively to other interest rates. Yet credit card spreads have actually trended upward over the past fifteen years (Chart 2). The spread shown in the chart is simply the difference between the credit card rate and the one-year Treasury bill rate, which measures the cost of funds to lenders. While the credit card rate has fallen in recent years, the spread is a more relevant measure because it reflects the compensation lenders require for the risks they are taking.[7] Apart from cyclical variation, the spread has

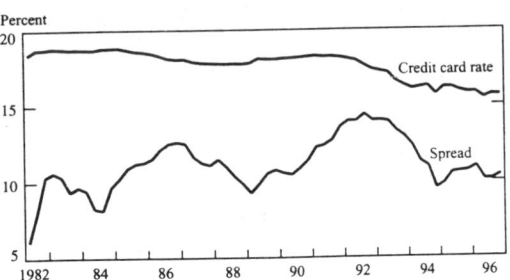

Chart 2
Credit Card Rate and Spread

Source: Board of Governors of the Federal Reserve System, G.19 Statistical Release "Terms of Credit at Commercial Banks and Finance Companies."

Note: The spread is the credit card rate less the one-year Treasury bill rate.

clearly moved upward—from 6.1 percentage points in the second quarter of 1982 to 11 percentage points in the first quarter of 1996. This trend parallels the climb in charge-offs shown in Chart 1, indicating that banks have been raising the spread to compensate for the rising risk of charge-offs.[8]

Another way to identify a supply shift in the credit card market is to examine charge-offs on non-credit-card consumer loans. If lenders have become more willing to gamble on credit card loans than on other consumer loans, credit card charge-offs should be rising at a faster rate. The charge-off rates on credit card loans and on other consumer loans, primarily installment loans, are shown in Chart 3. Contrary to the supply-side story, charge-offs on other consumer loans have risen at virtually the same rate as credit card charge-offs.

Although developments in the credit card market might lead one to suspect that a supply

Chart 3
Relative Charge-off Rates for Credit Card and Other Consumer Loans

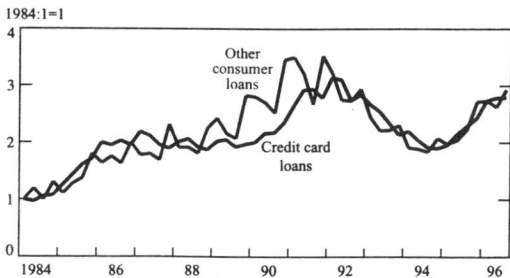

Source: Federal Financial Institutions Examination Council, Reports of Condition and Income.
Note: Series are scaled by their first-quarter 1984 values.

shift is causing the rise in charge-offs, the evidence presented here contradicts that story. Moreover, the uniform rise in all consumer charge-offs steers us toward another explanation: perhaps rising demand for credit is raising debt burdens, making borrowers riskier, and forcing up charge-offs across the board.

THE DEMAND-SIDE STORY

Our demand-side explanation draws on the two leading theories of household borrowing—the permanent income theory and the life-cycle theory. According to the permanent income theory, spending and the demand for credit will rise along with wealth. Suppose home values double. To consume some of this new wealth without selling their homes, homeowners can simply take out a loan. If debt increases more than current income, households' debt burden—the ratio of debt to income—rises.

The second theory relates the demand for credit to borrower's age. According to this life-cycle theory, people try to maintain a stable standard of living over time, even though incomes tend to rise over a person's working life. To smooth consumption, younger individuals borrow against future income and then work down their debt as they grow older and their income rises.

These two theories lead us to look for shifts in wealth and demographics that could be driving up the debt burden—and charge-offs. We measure wealth with net worth per capita in 1983 dollars. Our age variable is the percent of the population in the peak borrowing age of twenty-five to fifty-four. We identified these as the peak borrowing years on the basis of data from the Federal Reserve Board's periodic *Survey of Consumer Finances*; the surveys for 1989 and 1992 reveal that the debt burden is highest across those age groups (Canner, Kennickell, and Luckett 1995).

Although there have been several notable swings in the net worth and age variables over the last forty years, before 1983 the variables usually moved in opposite directions (Chart 4). Between 1956 and 1972, the share of the population at peak borrowing age was falling or level while net worth was rising or stable. When net worth began to fall in 1973, the share of heavy borrowers had already begun to rise. According to the theory, these counter movements should tend to offset the effect on credit demand and debt burdens. In the early 1980s, however, net worth turned up, and both variables have since risen

PART III Financial Institutions

Chart 4
Wealth and the Share of the U.S. Population Aged Twenty-Five to Fifty-Four

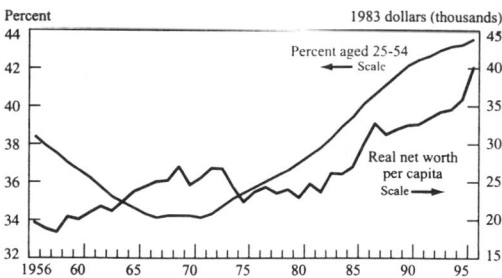

Sources: Board of Governors of the Federal Reserve System, Flow of Funds Accounts; U.S. Bureau of the Census.

Chart 5
Actual and Predicted Debt Burden, Based on Wealth and Age

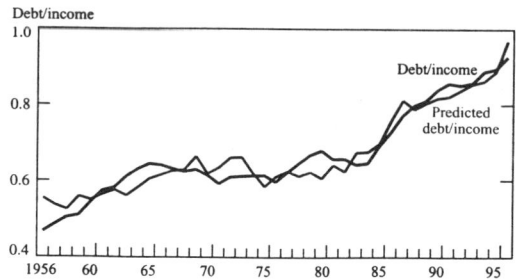

Sources: Board of Governors of the Federal Reserve System, Flow of Funds Accounts; U.S. Bureau of the Census; authors' forecasts.

together steadily.

The combination of rising net worth and the increasing share of heavy borrowers can account for the mounting debt burden. Indeed, these two variables predict most of the variation in the debt burden over the last forty years (Chart 5).[9] The debt burden increased only moderately between the late 1950s and the early 1980s, a period when the movements of the wealth and age variables partially offset one another. Since the early 1980s, the combined forces of rising net worth and an increasing share of heavy borrowers have driven up the household debt burden.

The debt burden predicted by the wealth and age variables can, in turn, explain the rise in charge-offs (Chart 6).[10] To demonstrate this relationship, we regressed the charge-off rate on the level of the debt burden we predicted using the wealth and age variables (shown in Chart 5). We included the annual rate of job growth in the regression to capture cyclical influences. If a supply shift had occurred, the charge-off rate would consistently exceed the rate we predicted using only the demand-side and cyclical variables.

Chart 6
Actual and Predicted Credit Card Charge-offs, Based on Predicted Debt Burden

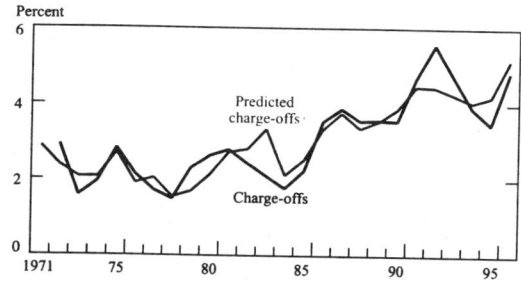

Sources: Federal Financial Institutions Examination Council, Reports of Condition and Income; Board of Governors of the Federal Reserve System, Flow of Funds Accounts; authors' forecasts.

Charge-offs *were* somewhat higher than predicted in the early 1990s, but that deviation likely reflects the added effect of the recession in 1990-91. Since 1993, however, charge-offs have actually been a bit lower than predicted. Overall, the predicted rate tracks the actual rate very closely, confirming the role of the demand-side factors in explaining the increase in charge-offs.[11]

CONCLUSION

Why are credit card charge-offs rising? Many analysts blame lenders for supplying cards to riskier borrowers without raising rates to compensate. Although we consider developments that could expand credit card lending, we find no evidence that the rise in charge-offs reflects a supply shift. Credit card spreads have risen along with charge-offs over the past fifteen years, suggesting that lenders are charging for the extra risk they face. Moreover, charge-offs on other consumer loans are rising just as fast as credit card charge-offs, suggesting that some other force is driving up bad debt.

Finding no evidence of a supply shift, we then consider demand-side developments that many analysts have overlooked. Two variables that drive household borrowing, wealth and the share of heavy borrowers in the population, moved in offsetting directions before the early 1980s, keeping demand in check. Since 1983, however, these two variables have moved in one direction—up. This convergence has fueled the demand for credit and has driven up debt burdens, making borrowers riskier. As a result, bad debt is on the rise.

ENDNOTES

1. The charge-off series in Chart 1 has two parts. The series since 1984 is from the Federal Financial Institutions Examination Council's Report of Condition and Income (commonly known as Call Reports), which are filed each quarter by all U.S. banks. The series before 1984 is from Lawrence Ausubel (1995), who derived it from publications by Visa International. The two series had a correlation of .97 in the period when they overlapped (1985-1991:2), so we simply combined them to generate the series in Chart 1.
2. Borrowers are subject, of course, to a minimum payment and a maximum credit limit. The revolving or open-ended feature distinguishes credit card lending from closed-end lending, such as installment loans, which require fixed payments over a specified term and do not allow additional borrowing.
3. The growth of credit card balances does not explain rising debt burdens because credit card debt remains a small portion of total household debt.
4. Not all analysts accept Ausubel's (1991) arguments; Ausubel (1995) addresses his critics.
5. Although this shifting of risk would appear to tempt lenders to offer cards to riskier borrowers, bankers report that the charge-off rate on the loans they hold is about the same as that on securitized loans (Board of Governors of the Federal Reserve System 1996).
6. Banks are required to hold capital against their assets; securitization reduces banks' assets and thus their required capital.
7. The credit card rate shown is the rate most commonly charged by banks. Because banks now seem to offer a wider range of rates, we were concerned that this mode rate might overstate the average rate in recent years. To address this

PART III Financial Institutions

concern, we calculated the average rate (interest income on credit card lending at all banks/credit card balances at all banks) using data available since 1986 and found that it tracked the mode rate very closely. Another consideration was that banks might be lowering fees rather than spreads. Although Ausubel (1991) notes that fees have declined steadily since the early 1980s, he also observes that lenders have raised late charges and other "hidden" fees to compensate.

8. We regressed the spread and the charge-off rate on a constant and a trend term. The trend coefficients, .189 and .195, were both significant (at 5 percent or lower) but did not differ significantly. By comparing the spread with charge-offs, we accounted for the loss of principal resulting from charge-offs but not the loss of interest. To account for both, we used the risk-adjusted spread = $r_c - r_t - p - p(r_c - r_r)$, where r_c denotes the credit card rate, r_t the Treasury bill rate, p the charge-off rate, and r_r the recovery rate on charge-offs, which is about 15 cents per dollar charged-off (according to the Call Reports). Using that figure, we calculated the risk-adjusted spread between 1982 and 1996 and found it was essentially trendless. This result is not sensitive to the assumption of a constant recovery rate, because the term pr_r is an order or two smaller than the other terms.

9. The ratio of debt to income was predicted using the following regression equation, estimated with the forty-one annual observations between the first quarter of 1956 and the first quarter of 1996: debt/income = -.064 + .007(share aged 25 to 54) + .019(real net worth per capita). The coefficients were both significant at 5 percent or lower. The adjusted R-squared is .91. If a trend is included, the age variable is insignificant, but wealth is still highly significant. We are inclined against including a trend, however, because the life-cycle theory suggests that the demographic variable should help explain the trend in the debt burden.

10. The equation used to predict charge-offs, estimated using annual observations between second-quarter 1971 and the first quarter 1996, was as follows: charge-offs = -2.61 + 8.39(predicted debt-to-income ratio) - .193(annual job growth). The predicted debt-to-income ratio is plotted in Chart 5, and the equation used to predict that ratio is described in note 9. all the coefficients are significant at 5 percent or lower and the adjusted R-squared is .80. Including lagged charge-offs eliminates the serial error in the forecast and raises the adjusted R-squared to .94.

11. If the demand for credit is increasing, wouldn't the risk-adjusted spread, described in note 8, be rising? Not necessarily, because the demand factors we have identified—wealth and age—should increase demand across the board, not just the demand for credit card loans. Even if the relative demand for credit card loans were increasing, the risk-adjusted spread would increase only if the supply of credit card loans were inelastic. If the supply is elastic, lenders can accommodate the increased demand for loans without raising the risk-adjusted spread.

REFERENCES

Ausubel, Lawrence. 1991. "The Failure of Competition in the Credit Card Industry." *American Economic Review*, March: 50-81.

———. 1995. "The Credit Market Revisited." Unpublished paper, University of Maryland, July.

———. 1997. "Credit Card Defaults and Credit Card Profits." *American Bankruptcy Law Journal*. Forthcoming.

Board of Governors of the Federal Reserve System. 1996. *Senior Loan Officer Opinion Survey on Bank Lending Practices*, May.

Canner, Glenn, Arthur Kennickell, and Charles Luckett. 1995. "Household Sector Borrowing and the Burden of Debt." *Federal Reserve Bulletin*, April: 323-38.

Laderman, Elizabeth. 1996. "What's Behind Problem Credit Card Loans?" Federal Reserve Bank of San Francisco *Economic Letter*, July 19.

READING 12 Bad Debt Rising

QUESTIONS

1. What supply changes have occurred in credit card lending that might lead one to hypothesize that supply shifts are responsible for the increased credit card charge-off rate? Why do Morgan and Toll reject the notion that these supply changes actually are the cause of the increased charge-off rate?

2. How do Morgan and Toll use the permanent income theory and the life-cycle theory to explain shifts in the demand for credit? How do they test the effect of these demand shifts on the credit card charge-off rate?

3. How do the shifts in the demand for credit identified in this reading affect the credit risk banks face? What steps might banks take to manage this risk?

READING 13

Loan Lending Magic

Laura Fortunato

Jeff Norris was all that a successful 30-something professional could hope to be. He had a thriving career as a computer systems engineer with Digital Equipment Corp., and had amassed investments and savings considered a basis for financial security. Norris thought he would have no problem getting a bank officer to lend him money for a real estate venture. Not so. The bank's long loan application process proved to be a major disappointment for Norris and his wife.

"I was a higher middle-class individual with all accounts at a very large [banking] institution. I was amazed at how inefficient [the loan process] was and how long it took for [bank officials] to make a decision," says Norris, 35.

That experience led Norris to develop a technology that is revolutionizing the loan industry. Today Norris is president and chief executive officer of Affinity Technology Group Inc. of South Carolina. Affinity has focused much of its efforts and resources on developing an electronic commerce system that automates consumer loans and other financial services. Affinity markets one product—the Affinity Automated Loan Machine (ALM). It does not make or guarantee loans, but derives fees from the setup and rental of the machines, and for recurring transactions.

USING ALMs

The ALM looks and operates much like an automatic teller machine. ATMs, which first appeared in banks in the 1970s, have long provided an option to waiting in long lines at the teller's window and the inconvenience of limited banking hours. These machines now are located any place where people are likely to need quick cash and easy transactions, including in grocery stores and malls.

Applying for a loan with an ALM is relatively quick—it takes about 10 minutes. A customer uses a credit card, charge card, or debit card to initiate the loan process. A customer activates the ALM by running the card along a special magnetic strip. The machine responds with a series of personal and financial questions geared toward assessing the loan application. The customer logs the answers using a touch screen.

Reprinted from Federal Reserve Bank of Richmond *Cross Sections* 13, 4 (Winter 1996/97), 12-15. The views expressed in *Cross Sections* are those of the contributors and not necessarily those of the Federal Reserve Bank of Richmond or the Federal Reserve System.

The ALMs, which are hooked into the bank's data phone lines, process this information and compare it to various data banks. A variety of additional sources also are used to verify a customer's credit history, employment, driver's license, Social Security number, and correct signature.

During the transaction, a camera snaps pictures several times a second, and cross-checks personal financial data banks to make sure the person getting the loan is the one filling out the application. When the background is completed, the machine will either approve or deny the application. If the loan application is approved, the machine will issue a check or deposit the funds into the customer's bank account of choice. A digital picture of the applicant is printed on the note. If denied a loan, the applicant is instructed to speak with a bank officer.

INTEREST FROM BANKING COMMUNITY

The new technology has sparked wide curiosity and interest from the banking industry, including the major players in the industry. Fifty financial institutions have nearly 200 automated loan machines located throughout the United States and Puerto Rico, says Norris. So far, ALMs have been placed in banks and grocery stores.

The Fifth District is home to 57 ALMs; 35 are located in Maryland, 12 in South Carolina, and 10 in West Virginia. North Carolina and Virginia have yet to pilot these machines.

Carolina First Corp. of Greenville, S.C., was the first to test the ALM technology and provided a loan to help the company get started. So far Carolina First has ALMs in seven different sites, including in banks and in grocery stores in Myrtle Beach, according to a bank spokesperson. The bank hopes to install eleven others within the next year.

"We are very excited about the technology and the impact on the loan industry," says Mack Whittle Jr., chairman and chief financial officer of Carolina First. "It makes the customer happy because it is an extension of services. It makes the banks happy because it is faster and cheaper."

A typical loan transaction with a bank teller requires more man hours and overhead, Whittle says. He estimates costs for processing a teller-assisted loan at $100, while the cost of processing an ALM loan at $20.

Affinity's customers also include several regional and super-regional financial institutions: Banc One Corp., Banco Popular, Deposit Guaranty Corp., and Union Planters Corp. The company currently is working on a deal with NationsBank—the country's fifth-largest bank—and is negotiating with six of the top ten banks in the country. Major banking institutions, including Carolina First, Horizon Bancorp Indiana, Susquehanna Bancshares, and Union Planters Corp., accounted for 83 percent of Affinity's revenues in 1995.

Banks are attracted to ALMs for a variety of reasons. The ALMs provide convenience to their customers, and the various locations boost business for banks, says Norris. Affinity research shows that "when you put an ALM in a branch office then you are servicing people

PART III Financial Institutions

who are already customers," Norris explains. "When you put it outside the bank, 78 percent of the users are not your customers."

In the future, the technology will not be limited to ALMs. The technology will be delivered via the Internet and other home computer programs, as well as stand-alone kiosks in automotive dealerships, promises Norris. And ALMs will be able to set up checking and savings accounts, handle credit card applications, and consolidate loans. "The ALM is just one piece of a multi-legged stool," Norris says. Each facet of the technology stool is geared toward making banking an easy and convenient experience for customers.

CUSTOMER SERVICE

ALM loans are primarily unsecured loans of between $1,000 and $10,000; the average loan is about $2,500. But the amounts can vary greatly. One Puerto Rican bank is offering unsecured loans up to $25,000, says Norris. Typically, interest rates for ALM loans are comparable to credit card rates and require a payback period of less than five years. Generally, each financial institution's loan standards, amounts, interest rates, and payback schedules are tailor-made. And an applicant need not have an account with the institution to apply for its ALM loan.

In the coming year, Affinity plans to offer technology that will provide customers with secured loans, such as auto and home equity loans. For instance, home buyers will be able to obtain a mortgage in a few days—not 30 to 45 days as is now customary, says Norris.

"Initially, this service will be available in states that do not require an attorney for [real estate] closings," Norris says. "Consumers will be able to close in minutes."

Earl Jackson, president of Richmond Association of Realtors, doubts that ALM-type mortgage technology will be embraced any time soon. "Customers [still] want to be face-to-face when applying for a mortgage."

Jackson does see such technology helpful as an information tool. He believes that consumers would benefit if they could receive mortgage and real estate information via the computer. The main problem, though, would be managing the information and the financial organizations, says Jackson. "How are we going to bring all these lenders together?"

Norris holds out hope that the technology will continue to develop and that it will eventually be received well by the public. "We manifested ALM technology because we thought consumers would use it," says Norris.

John Brennan, senior vice president and automated banking manager for NationsBank in Charlotte, N.C., agrees. NationsBank hopes to pilot ALMs sometime in 1997. The attraction to the technology, says Brennan, is its ability to meet customers' demands for service and convenience. "Our customers have redefined convenience," Brennan says. "They want service seven days a week, 24 hours a day, when they want it, and where they want it."

He says that the convenience of use may make ALMs as popular as ATMs. However, he notes, NationsBank has not decided whether this service is something customers really want. "There are a lot of questions we need to answer."

CONCERNS

Whether consumers want—or need—such a luxury also is a concern for at least one consumer group. The United States Public Interest Research Group has been following developments in computer banking, including the use of ALMs, according to the group's consumer research director, Janice Shields. ALM technology, Shields says, sends up a red flag for several reasons.

First, the group questions the "numerical formula" ALMs use to make decisions about who qualifies for a loan. The applicant doesn't have the opportunity to explain additional resources, such as the possibility of family members as cosigners. "The formula may not be adequate or applicable for everyone," says Shields. "The applicant can't explain family relationships."

And then there are questions about how the ALM handles credit histories. In some cases, applicants can be denied a loan because of errors in data used to scan credit history. By working with a loan officer, the applicant can discover credit errors and explain past credit problems. On the other hand, Shields says her research shows that those typically drawn to the use of ALMs are people living paycheck to paycheck. "This is one more case where they're [financial institutions] making it easier for someone to take on more debt," Shields says.

Carolina First spokesperson Mary Gentry acknowledges the concerns associated with granting ALM loans to individuals who have experienced chronic financial problems. However, she notes, any bank customer is likely to find ALM loans attractive. "People want to use it because it's immediate, convenient, and provides an alternative when no access to credit card lines is available," Gentry says.

Even if the criteria and credit history kinks in the system are worked out, privacy and security issues remain paramount. Shields says consumers need to be careful about giving personal data to computers at a time when computer hacking is commonplace. A big question, says Shields, is "who has access to this personal, private information that the consumers provide via the machines?"

OUTLOOK

Despite concerns, enthusiasm for ALM technology is growing, although how quickly the technology will be embraced remains to be seen.

A recent report by Donaldson, Lufkin & Jenrette of New York indicates long-term success for Affinity. "From a technology standpoint, I think [Affinity] will be an effective and widely used technology," says senior analyst Thomas Brown. "It is consistent with the change in our country. Customers want increased convenience and services."

Vernon Plack, financial institutions analyst with Scott & Stringfellow Inc. of Richmond, notes that ALM technology in theory "sounds great," but there may not be a big need for it right now. And, analysts agree, banks are traditionally slower to implement new technology until it has been tried successfully. For Affinity, the acceptance cycle for the new technology is likely to take longer than expected, says Stephen Krug, an associate

PART III Financial Institutions

analyst with Donaldson, Lufkin & Jenrette. "It's a matter of riding out the wave," says Krug.

> **QUESTIONS**
>
> 1. How do people use ALMs to obtain loans? What are the size and other characteristics of a typical ALM loan?
>
> 2. What advantages do ALMs offer banks and their customers? Are there any disadvantages?
>
> 3. Explain the development and spread of ALM technology using Mishkin's model of financial innovation.

READING 14

Efficiency of U.S. Banking Firms—An Overview

Simon Kwan

INTRODUCTION

Bank managers, policymakers, and bank investors all are concerned with how efficiently a bank uses its labor and capital inputs to produce the cluster of financial products. Is a bank using the right level and mix of inputs? Is it producing the right output mix? Is it operating at the optimal scale? Since a bank's profitability is directly driven by its operating efficiency, the bank manager who is hired by the shareholders to maximize their wealth should be concerned with these questions; an under-performing bank would be penalized by the capital market by depressing its share price and subjecting it to takeover. Banking supervisors also pay attention to operating efficiency because a bank's safety and soundness is dependent on the quality of its management. In fact, managerial quality is one of the five components of the so-called CAMEL (Capital, Assets, Management, Earnings, and Leverage) rating in the bank examination process. In an attempt to explore the economics underlying these questions, economists have applied advance production theory and sophisticated econometric techniques to estimate bank efficiency, and a great deal of progress has been made in the past twenty years. This *Economic Letter* provides an overview of the findings of the research on the efficiency of U.S. banks.

SCALE EFFICIENCY

One dimension of banking efficiency that draws a lot of researchers' attention is scale efficiency, which refers to the relationship between a firm's per unit average production cost and production volume. For example, a firm that increases its production of outputs can see its unit cost of production decline, because the cost of some elements of inputs are fixed, such as administrative and overhead expenses. This is called economies of scale. However, diseconomies of scale also are possible if the average production cost starts to rise with outputs beyond a certain volume of production. Scale diseconomies may arise because it may be more costly to manage a very large firm, or because the management of a very large firm becomes entrenched and therefore concerned more about maximizing

---

Reprinted from Federal Reserve Bank of San Francisco *Economic Letter* No. 97-06, February 28, 1997. The opinions expressed in this article do not necessarily reflect the views of the management of the Federal Reserve Bank of San Francisco, or of the Board of Governors of the Federal Reserve System.

their own welfare than that of shareholders. If the average cost curve is U-shaped—due to economies of scale at a low output level and diseconomies of scale at a high output level—it implies that there is an optimal scale of production at which the per unit average production cost is minimized.

For banking, prior research on scale efficiency found that the average cost curve was a relatively flat U-shape (see the survey by Humphrey 1990). However, the location of the optimal production scale remains unclear. In the U.S., there are a small number of very large banks that operate alongside a large number of smaller banks. The huge disparity in sizes among U.S. banking firms makes it difficult to estimate the average cost curve precisely. Furthermore, in general, the product mix at large banks is very different from the product mix at smaller banks, suggesting that it may not be appropriate to combine large banks with smaller ones when doing cost analysis. Consistent with this, studies that exclude large banks reported that average costs appear to be minimized at about $100 million to $300 million in total assets, while research that focused exclusively on large banks found that their optimal scale seems to be between $2 and $10 billion in total assets.

Recently, a major wave of consolidation has swept through the U.S. banking industry, affecting firms in almost all size classes. With respect to mergers between large institutions, the marriage of Chase Manhattan Corporation and Chemical Banking Corporation created the largest banking company ($297 billion in total assets) in the U.S., while the acquisition of First Interstate Bancorp by Wells Fargo & Company ($108 billion in combined total assets) represented the largest bank merger (in a deal valued at $11.6 billion). In both cases, cost reduction is cited as a very important motivation for the merger. However, if the average cost curve is truly U-shaped, the fact that the already very large banks were getting much larger would be inconsistent with cost minimization.

Apparently, bankers think that the optimal scale is much bigger than prior research suggests. This can be justified by the recent changes in the banking industry. First, the passage of the Riegle-Neal Interstate Banking and Branches Efficiency Act, which permits interstate branching effective 1997, may have changed the underlying production function of banking firms. Since banking firms do not need to set up separately capitalized banks in different states to deliver their financial products, it would be less costly to expand outputs. Second, the rapid change in information technology and the sharp drop in the cost of computers may have shifted the average cost curve. Third, banking firms have successfully cultivated alternative delivery channels for certain financial products, for example, through supermarkets, telephone lines, and the Internet, which may permanently alter the cost of providing certain banking products. As a result of fewer geographic barriers, rapid technological breakthroughs, and advances in distribution systems, it is quite plausible that the optimal scale of production may have increased. Moreover, the largest U.S. banking firm today is still not even in the worldwide top ten largest banks list based on 1995 total assets, suggesting that there may be room for further consolidation among large U.S. banks. Nevertheless, one cannot rule out the alternative hypothesis that entrenched managers use mergers and acquisitions to increase the size of the firm with the objective of enhancing their own welfare.

X-EFFICIENCY

While scale efficiency is about whether a banking firm has the right size, a potentially more important question is whether a firm produces as efficiently as it possibly can, given its size. This question can be answered by measuring X-efficiency, which in technical terms refers to deviations from the cost-efficient frontier that depicts the lowest production cost for a given level of output. X-efficiency stems from technical efficiency, which measures the degree of friction and waste in the production process, and allocative efficiency, which measures whether the right levels of various inputs are used.

A number of studies have investigated the X-efficiency of U.S. banks (see the survey by Berger, Hunter, and Timme 1993). Most of the research done to date focused on the following question: Given the level of outputs and the price of capital, labor, and funds faced by the bank, does the bank minimize its total operating costs? If the observed total operating cost is higher than the minimized cost, the difference represents the bank's X-efficiency.

Researchers find that X-efficiency appears to vary substantially across banks. On average, the deviation from the minimum cost is found to be quite large, in the neighborhood of 20 to 25 percent of total costs, and it seems to dominate the effect of scale inefficiency. The findings suggest that for an average bank, the biggest room for efficiency gains lies in improving its operating efficiency, that is, doing things right, rather than on scale efficiency, that is, being the right size.

After identifying X-efficiency in banking firms, it is important to find out what may cause this type of inefficiency. While we do not have a conclusive answer to this question, preliminary evidence suggests that X-efficiency seems to be related to at least three things. First is size; on average, operating costs of larger banks are found to be closer to their minimum cost curve than those of smaller banks to their respective cost frontier. To the extent that large banks, which operate in metropolitan markets, face stronger competition than smaller banks, many of which operate in suburban or rural areas, it is not surprising that competition forces large banks to operate more efficiently. Second is risk-taking; inefficient firms are found to take on a higher level of risk. It is possible that managers of inefficient banks make loans with higher yields and higher risks in an attempt to compensate for their operating inefficiency. Furthermore, an inefficient firm, which has lower market valuation, has less to lose in taking a risky gamble than an efficient firm. Third is financial condition; banking firms with relatively more problem loans (that is, past due loans and non-accrual loans), tend to be less efficient than those with fewer problem loans. The correlation between poor asset quality and inefficiency may be an indication of poor management, or a direct consequence of the tendency of inefficient firms to make risky loans; alternatively, it may reflect the high operating cost of managing problem loans.

However, several caveats are in order. First, there are a number of methods of estimating X-efficiency, and the results are quite sensitive to the choice of method. Not only is the level of X-efficiency found to vary from method to method, but the ranking of X-efficiency of individual banks also is found to be somewhat inconsistent across methods. Second, by focusing solely on the cost function, researchers implicitly assumed that banking products are homogeneous. Since the cost function approach fails to trade off between product quality and production cost, a banking product that has more value-added to the customer but is more costly to produce will be treated as cost inefficient under this approach, despite the fact that a customer may be willing to pay more for a high quality product. Whereas the cost function approach is acceptable for analyzing commodity-type banking products, it is unacceptable when product differentiation is significant. To allow for variations in product quality, researchers have started to move away from the cost function approach and towards the revenue or profit function approach. Third, X-efficiency analyses were done in a static setting. They failed to capture changes in the regulatory environment and in the marketplace, which may have altered the underlying production process and the associated cost function. Based on these considerations, the research finding in X-efficiency studies should be interpreted with caution. These results are best treated as indicative rather than definitive, assisting decisionmakers in identifying potential problems instead of rendering judgment.

CONCLUSION

In the U.S. banking industry, researchers detected economies of scale, though the optimal scale appears to differ for large banks and smaller banks due to their very different product mix. They also suggest that the optimal size of large banks is well below that of today's megabanks. However, that finding may be obsolete given the dynamics of the banking industry. With significant regulatory changes, rapid technological breakthroughs, and constant product innovations, the right size for yesterday's environment may no longer be optimal today, much less for the future. More importantly, researchers find that X-efficiencies, that is, deviations from the cost-efficient frontier, on average are large and dominate scale efficiency. Hence, it may be more fruitful to achieve efficiency gains by doing things right rather than by searching for the right scale.

READING 14   Efficiency of U.S. Banking Firms—An Overview

REFERENCES

Berger, A. N., W. C. Hunter, and S. G. Timme. 1993. "The Efficiency of Financial Institutions: A Review and Preview of Research Past, Present, and Future." *Journal of Banking and Finance* 17, pp. 221-249.

Humphrey, D.B. 1990. "Why Do Estimates of Bank Scale Economies Differ?" Federal Reserve Bank of Richmond *Economic Review* 76 (Sept./Oct.), pp. 38-50. The opinions expressed in this article do not necessarily reflect the views of the management of the Federal Reserve Bank of San Francisco, or of the Board of Governors of the Federal Reserve System.

QUESTIONS

1. Why is bank efficiency important to bank managers, investors, and policymakers?

2. What is *scale efficiency*? What do past studies of scale efficiency indicate about optimal banking firm asset size?

3. Are "megabanks" too big? Explain.

4. How does *X-efficiency* differ from scale efficiency? Based on this concept, what factors appear to be important influences on banking *in*efficiency?

READING 15

Small Business Lending and Bank Consolidation: Is There Cause for Concern?

Philip E. Strahan and James Weston

In May 1995, Texas became the first state to opt out of the interstate branching provision of the Riegle-Neal Interstate Banking and Branching Act of 1994. In Texas, foes of interstate banking and branching voiced a concern over how consolidation might affect small business lending and community development. If small banks are increasingly acquired by large, superregional banking companies, they argued, consolidation will have a negative effect on the availability of credit to small businesses and communities. Proponents countered by arguing that despite consolidation, the need for independent community banks will remain, leaving an important niche for the small banker to fill.

Who's right? The answer's implications go well beyond the welfare of one state. We can probably anticipate further consolidation in the banking system nationwide as bank holding companies (BHCs) continue to purchase banks and as banks themselves continue to merge. In this edition of *Current Issues*, we use recent information to analyze the likely consequence of that consolidation for small business lending. The preponderance of our evidence suggests that consolidation will not adversely affect credit availability to small businesses and communities.

LENDING PATTERNS OF SMALL AND LARGE BANKS

Small banks are a primary source of credit for small businesses. Unlike large, publicly traded firms, which have access to capital markets, small businesses rely heavily on banks.[1] These businesses often concentrate their borrowing at institutions with which they have long-term relationships—relationships that prove mutually beneficial: They enable banks to collect information about the borrower's ability to repay, reducing the cost of providing credit. Borrowers, in turn, enjoy better access to credit and lower borrowing costs. Small banks make more of these "relationship" loans than do large banks, which are more likely to make generic loans based on financial ratios and credit checks.[2]

Large banks may have an advantage in lending to large businesses because they typically offer a wider array of the products

Reprinted from Federal Reserve Bank of New York *Current Issues in Economics and Finance*, March 1996.

READING 15 Small Business Lending and Bank Consolidation

and services demanded by their large clients. For instance, large banks can provide more transaction-based services than small banks can. Moreover, large banks are less likely to be constrained by regulatory lending limits.[3] Even absent explicit lending limits, small banks generally avoid very large loans in order to preserve adequate diversification.

With these considerations in mind, we ask whether consolidation in banking will reduce relationship lending and therefore small business lending. According to one view, relationship loans require tighter control and oversight over loan officers by senior management than do loans based on simple ratio analyses or credit scoring models. As a consequence, the complexity of large banks makes relationship loans infeasible (or at least more difficult). Since senior management of small banks can monitor lending decisions closely, they can authorize more non-standard, relationship loans. Therefore, critics of interstate banking and consolidation argue, as small banks disappear no one will be willing to engage in relationship loans upon which small businesses depend.

Others argue, however, that relationship lending will survive bank consolidation because it will continue to be profitable. As large banks acquire smaller banks, they will have a financial incentive to continue to make relationship loans to small businesses. Moreover, if small banks have a cost advantage in providing relationship loans to small businesses, consolidation will *not* lead to the disappearance of small banks; they will continue to play a vital role at the small end of the lending market.

A PROFILE OF SMALL BUSINESS LENDING

In June 1993, the federal banking agencies began collecting data on small business loans. This information appears annually in the June *Report of Condition and Income* (the Call Report) filed by all commercial banks. The data are collected for three size categories of loans: those whose "original amounts" are $100,000 or less, $100,001 to $250,000, and $250,001 to $1,000,000. For our analysis, we refer to all commercial and industrial (C&I) loans under $1 million as small business loans. The loan's original amount provides a measure of the total amount of credit extended to the borrower and therefore provides a good proxy for borrower size.[4]

The Call Report data for 1995 enable us to compare the recent small business lending activity of large and small banks.[5] Large banks make a substantial contribution—35 percent—to the market for loans to small businesses, although this share falls well below their 82 percent share of the large C&I loan market (Table 1, panel A).[6] In contrast, small banks focus primarily on small business lending. Banks with assets under $300 million hold less than 2 percent of the large C&I loan market but hold about 35 percent of the small business loan market.

Despite their size difference, small banks can accomplish the same volume of small business lending as large banks because they focus almost completely at this end of the market. The smallest banks held almost 97 percent of their total C&I loans in small business loans in 1995 (Table 1, panel B).

PART III Financial Institutions

TABLE 1
PROFILE OF SMALL BUSINESS LENDING BY BANK SIZE

Panel A: Market Shares of C&I Loans[a]

Banks by Asset Size	Small C&I Loans	Large C&I Loans
Less Than $100 million	16.3	0.3
$100 million-$300 million	18.3	1.5
$300 million-$1 billion	13.4	3.7
$1 billion-$5 billion	16.5	12.7
Greater than $5 billion	35.4	81.9
Totals	100.0	100.0

Panel B: Portfolio Shares of Small C&I Loans[b]

Banks by Asset Size	Small C&I Loans/ Total C&I Loans	Small C&I Loans/ Total Assets
Less than $100 million	96.7	8.9
$100 million-$300 million	85.2	8.8
$300 million-$1 billion	63.2	6.9
$1 billion-$5 billion	37.8	4.9
Greater than $5 billion	16.9	2.9

Source: June 1995 *Report of Condition and Income*.
Notes: All Figures are in percent. Data for small C&I loans (those under $1 million) are based on the original amounts. For large C&I loans, the figures are computed by subtracting the original amount for small C&I loans from the book value of all C&I loans.
[a] Market shares equal the sum of all small (large) C&I loans held by banks in that size category divided by the sum of all small (large) C&I loans made by all banks.
[b] Portfolio shares equal the sum of all small C&I loans held by banks in that size category divided by all C&I loans (assets) held by banks in that size category. These figures are equivalent to weighted averages of the small C&I loans to total C&I loans (assets) ratio, weighted by total C&I loans (assets).

This portfolio share declines as bank size increases; the largest banks devote only about 17 percent of total C&I lending to small businesses. The share of total assets devoted to small business loans also falls as bank size increases.[7]

These portfolio shares seem to be the main force propelling the foes of interstate banking and bank consolidation. If the portfolio shares remain fixed as the size distribution evolves toward one dominated by large banks, the total availability of small business loans will indeed fall. To see why, imagine shifting $100 million in banking assets from the smallest to the largest end of the size distribution (which would occur if a $10 billion bank bought a $100 million bank). Taking $100 million in assets away from the smallest banks would lower small business lending by $8.9 million (8.9 percent times $100 million). Adding that $100 million to the largest end of the size distribution would raise small business lending by only $2.9 million. The net loss would be $6 million.[8]

Note, however, that this experiment does not take into account the dynamic responses of the marketplace to changes in loan availability. Two types of adjustments are likely. First, if small businesses are not being served because small banks have been acquired, large banks will have a strong profit motive to expand their small business lending. Second, if it turns out that small banks have a cost advantage in providing credit to small businesses (because of their ability to originate and monitor relationship loans), small banking will remain profitable. If this is the case, we should expect that a significant number of small banks will remain viable in the long run and that surviving small banks will increase their emphasis on small business lending. In fact, we see some evidence of this kind of dynamic market adjustment. Between 1993 and 1995, a period of rapid consolidation, the share of total assets invested in small business loans rose by about 5 percent for banks with assets under $100 million (from 8.5 percent to 8.9 percent of total assets).

BANK CONSOLIDATION AND SMALL BUSINESS LENDING

To determine whether consolidation will reduce the availability of small business lending, we consider whether the size and location of bank holding companies affect the propensity of their subsidiary banks to hold small business loans. We also consider whether bank mergers have reduced small business lending.

BHC Ownership and Small Business Lending

The acquisition of banks by large BHCs may reduce small business lending, at least when small banks are acquired by large BHCs. As Table 2 shows, banks with under $1 billion in assets hold fewer small business loans when owned by large BHCs. For instance, the typical independent bank with assets under $100 million holds 8.7 percent of assets in small business loans, compared with only 6.2 percent for the typical small bank owned by a large BHC. By contrast, banks with more than $1 billion in assets hold more small business loans when owned by large BHCs.[9]

Whether a bank is owned by an out-of-state or an in-state BHC does not substantially affect the extent of its small business lending. In four of the five bank asset size categories, banks owned by out-of-state BHCs held fewer

TABLE 2
SMALL BUSINESS LOANS AS A PERCENTAGE OF TOTAL ASSETS BY BHC AFFILIATION AND LOCATION

Banks by Asset Size	Independent Banks and Banks Owned by Small BHCs	Banks Owned by Large BHCs	Difference (T-statistic)	Banks Owned by Large BHCs		
				Banks Owned by In-State BHCs	Banks Owned by Out-of-State BHCs	Difference (T-statistic)
Less than $100 million	8.66	6.15	2.52 (9.79)[a]	6.38	5.83	0.55 (1.11)
$100 million-$300 million	9.27	7.38	1.89 (6.97)[a]	7.20	7.62	-0.42 (-0.91)
$300 million-$1 billion	7.94	6.25	1.69 (4.44)[a]	6.50	5.96	0.53 (1.02)
$1 billion-$5 billion	3.64	5.61	-1.96 (-2.88)[a]	5.97	5.15	0.82 (1.64)
Greater than $5 billion	2.89	3.51	-0.62 (-0.68)	3.78	3.12	0.67 (1.62)

Source: June 1995 *Report of Condition and Income*.
Notes: This table presents the simple (unweighted) average share of total assets invested in small business loans for banks in different size categories. All figures are in percent. Data for small business loans (those under $1 million) are based on the original amounts for C&I loans. T-statistics in columns 3 and 6 test the null hypothesis that the means in each of the preceding two columns are equal. Large BHCs are defined as bank holding companies with assets greater than $1 billion.
[a] Statistically significant at the 1 percent level.

small business loans. Nevertheless, the difference between the average ratio of small business loans to assets for the two groups of banks is not statistically significant in any of those cases. Overall, it appears that small banks may make fewer small business loans when owned by large banking companies, although the location of the owner relative to the bank seems to have little bearing on small business lending.[10]

Bank Mergers and Small Business Lending

To analyze the effects of consolidation through mergers, we construct a sample of 180 bank mergers that occurred between June 1993 and June 1994. Since only the newly merged bank is observable in 1994 or 1995, we construct a pro forma bank for each merger by summing the assets and liabilities of the acquiring and target banks in June 1993 (before the merger actually occurred). This pro forma bank provides the benchmark to which we compare the percentage of total assets devoted to small business lending before and after the merger.[11] A simple before-and-after comparison of small business lending, however, could be misleading because aggregate trends in demand for credit by small borrowers will affect changes in the ratio of small business loans to assets for all banks, apart from the effects of mergers. To isolate these effects, we compare changes in this ratio for the merger sample with a sample of nonmerged banks (the control group). For each merger, we randomly select one nonmerging bank with the same total assets as the pro forma bank in 1993.

Overall Changes After Mergers. The top panel of Table 3 compares the average change in the ratio of small business loans to assets at banks involved in a merger between June 1993 and June 1994 with the change for the control group. The changes for banks involved in mergers represent the average difference between the pro forma bank's ratio of small business loans to assets in June 1993 and the newly merged bank's actual ratio of small business loans to assets in June 1995.[12] The ratio of small business loans to assets for the pro forma bank in 1993 is a measure of the expected amount of small business lending for the newly merged bank *provided that no change occurs in the target bank's propensity to engage in small business lending*. If the new management of the target bank reduces its small business lending following the merger, the ratio of small business loans to assets will decline from 1993 to 1995; if management increases small business lending, we should see an increase in that ratio.

As shown, the average ratio of small business loans to assets rose from 8.3 percent in June 1993 for the pro forma banks to 8.5 percent in June 1995 for the newly merged banks. By contrast, the average ratio *fell* from 7.4 percent to 6.9 percent for banks not involved in mergers.[13]

The same test was performed using three different size classifications for the pro forma bank. Here we found a significant increase in small business lending for small mergers, and no significant difference between the newly merged banks and the control group for medium-size and large mergers.[14]

Changes By Merger Type. Although our evidence suggests that bank mergers do not

TABLE 3
BANK MERGERS AND SMALL BUSINESS LENDING

Panel A: Comparison of Small-Loans-to-Assets Ratio for Newly Merged Banks and Control Group by Size of Pro Forma Bank

Pro Forma Bank Asset Size	Number of Banks	1993 Small-Loans-to-Assets		1995 Small-Loans-to-Assets		1993-95 Change in Small-Loans-to-Assets		T-statistic
		Pro Forma Banks	Control Banks	Merged Banks	Control Banks	Merged Banks	Control Banks	
Less than $300 million	102	9.12	8.15	10.12	8.20	1.00	0.05	1.90[a]
$300 million–$1 billion	39	9.10	8.03	7.64	6.66	-1.46	-1.38	-0.10
Greater than $1 billion	39	5.25	4.70	5.13	3.19	-0.11	-0.78	2.23
All Banks	180	8.28	7.38	8.50	6.94	0.22	-0.44	1.82[a]

Panel B: Changes in Small-Loans-to-Assets Ratio for Newly Merged Banks Relative to Control Group by Size of Target and Acquiring Banks

Target Bank	Acquiring Bank is Small	Acquiring Bank is Medium-Size	Acquiring Bank is Large
Small	2.17 (2.17)[a] [53]	0.06 (0.09) [52]	-0.13 (-0.33) [14]
Medium-Size	NA	-0.50 (-0.29) [15]	1.09 (0.85) [7]

Source: June 1993-95 *Reports of Condition and Income*.

Notes: All figures are in percent. Differences are percentage point differences (not percentage changes). In panel B, medium-size banks have total assets between $100 million and $1 billion, and large banks have assets above $1 billion. The average percentage point change in the ratio of small business loans to assets relative to the control group is presented first; the T-statistic testing that the average change equals zero appears in parentheses and the number of observations appears in brackets.

[a] Statistically significant at the 10 percent level.

reduce small business lending on average, certain types of mergers may work to reduce banks' propensity to serve the credit needs of small businesses. For instance, when two medium-size banks combine to form one large bank, the new bank may be so large and complex that relationship loans become more costly. The new, large bank may therefore provide less credit to small borrowers than the two medium-size banks did.

The bottom panel of Table 3 reports changes in the ratio of small business loans to assets (relative to the control group) for our sample of mergers broken down by the size of the target and acquiring banks.[15] For instance, the first column presents changes in the ratio of small business loans to assets from 1993 (pro forma) to 1995 when the acquiring bank is small. When two small banks merge, we find significant increases in small business lending; otherwise, we find no significant change.[16]

Overall, our research provides no support for the idea that consolidation from bank mergers reduces the portfolio share of a bank's small business loans. If anything, mergers seem to *increase* banks' propensity to hold these loans. Even when a marked change in the size of the target bank occurs post-merger (for example, when a large bank buys a small one or when two medium-size banks merge), we see no significant decline in the share of resources devoted to small business lending.

CONCLUSIONS

The availability of small business loans has recently received considerable attention in political and academic spheres. The new Call Report data show that small businesses receive credit from banks of all sizes. Both large and small banks are responsible for small business lending, although small banks' C&I lending is almost completely devoted to small businesses.

Looking ahead, we can probably anticipate further consolidation in the banking industry. Can we conclude that a decline in the presence of independently owned, small banks would have an adverse impact on the credit available to small businesses? The preponderance of our evidence suggests no. Although small banks hold more small business loans as a percentage of total assets than do large banks, the largest banks currently hold more than one-third of all small business loans. Evidently, some large banks find small business lending profitable. We also find that the share of small banks' assets invested in small business loans has risen over the past two years, at least partially offsetting the decline in the number of small banks.

We do find, however, that small banks owned by large banking companies hold fewer small business loans than do independent banks. This may mean that the costs of providing credit to small borrowers are lowest in small banking companies. If so, we would expect at least some small banking companies to survive the wave of consolidation and continue to serve the credit needs of small businesses. Finally, banks involved in mergers, on average, hold more small business loans two years after the merger.

PART III Financial Institutions

Since small business loan data only became available in June 1993, this merger analysis is necessarily limited. As more data become available, the long-run effects of bank mergers on small business loans will likely become clearer.

ENDNOTES

1. According to the 1993 National Survey of Small Business Finances, commercial banks are the most important single source of credit to small firms (Cole and Wolken 1995).
2. Following Berger and Udell (1996), we use the term relationship loan to refer to loans that require borrowers to have established a relationship with the lender before receiving credit. By contrast, standard loans do not require such a relationship. Non-relationship borrowers can be approved if they pass a formal set of criteria based, for instance, on financial ratios, appraisals, and credit scores. See Peterson and Rajan (1994) for evidence on the importance of relationship lending. See Berger and Udell (1996) for evidence that small banks engage in more relationship lending than do large banks.
3. Nationally chartered banks are restricted from making loans greater than 15 percent of capital to a single borrower. State-chartered banks face similar lending limits, although these vary somewhat based on state regulations (Spong 1994).
4. We define small business loans by the loan's original amount, rather than by actual borrower size, since this is how the data are collected. The original amount is defined under the following guidelines: For loans drawn under commitment, the original amount is the size of the line of credit or loan commitment when the line of credit or loan commitment was most recently approved, extended, or renewed before the report date. If the amount outstanding as of the report date exceeds this size, however, the original amount is the amount currently outstanding on the report date. For loan participations and syndications, the original amount is the entire amount of credit originated by the lead lender. For all other loans, the original amount is the total amount of the loan at origination or the amount outstanding as of the report date, whichever is larger.
5. The figures reported for June 1995 in Table 1 are representative of those that prevailed in June 1993 and June 1994.
6. The original amounts for large C&I loans (that is, loans greater than $1 million) are not collected in the June *Report of Condition and Income*. The figures in Tables 1-3 using large C&I loans are computed by subtracting the original amount of small C&I loans from the book value of all C&I loans. Moreover, we do not have original amounts for banks that report that "all or substantially all" of their loans are below $100,000. For these banks, we use the book value of their C&I loans and assume that 100 percent of these loans are small.
7. Levonian and Soller (1996) also find that small banks concentrate on small business lending but large banks hold a significant share of the small business loan market.
8. Berger, Kashyap, and Scalise (1995) simulate the impact of future consolidation on small business lending holding bank portfolio shares constant. They find a large decline in small business lending, but this simulation experiment does not account for the dynamic market adjustments described in the text.
9. Keeton (1995) finds that multi-office banking companies hold fewer small business loans than single-office banking companies.
10. Whalen (1995) also finds no adverse effects of out-of-state ownership on small business lending by banks in Illinois, Kentucky, and Montana.
11. We construct a sample of 180 mergers completed between June 1993 and June 1994 from the Federal Reserve System's National Information Center transformation table (a summary of structural changes in the banking industry). We exclude mergers of banks held by the same BHC.
12. We consider the two-year change to allow enough time for significant changes to have been made in the new, merged bank's focus on small business lending. We can look only at two-year changes because we only have small business loan

data available in 1993, 1994, and 1995. Note that the amount of time that has passed from the time of the merger to June 1995 can range from a maximum of two years (if the merger occurred on June 30, 1993) to a minimum of one year (if the merger occurred on June 30, 1994).

13. Peek and Rosengren (1996), however, find that small lending falls following mergers, based on a small sample of mergers that occurred in New England during 1993-94. They do not compare the change in small business lending with a control group, nor do they present statistical tests of their findings.

14. We also compared the average change in the ratio of small business loans to assets for the merger sample with a second control group of banks that began the period with similar assets and grew at roughly the same rate over the next two years. We compared the behavior of the merged banks with this second control group because the typical bank involved in a merger may also be a rapidly growing bank. If rapidly growing banks differ systematically from other banks, the comparison of the merged banks with the control group in Table 3 may be misleading. After controlling for asset growth following the merger, however, we found even stronger evidence that mergers increase small business lending.

15. Note that Table 3, panel B, includes only mergers in which the acquiring bank merged with a single target bank during the 1993-94 period.

16. The results in Table 3 were also computed using $300 million in assets as the cutoff for the definition of a small bank. These results are almost identical to those presented in Table 3.

REFERENCES

Berger, Allen N., and Gregory Udell. 1996. "Universal Banking and the Future of Small Business Lending." In Anthony Saunders and Ingo Walter, eds., *Universal Banking: Financial System Design Reconsidered*. Burr Ridge, Illinois: Irwin Publishing (forthcoming).

Berger, Allen N., Anil K. Kashyap, and Joseph M. Scalise. 1995. "The Transformation of the U.S. Banking Industry: What a Long Strange Trip It's Been." *Brookings Papers on Economic Activity* 2.

Cole, Rebel, and John D. Wolken. 1995. "Financial Services Used by Small Businesses: Evidence from the 1993 National Survey of Small Business Finances." *Federal Reserve Bulletin* 81: 629-67.

Keeton, William R. 1995. "Multi-Office Bank Lending to Small Businesses: Some New Evidence." *Federal Reserve Bank of Kansas City Economic Review* 80(2): 45-57.

Levonian, Mark, and Jennifer Soller. 1996. "Small Banks, Small Loans, Small Business." *FRBSF Weekly Letter* no. 96-02.

Peek, Joe, and Eric S. Rosengren. 1996. "Small Business Credit Availability: How Important Is the Size of the Lender?" In Anthony Saunders and Ingo Walter, eds., *Universal Banking: Financial System Design Reconsidered*. Burr Ridge, Illinois: Irwin Publishing (forthcoming).

Petersen, Mitchell A., and Raghuram G. Rajan. 1994. "The Benefits of Lending Relationships: Evidence from the Small Business Data." *Journal of Finance* 49: 3-37.

Spong, Kenneth. 1994. *Banking Regulation: Its Purposes, Implementation and Effects*. Federal Reserve Bank of Kansas City.

Whalen, Gary. 1995. "Out-of-State Holding Company Affiliation and Small Business Lending." Comptroller of the Currency Economic & Policy Analysis Working Paper no. 95-4.

PART III   Financial Institutions

QUESTIONS

1. What is the distinction between a "relationship" loan and a standard or non-relationship one? What size business firms depend most heavily on the former? Why?

2. What are the main opposing views regarding the effect banking consolidation will have on small business lending? What arguments support each view?

3. Large banks devote a smaller share of their assets to small business loans than smaller banks do. Does this imply that consolidation which shifts assets from small to large banks will cause the total amount of small business lending to decline? Why?

4. What tests do Strahan and Weston perform to determine how bank holding company affiliation and location and bank mergers affect small business lending? What do they conclude?

READING 16

Bank Branches in Supermarkets

Lawrence J. Radecki, John Wenninger, and Daniel K. Orlow

Although the largest U.S. commercial banks have enjoyed strong earnings in recent years, they are under considerable pressure to restructure their retail operations. A stagnant deposit base and stiffer competition in the marketplace for financial services have made the overhead costs of an extensive branch network increasingly onerous. To cut costs and remain competitive, these banks are deploying phone centers, introducing the next generation of automated teller machines (ATMs), and offering customers the option to bank at home or the office from a personal computer. These electronic channels for the delivery of banking services are making visits to the branch increasingly unnecessary for routine transactions.

As part of their restructuring efforts, commercial banks are rethinking the concept of a branch office. An alternative to the traditional office is a scaled-down, full-service branch located within a large retail outlet, often called a "supermarket," or "in-store," branch. This new type of office enables banks to improve the efficiency of the branch network and realize savings from their investment in phone centers and ATMs.[1]

According to industry analysts, about 3,500 supermarkets branches are now in operation out of a total of 50,000 commercial bank branch offices.[2] Some of the largest bank holding companies have taken the lead in introducing supermarket branches (see table). Moreover, supermarket branches will become increasingly common in the next two to three years as several large banks carry out their announced plans to open hundreds more such offices.

In this edition of *Current Issues*, we describe the operational and strategic considerations that have prompted banks to use this new branch design, including the potential to reduce costs and expand customer bases. We then review some relevant policy issues that emerge from this new and growing approach to retail banking.[3]

BANKS' COST DISADVANTAGE

Banks' declining role as holders of household savings has resulted in a high cost structure for their branch operations. After rising to a peak of 38 percent at year-end 1974, deposits at banks, thrifts, and credit unions—measured as a share of the household sector's financial wealth—have fallen by a

Reprinted from Federal Reserve Bank of New York *Current Issues in Economics and Finance* 2, no. 13 (December 1996).

PART III Financial Institutions

Leading Banks in Supermarket Branching as of June 30, 1995

Bank Holding Company	Number of Supermarket Branches	Supermarket Branches as a Percentage of the Bank's Total Branches
BankAmerica Corporation	126	6.1
Wells Fargo & Company	88	4.6
Fifth Third Bancorp	82	16.9
BancOne Corporation	71	4.5
NationsBank Corporation	68	3.1
National Commerce Bancorp	47	58.0
Mellon Bank Corporation	35	7.9
National City Corporation	29	3.1
Bank of Tokyo	27	9.5
Zions Bancorp	25	19.1

Source: SNL Branch Migration DataSource, version 1.5.
[a]Includes branches with zero deposits.

little more than half, to 17 percent at year-end 1995 (see chart).

The cost of a typical branch office can be used to illustrate how a static deposit base creates a competitive disadvantage for banks relative to other financial intermediaries. A typical branch has total annual direct expenses on the order of $700,000, of which the largest component is staff compensation (for twelve or so full-time equivalent employees).[4] The cost of the building itself represents the next largest component of these total direct expenses, and the remainder comprises such items as electricity, supplies, and property maintenance. On top of direct expenses are indirect operating expenses, incurred by the head office or other centralized functions for such items as computing, preparation and mailing of monthly statements, and advertising. These indirect expenses are

READING 16 Bank Branches in Supermarkets

Distribution of Total Financial Assets Held by the Household Sector
1952-95

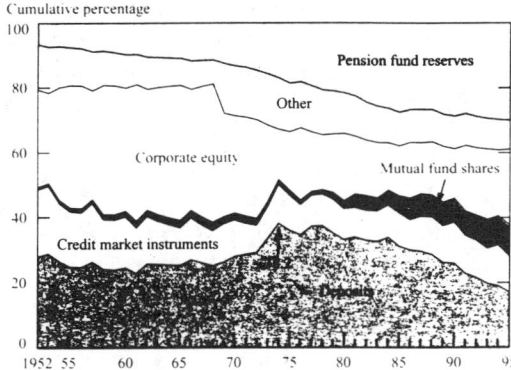

Source: Board of Governors of the Federal Reserve System, Flow of Funds Accounts.

Notes: The chart reports fourth-quarter data for each year. For the percentage share of deposits, the numerator is the sum of demand, savings, and time deposits at commercial banks, thrifts, and credit unions, plus currency in the hands of the household sector; the denominator is the total financial assets of the household sector less equity in unincorporated business and security credit. The household sector includes nonprofit organizations. "Other" includes life insurance reserves, investments in bank personal trusts, equity in unincorporated business and security credit, and miscellaneous assets.

roughly equal to direct expenses, bringing the total annual operating expenses of a branch to $1.4 million.[5]

The dollar volume of deposits at a typical branch is about $50 million, over which the $1.4 million of non-interest expenses must be spread. In percentage terms, annual operating or noninterest expenses therefore equal 2.8 percentage points of deposits. To cover these costs, a margin of 280 basis points must be maintained between interest expense and interest earnings, less noninterest revenue received from account fees and other charges.[6] In contrast, a typical money market mutual fund, a close substitute for a savings deposit, has an expense ratio of around 50 basis points. Thus, a bank's cost disadvantage here is substantial and could be as much as 200 basis points. Similarly, a short-term bond mutual fund, a possible substitute for a time deposit, has an expense ratio of 80 to 100 basis points, but also a higher expected rate of return. Again, a bank appears to be working under a serious cost disadvantage. If a bank had a larger pool of deposits over which to spread its fixed expenses, the cost of the branch system would be proportionately less burdensome.

Banks have tried to reduce their cost disadvantage by identifying and reducing inefficiencies in their retail operations. For instance, branch managers track the volume of teller-window transactions at each office by day of the month, day of the week, and hour of the day. The anticipated volume of customer traffic is used to set schedules for full- and part-time teller staff at each branch location. Retail management indicates, however, that it has squeezed out nearly all the costs it can from the existing system while still providing a high level of customer service.[7]

SUPERMARKET BRANCHES

To cut costs, expand market share, and offer customers greater convenience, banks are testing new designs and locations for their branches. One new type of branch office is a supermarket, or in-store, branch—a full-service office operating in leased space, usually located within a giant supermarket of

50,000 or more square feet attracting 15,000 or more shoppers each week. For the convenience of bank customers, it is open seven days a week and most evenings, like the supermarket.

An in-store branch occupies 400 to 600 square feet, compared with a traditional branch's 5,000. A typical unit is located near the store entrance or checkout lanes and features two teller windows, two stations at a counter to open accounts, one or two ATMs, and direction connections to the phone center. It often has a single office to hold private consultations. Some banks also equip their in-store branches with high-tech devices such as a video phone or an automated loan machine.

Supermarket branches can be built and installed at a comparatively low cost—$200,000 to $300,000, or one-fifth the cost of setting up a conventional branch. About $60,000 to $100,000 of this amount covers construction costs, and the remainder is for equipment, most of which can be removed and reinstalled elsewhere. Hence, only the construction costs represent a sunk expense. The operating expenses are estimated to be $350,000 annually, compared with $700,000 or more for a traditional branch, even though the supermarket branch is open many more hours each week. A supermarket branch can therefore attain the same level of profitability as a conventional branch with slightly less than half the account and deposit volumes.

Selling and Staffing

The foot-traffic passing through the supermarket is a critical element of what makes an in-store branch work. Members of a broad cross-section of households residing within six miles of a large suburban supermarket come in to shop two or three times a week. Frequent shopping trips thus create opportunities for a bank to open accounts with and offer services to individuals who would otherwise not enter one of its traditional branches. Opportunities also arise to sell additional services to existing customers, who typically visit a supermarket more often than a conventional branch. To take full advantage of these opportunities, branch staff will circulate through the store in order to win new accounts and sell banking products.

Banks realize that they must develop a more sales-oriented culture among their staff if the in-store branches are to succeed. To find employees who thrive on customer contact, personnel departments are reportedly adjusting their search procedures and increasingly emphasizing a background in retail sales and customer relations. To sustain the staff's efforts to generate sales and new accounts, management uses compensation packages that include commissions or bonuses linked to individual or branch performance.

In addition to providing more selling opportunities, supermarket branches offer greater operational efficiencies. For example, in-store branches are less expensive to operate in part because they use fewer employees—about six full-time equivalents in contrast to twelve at a conventional branch.

Staff members cover for each other and are largely interchangeable. This flexibility is necessary because at many times only two employees will be working at the branch. Consequently, there is no sharp division of tasks among tellers, platform personnel, and branch management. Moreover, the branch manager typically has less management responsibility and a smaller range of duties than at a traditional branch. As a result, there is essentially one job at a supermarket branch.

Strategic Considerations

The supermarket and the bank see in-store branches as mutually beneficial. The supermarket chain expects increased sales as more of the bank's customers choose to shop at a store housing a branch: the greater the bank's market share in the region served by the supermarket chain, the larger the potential boost to sales. The revenue received from renting space to the bank is usually viewed as somewhat incidental. From its side of the alliance, the bank expects to gain from the supermarket's flow of shoppers. Banks seek out chains that have a high proportion of super-size stores: the larger the store, the greater the flow of potential bank customers.

The supermarket-bank alliances tend to be exclusive within a state or metropolitan area. The supermarket chain prefers a single large bank to put branches in its stores because negotiating with one bank is much simpler than negotiating with several, and the chain can more effectively promote the addition of a single partner's branches at all its locations. The bank, in turn, is looking for a supermarket chain with a presence throughout a marketing area so that it too can more efficiently advertise the combination. As a result, agreements between the largest players in a geographic area—both supermarket chains and banks—are becoming somewhat common.

Supermarket branching can be used by banks as both an offensive and a defensive strategy. On the offensive side, a bank opening in-store branches can enter a market or expand at relatively low cost. In-store branching can also serve as a defensive strategy because only a very limited number of large supermarket chains operate in any one state or metropolitan area. By forming an exclusive arrangement with one chain, a bank may hinder local competitors and potential out-of-state entrants from following the same low-cost strategy for penetrating a market area on a large scale.

Banking Kiosks

In addition to opening full-service, in-store branches, banks are installing limited-service kiosks inside supermarkets and giant discount stores. A kiosk, occupying less than 100 square feet of space, consists of one or two ATMs, a dedicated connection to the phone center, and occasionally some other self-service device, but it has no teller window. During peak shopping hours, the kiosk is staffed by one or two employees, who spend much of their time circulating among shoppers to provide information and assist in the opening of new accounts. Some large retail banks will soon have numerous kiosks in place to supplement their network of full-service, in-store branches. Kiosks are often installed in the smaller supermarkets that do not generate the shopper flows necessary to sustain a true in-store branch. This practice allows both partners to promote the bank's presence, in the form of either a full- or a limited-service location, at every store in the chain.

Kiosks, which go by names such as express centers, express branches, or in-store sales kiosks, are classified by the banking agencies as off-site ATM locations; they are *not* officially considered to be branches. Press reports, however, often refer to them as supermarket branches, failing to distinguish them from full-service locations.

POLICY ISSUES

The advent of supermarket branches raises several issues, some theoretical or long-run in nature, others more practical and immediate. Among the long-run issues is the impact this new type of branch office will have on the economies of scale, scope, and distribution in retail banking. The switch to lower cost, in-store branches raises efficiency, which should benefit bank customers. At the same time, the new type of branch office and the alliances with the largest supermarket chains together imply a shift in a bank's cost structure and possibly an increase in the size of a bank necessary to achieve the greatest cost efficiency now attainable. If such a shift were to occur as supermarket branching gains in popularity, the size distribution of institutions in the banking industry could eventually tilt toward larger institutions.

The shift to supermarket branches also raises a number of more immediate issues, including the effects on competition and the public's access to financial services.

The Effects on Competition.

As part of its assessment of the effects of proposed mergers and acquisitions on competition, the Federal Reserve calculates an index of market concentration (the Herfindahl-Hirschman Index, or HHI) for each geographical market in which the combining banks operate. A higher HHI suggests a less competitive market. The competitive effects of a proposed merger that produces a high value of the HHI or increases the HHI significantly are subject to careful analysis by the Federal Reserve.[8]

In principle, the popularization of supermarket branching should make markets more competitive for any given value of the HHI (Neill and Danforth 1996). The lower cost structure of an in-store branch implies a lower barrier to entry or expansion. The heightened threat of entry or expansion by other banks should encourage the banks already serving a market to behave more competitively.

Banks are, in fact, using the new lower cost branch design to increase the density of their branch networks and expand their geographical reach. For example, People's Bank, most of whose branch offices are located in Fairfield County, Connecticut, has announced plans in alliance with the Stop & Shop chain to open forty-five in-store branches during a two-and-a-half-year period in all parts of the state, including those counties where it does not currently have a presence (People's Bank 1996). This expansion would tend to increase competition both in areas in which People's Bank is already operating, as rival banks strive to maintain market share, and in those areas it is entering, where the HHI should fall as a result of its entry.

Another example of this strategy is BankAmerica's long-distance de novo entry into Chicago. By forming an alliance with Jewel-Osco, the largest supermarket chain in metropolitan Chicago, BankAmerica will open fifty supermarket branches before the year-end 1996 (*American Banker* 1996). The large-scale entry of BankAmerica would also be expected to cause the HHI to fall and the level of competition to rise in the Chicago market.

In the longer run, however, increases in the level of competition in local banking markets brought about by supermarket branching may not be sustained. For example, if the two or three largest banks in a particular area open a large number of supermarket branches and their deposit shares increase proportionately with the expansion of their branch networks, the resulting increase in retail deposit concentration in the local market could eventually lead to a higher HHI and subdued competition.

Moreover, local markets could even become much more concentrated over time. If the new type of branch office proves to be cost-effective and popular with the public, smaller banks may lose deposits and see average deposits per branch fall below their break-even point. The profitability of these smaller banks may decline enough to convince them to exit the industry, a development that could result in more concentrated and less competitive markets. Furthermore, by allying with the two or three dominant supermarket chains in an area, the largest banks could prevent potential competition from expanding through the in-store branch strategy.

Meeting the Public's Need for Banking Services

In evaluating merger and acquisition applications, the Federal Reserve considers how well the public's banking needs are being met. As part of the review process, it seeks comments from residents of the communities that the applying banks serve. In fact, community representatives have opposed several proposed mergers in recent years on the grounds that prospective branch office closings would seriously reduce the availability of banking services to residents of certain low- and moderate-income communities.

The switch to supermarket branches and kiosks is a development that could help maintain or even increase the availability of banking services in these communities. Supermarket branches reduce a bank's fixed and operating costs substantially. A bank may therefore be willing to operate in-store branches and kiosks in those areas that could not sustain a traditional branch. A potential stumbling block, however, is the shortage of large supermarkets in urban areas. Hence, in deciding whether to offer tax incentives, zoning variances, or other inducements to attract large supermarkets to low- and

CONCLUSION

In restructuring their retail operations, many large commercial banks are adopting a promising new design for a branch office: the supermarket, or in-store, branch. By opening scaled-down branches in retail outlets, banks are attempting to reduce costs and afford greater convenience to their household customers. This approach offers potential benefits to both the bank and the supermarket chain in the form of increased customer traffic and joint promotions. At the same time, supermarket branching raises important public policy issues, such as those concerning its effects on competition in local banking markets and on the public's access to banking services.

Moderate-income areas, local governments may also wish to consider the opportunities that these large retail outlets offer to increase the availability of banking services.

ENDNOTES

1. Orlow, Radecki, and Wenninger (1996) discuss in detail the movement to electronic delivery channels for retail banking services and how it is integrated strategically with the introduction of supermarket branches.
2. The data collected by the banking agencies do not distinguish in-store branches from traditional branches.
3. Our discussion of supermarket branches is from the perspective of broad industry trends. Many individual institutions will not, of course, follow the general patterns.
4. Much of the information on in-store branches was obtained at an industry conference on "Advances in Supermarket Branching" held on April 24-26, 1996, in Chicago. In-store branching has also been the subject of numerous articles in the *American Banker* during the past few years.
5. The costs of branch operations cannot be allocated precisely because most of a bank's noninterest expenses are shared by two or more units.
6. Most estimates of the total expenses of branch operations fall in the range of 200 to 300 basis points. The variance seems to be attributable to differences in operational efficiency and cost-accounting methodology. It is unclear whether each estimate captures all direct and indirect expenses attributable to branch operations.
7. The public disclosure of results by line of business in 1995 annual reports indicates that, among the few banks that specifically break them out, branch-based operations are not particularly profitable, in some cases earning a lower return on equity than other major segments such as corporate banking and national consumer finance.
8. The calculation of the HHI involves three steps: obtaining the percentage shares of total deposits in the market held by each bank (or bank holding company), squaring these numbers, and summing the results. For example, a market served by five banks, each with a 20 percent share of total deposits, would have an HHI value of $(5) \times (20)^2$, or 2000. The Federal Reserve reviews the competitive effects of proposed mergers that produce a value of the HHI greater than 1800 or increase the HHI by more than 200 points. See Jayaratne and Hall (1996) for more information on the HHI.

REFERENCES

American Banker, 1996. "B of A Blitz to Put 50 Banks in Chicago Groceries." July 26.

READING 16 Bank Branches in Supermarkets

Jayaratne, Jith, and Christine Hall. 1996. "Consolidation and Competition in Second District Banking Markets." Federal Reserve Bank of New York *Current Issues in Economics and Finance* 2, no. 8 (July).

Neill, Daniel S., and John P. Danforth. 1996. "Bank Merger Impact on Small Business Services Is Changing." *Banking Policy Report* 15, no. 8 (April 15).

Orlow, Daniel K., Lawrence J. Radecki, and John Wenninger. 1996. "Ongoing Restructuring of Retail Banking." Federal Reserve Bank of New York Research Paper no. 9634.

People's Bank. 1996. *1995 Annual Report*.

QUESTIONS

1. Describe the cost advantages for banks of opening and operating in-store branches rather than traditional branches.

2. How do operations at a supermarket branch differ from those at a traditional branch?

3. Supermarket branching will increase competition in banking." Is this statement true, false, or uncertain? Explain.

4. How is supermarket branching likely to affect efficiency and the size distribution of banks? How might it affect the public's access to banking services?

READING 17

Cracking the Glass-Steagall Barriers

Simon Kwan

Since 1933, the Glass-Steagall Act has stood as a wall between commercial banking and investment banking in the U.S. financial system. But the wall is not perfectly solid. The act does allow commercial banks to underwrite and deal in certain classes of securities, the so-called "bank eligible securities." Furthermore, it states only that commercial banks cannot be affiliated with any organization that is engaged *principally* in underwriting and dealing in securities, without giving a clear indication of the degree of integration that would be permissible. As a result, commercial banking organizations have made inroads into investment banking via their so-called "Section 20 subsidiaries," which are bank holding company subsidiaries authorized by the Federal Reserve to engage in a limited amount of bank-ineligible securities activities. In this *Economic Letter*, I discuss the creation of Section 20 subsidiaries, their economic role in the financial markets, and the latest developments and future outlook for banking organizations' securities activities.

CREATION OF SECTION 20 SUBSIDIARIES

The provisions of the Glass-Steagall Act that separated commercial banking from investment banking are in Sections 16, 20, 21, and 32 of the Act. Section 16 bars national banks from investing in shares of stocks, limits them to buying and selling securities as an agent, and prohibits them from underwriting and dealing in securities. Section 20 prohibits Federal Reserve member banks from being affiliated with any organization that is "engaged principally" in underwriting or dealing in securities. Section 21 makes it unlawful for securities firms to accept deposits. Section 32 prohibits officer, director, or employee interlocks between a Federal Reserve member bank and any organization "primarily engaged" in underwriting or dealing in securities.

Certain securities are exempted from the act. They include municipal general obligation bonds, U.S. government bonds, private placement of commercial paper, and real estate bonds, which collectively are referred to as bank eligible securities. All other securities

Reprinted from Federal Reserve Bank of San Francisco *Economic Letter*, No. 97-08, March 21, 1997. The opinions expressed in this article do not necessarily reflect the views of the management of the Federal Reserve Bank of San Francisco, or of the Board of Governors of the Federal Reserve System.

are deemed "bank ineligible." More importantly, since the terms "engaged principally" and "primarily engaged" were not defined in the Act, both the courts and the regulators have had to determine the meaning of these terms in enforcing the law.

In 1986, the Federal Reserve made a new ruling on Section 20 of the Act. It allowed securities subsidiaries of bank holding companies to underwrite and deal in certain bank ineligible securities for the first time. To comply with the Glass-Steagall concept of not "engaging primarily" in ineligible securities, the initial limits on revenues from these activities were set at no more than 5% of the subsidiary's total gross revenues on an eight-quarter moving average basis. The securities affiliates established under this authorization are commonly referred to as Section 20 subsidiaries.

On several occasions, the Fed has expanded the securities power of Section 20 subsidiaries, including enlarging the set of permissible bank ineligible securities, increasing the revenue limit on ineligible securities activities, and allowing an alternative method to calculate ineligible revenues. Today, the classes of ineligible securities that are permissible in Section 20 affiliates include corporate debt and equity, commercial paper, municipal revenue bonds, mortgage-backed securities, and asset-backed securities. The ineligible revenue limit was raised to 10% in 1989 and further increased to 25% recently. Furthermore, Section 20 subsidiaries have been given the option to index the revenue test for interest rate changes.

In requiring all ineligible securities activities to be conducted in a subsidiary of the holding company that is separate from the commercial bank, the Fed also erected a number of "firewalls" between the securities subsidiary and the bank owned by the same holding company. For example, a bank may not make loans to securities issuers to support or enhance the securities underwritten by its securities affiliate, or to finance the purchase of securities underwritten by its securities affiliate; a bank may not purchase financial assets from, or sell such assets to, its securities affiliate; the securities and bank affiliates may not have common officers, directors, or employees, nor may they cross-market each other's financial services; the securities affiliate may not have full access to customer records of the commercial bank. These firewalls are aimed at preventing conflicts of interest between the securities subsidiary and the commercial bank, the primary concerns that led to the passage of the Glass-Steagall Act in the first place. By restricting transactions, information flows, and shared management between the securities subsidiary and the commercial bank, the firewalls also safeguard the banking system and prevent securities affiliates from tapping the safety net that is available exclusively to commercial banks.

ECONOMIC ROLE OF SECTION 20 SUBSIDIARIES

To date, 40 bank holding companies have Section 20 subsidiaries. Banking organizations have traditionally been major competitors in the underwriting of municipal securities. Once their securities affiliates were allowed to deal in and underwrite bank ineligible securities, a number of Section 20 subsidiaries successfully challenged the corporate underwriting market, despite the limit on ineligible revenues. For example, during the first six months of 1996, two of the top ten underwriters of U.S. corporate debt by dollar volume and two of the top ten underwriters of municipal bonds are affiliated with banking organizations.

Banking organizations have been fairly successful in entering the market for corporate bond-underwriting partly because of their expertise in providing credit services. Both bond-underwriting and loan-making involve credit analysis and pricing. The main difference is that in providing credit, banks hold and fund the loans until they mature, whereas in underwriting, the underwriters hold the bonds for a very short period of time and quickly resell them in the open market. Hence, in order for banks to be successful in underwriting, they must be able to set up their own distribution channel and network of potential buyers. This is exactly what banks have been practicing when they securitize their loans. As banks become more prominent in underwriting corporate securities, the ability to provide both credit and underwriting services within the same organization allows banking firms to offer one-stop shopping in corporate finance. Bank customers may even enjoy lower prices when the efficiency gains from scope economies are passed on to them.

Although banking firms have acquired a significant share of the bond underwriting market, they have not been able to capture

Figure 1
Average Ratio of Ineligible Revenue to Total Revenue of Section 20 Subsidiaries

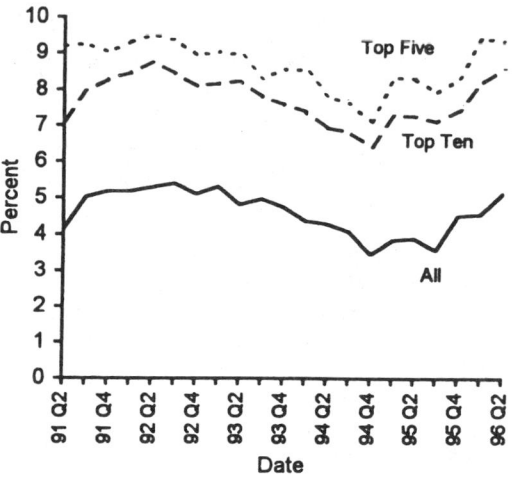

much of the action in equity underwriting, which garners much higher fees than bond underwriting. The infrastructure for underwriting equity securities is not the same as that for underwriting bonds, because it requires different expertise in the areas of research, client contact, and sales support. While building up an equity underwriting department involves substantial investment by the holding company, the most active Section 20 subsidiaries were operating close to the 10% then ineligible revenue limit (see Figure 1), which could have hindered their expansion into equity underwriting.

RECENT DEVELOPMENTS AND FUTURE OUTLOOK

Following the recent failure to repeal the Glass-Steagall Act by the Congress, the Federal Reserve submitted proposals to ease some of the restrictions on Section 20 subsidiaries. Based on the responses, in October 1996, the Fed relaxed three firewalls between securities affiliates and their banks. First, officers and directors may work for both the Section 20 subsidiary and the bank, provided that the directors of one may not comprise more than 49% of the board of the other. Also, the CEO of the bank may not be a director, officer or employee of the securities affiliate, and vice versa. Second, the restrictions on cross-marketing between the bank and its Section 20 subsidiary are repealed. Third, intercompany transactions between a bank and its Section 20 affiliate are expanded to include any assets that have a readily identifiable and publicly available market quotation.

In addition to liberalizing the above restrictions, in December 1996, the Fed lifted the ineligible revenue limit on Section 20 subsidiaries from 10% to 25%. From a capital budgeting perspective, raising the revenue cap can lower the hurdle in recovering the initial investment in the Section 20 subsidiary, thus enticing more banking firms to enter the securities business. By the same token, it also encourages existing securities affiliates to make capital investments in the equity underwriting business. To the extent that the previous 10% revenue cap represented a binding constraint on active Section 20 affiliates and hence limited their ability to expand into equity underwriting, the recent ruling allows banking organizations to launch a serious challenge at equity underwriting. Furthermore, under the 10% revenue cap, banking firms had little choice but to build up their securities affiliates from scratch. Entering the securities business by acquisition was either infeasible due to the cap, or unattractive because of limited growth potential. The boost in permissible ineligible revenues makes the acquisition of an established securities firm a more viable alternative.

In January 1997, the Fed submitted for public comment another proposal that further relaxes the restrictions between Section 20 subsidiaries and their bank affiliates. Since 1987 when the original Section 20 firewalls were prescribed, the Fed implemented Section 23B of the Federal Reserve Act, which requires all inter-affiliate transactions to be on arm's-length terms. Also, Section 23B prohibits representing that a bank is responsible for a Section 20 affiliate's obligations, and prohibits a bank from purchasing certain products from a Section 20 affiliate. Thus, Section 23B makes many of the firewalls specifically designed for the securities affiliates redundant. In addition, as the Fed has gained experience in regulating banks' securities affiliates, it has become apparent that some of the Section 20 firewalls are too conservative and impede their ability to operate efficiently and effectively. Modifying these restrictions would allow the bank and the securities affiliate to maximize synergies, enhance services, and possibly reduce costs.

Nevertheless, important policy questions remain to be addressed. While policymakers seem to be in general agreement that the Glass-Steagall Act should be repealed, there is vigorous debate on how to integrate commercial and investment banking. At issue are: How can the financial services industry be modernized without compromising the safety and soundness of the banking system? What degree of integration among financial services providers, and between financial and non-financial firms, would be socially desirable? How should the new financial services firms be organized and regulated?

CONCLUSION

Although the Glass-Steagall Act, which separates commercial banking from investment banking, has been targeted for repeal for many years, the reform effort has failed each time. However, in enforcing the law, banking regulators have some leeway in providing limited relief for banking firms to engage in ineligible securities activities through their Section 20 subsidiaries. Despite being hamstrung by numerous restrictions, banks' securities affiliates have been able to foster meaningful competition in the somewhat concentrated investment banking market. As financial services customers are benefiting from banking firms' penetration into the securities market, the restrictions on Section 20 securities affiliates are being gradually relaxed. Nevertheless, true financial modernization can be accomplished only by reforming the Glass-Steagall Act, rather than by loosening banking regulations. The success of banks' securities affiliates should be viewed as convincing economic evidence to support such reform.

QUESTIONS

1. What are "Section 20" subsidiaries? What powers do they have?

2. What "firewalls" separate the activities of Section 20 subsidiaries from banks? What is their purpose?

3. What are the similarities and differences between banks' lending and underwriting activities?

4. How has the Fed facilitated banks' increasing expansion into underwriting "ineligible" securities?

PART FOUR

CENTRAL BANKING AND THE CONDUCT OF MONETARY POLICY

Central banks play a major role in determining the money supply. Like central banks elsewhere, the Federal Reserve conducts monetary policy in the midst of on-going public debate over how much independence it should have, what policy objectives it should pursue, and what economic indicators it should target. International considerations also influence a central bank's monetary policy. These issues are treated in the readings for Part Four.

Former Fed Board of Governors Vice Chairman Alan Blinder discusses the Fed's structure, independence, and responsibilities in Reading 18, **"Central Banking in a Democracy."** He argues that the Fed should pursue both low unemployment and low inflation and that its independence is consistent with political democracy, provided that its power is checked by the constraints of openness and credibility and limited to deciding how to reach monetary policy goals rather than selecting which goals to pursue. This reading goes with Chapter 15's coverage of Federal Reserve structure and independence.

Reading 19, **"Why Central Bank Independence Helps to Mitigate Inflationary Bias"** by Timothy Cogley, describes the effects of unexpected inflation on debtors and creditors. Cogley argues that unchecked factional politics leads to high inflation because of debtors' numerical superiority and that having an independent central bank publicly commits monetary authorities to a low-inflation policy. This reading is suggested for use with Chapter 15's discussion of Federal Reserve structure and independence; it could be used also with Chapter 28's treatment of policy credibility.

Arguments supporting central bank independence notwithstanding, the Fed is always criticized by some for being *too* independent. Reading 20, **"Fed's Huge Empire, Set Up Years Ago, Is Costly and Inefficient"** by John R. Wilke, provides a context for these conflicting views by investigating the Fed's changing role in check clearing as it faces competition from private companies. In light of this competition and changes in technology, many observers favor the downsizing of Fed check-clearing operations and even eliminating some Fed branches, moves which the Fed has opposed. This reading provides an excellent supplement to Chapter 15's discussion of the theory of bureaucratic behavior.

The money supply model developed in Chapter 17 helps students identify an assortment of factors which influence the money supply and cause it to change. One of those factors is currency in circulation. Reading 21, **"Where Is All the U.S. Currency Hiding?"** by John B. Carlson and Benjamin D. Keen, focuses on currency held outside the U.S., examining why foreigners hold U.S. dollars and how their holdings affect economic policy.

Reading 22, **"Falling Reserve Balances and the Federal Funds Rate"** by Paul Bennett and Spence Hilton, describes how banks determine and meet their required reserve and clearing balances. It then examines a number of factors, including the growth of sweep accounts, that have caused banks' reserve balances at the Fed to shrink. The authors conclude that while the downward trend in required balances could destabilize the federal funds market, there is little evidence that it has done so. This reading can be used with Chapter 18's discussion of reserve requirements.

"Never Mind Those Ms," Reading 23, argues that a new European central bank should forsake the use of monetary targets in its conduct of monetary policy because evidence suggests that the relationships between monetary aggregates and inflation and income are weak. It is intended for use with Chapter 19's coverage of policy target selection.

Also for use with Chapter 19 is Reading 24, **"Inflation Targeting: A New Framework for Monetary Policy?"** by Ben S. Bernanke and Frederic S. Mishkin. Bernanke and Mishkin survey the use of inflation targeting by a number of central banks, explaining how it works and why it has been adopted.

They advocate its use as a framework for monetary policy because it leads to increased accountability and open discussion of long-run policy consequences. They also discuss issues such as which inflation measure to use and what value of it to target.

The next two readings supplement Chapter 20's discussion of Mexico's peso crisis. In Reading 25, **"A Predictable and Avoidable Mexican Meltdown,"** Joseph A. Whitt, Jr. argues that there were several warning signs of impending financial crisis—large short-term liabilities, an overvalued exchange rate for the peso, and a succession of current account deficits—and sees the crisis as resulting from the Mexican government's failure to take appropriate responses to these signs.

Marco Espinosa and Steven Russell offer an alternative explanation in **"Mexico's Liquidity-Driven Financial Panic,"** Reading 26. They emphasize the short-term nature of Mexico's foreign liabilities, arguing that Mexican financial institutions became vulnerable to huge withdrawals when political shocks diminished foreign investors' confidence. They examine why short-term loans played such a large role in Mexico's foreign borrowing and offer a variety of suggestions for increasing longer-term borrowing.

"The EMU: A Groundbreaking Monetary Experiment" by Fiona Sigalla and David Gould is Reading 27. Sigalla and Gould describe the advantages and disadvantages that are foreseen for Europe with the adoption of the European monetary union and the *euro* currency and the effects that EMU and the euro may have on the dollar and U.S. interest rates. This reading is suggested for use with Chapter 20.

READING 18

Central Banking in a Democracy

Alan S. Blinder

It is a pleasure to welcome all of you this afternoon for this latest program in our series of occasional lectures by distinguished economists on major economic policy issues. Largely for convenience, we hold these programs here at the Richmond Fed, and we are delighted to host them. But let me remind you that they are jointly planned and funded with the three university business schools here in Richmond. I'd like to introduce my colleagues in this endeavor: Dr. Al Altimus, Dean of the Lewis School of Business at Virginia Union University; Dr. Randolph New, Dean of the Robins School of Business at the University of Richmond; and Dr. Howard Tuckman, Dean of the School of Business at Virginia Commonwealth University. It's been a great pleasure working with these folks over the years and I think it's been a very productive collaboration. I would also like to recognize my colleague, Marvin Goodfriend, who is Senior Vice President and Director of Research here at the bank. Marvin is my principal adviser and has played a leading role in planning and putting on these programs in recent years.

It's a particular personal pleasure and an honor to introduce our speaker. Alan Blinder, to put it bluntly but accurately, is one of the most distinguished macroeconomists in the world today. He has done about everything any economist and even a leading economist would do. He earned a Ph.D. from a leading economics department, MIT. He has taught and is teaching at a top university, Princeton, which also happens to be his undergraduate alma mater. He has published numerous scholarly articles in professional journals, a leading economics textbook, and a number of other books, including a little gem on major economic policy issues called Hard Heads, Soft Hearts. Finally, he has served as an economic policymaker at the highest level. Early in his career, in the mid-'70s, he was briefly Deputy Assistant Director of the Congressional Budget Office when it was just getting started. More recently, of course, he was a member of the President's Council of Economic Advisers in the first year and a half of the Clinton Administration. In that capacity, he was a leading economic policy advisor to the Administration. Subsequently he was our colleague at the Fed, serving as

---

Reprinted from Federal Reserve Bank of Richmond *Economic Quarterly*, 82, 4 (Fall 1996): 1-14. Opinions expressed herein are those of the authors and not necessarily those of the Federal Reserve Bank of Richmond or the Federal Reserve System.

PART IV Central Banking and the Conduct of Monetary Policy

Vice Chairman of the Board of Governors of the Federal Reserve System from June 1994 until he departed early this year to return to Princeton, where he is the Gordon S. Rentschler Memorial Professor of Economics. Some of you who have been attending these lectures regularly will remember that we had Alice Rivlin here not too long ago. She has now become the Vice Chairman of the Board of Governors. We wanted to give an equal opportunity to former Vice Chairmen of the Federal Reserve Board.

It's not an idle compliment when I say that as a veteran Fed employee, I greatly enjoyed Alan's all-too-brief tenure at the Fed. Let me share with you a little Fed secret. It's not about interest rates, but about the Federal Open Market Committee, which as you know is the main policymaking body in the Fed. It's a strong and I believe effective committee, but it is not always a terribly lively committee. It was, however, a much livelier committee when Alan was part of it. He challenged us—and also helped us—to confront issues objectively with careful and solid economic analysis. He helped take the edge off the debates that we had in the committee during his tenure with keen and well-timed humor. And he raised the level of discussion in the committee during his tenure. I miss his input very much. It's good to have him back in Richmond. He was here about a year-and-a-half ago and gave a great lecture to the Virginia Bond Club. Please join me in welcoming back Dr. Alan Blinder.

Al, I thank you very much for that fine introduction. I want to talk this afternoon about the role of the Federal Reserve in society in very broad terms and, along the way, to make a few rather more specific points. Then I will be glad to entertain questions about what interest rates will do next week, a subject about which I know nothing! But neither does anyone else, so we are all on an equal footing on the subject.

WHO DOES THE FED SERVE?

Relative to their economic and therefore social importance, central banks must be among the least well understood institutions in the entire world. For example, I have been told that millions of Americans still think that the Federal Reserve System is a system of government-owned forests and wildlife preserves where, presumably, bulls and bears and hawks and doves frolic together in blissful harmony. Having spent 19 months there, I can assure you that that is not the case. The Federal Reserve is an institution that touches almost everyone in America, plus many people outside America, but is itself touched or even seen by relatively few. But its traces are everywhere. Every time you pay or receive paper currency, you are using a "Federal Reserve Note"—a debt obligation of the Fed. Unbeknownst to most of you, your checks are also probably cleared through a regional Federal Reserve Bank; and, if you bank here in Richmond, through this regional Federal Reserve Bank.

When you read in a newspaper ad that a certain bank will pay you 5.7 percent on a certificate of deposit or you hear on television that an automobile company this week is

READING 18 Central Banking in a Democracy

offering 4.9 percent financing, you are seeing tangible evidence of the Fed's regulatory hand at work. Very few people have any idea that it is the Fed that tells banks and auto finance companies how to calculate and advertise those numbers. And even fewer know that the Fed doesn't always get it right!

The interest rates themselves, while set in free markets, are heavily influenced by the Fed's monetary policy. Most Americans these days know that, but few can tell you how that black magic is performed. Even fewer people understand how the Fed's interest rate decisions impact on the overall economy and therefore influence how many people will find jobs, how many will be laid off, how many businesses will succeed, how many will fail. Most economists will attest to the fact that the Fed has far more influence over these matters than the President and Congress.

The Federal Reserve System has a governance structure that is at least odd and perhaps even byzantine. While most countries in the world have one central bank, we have 12—the one here in Richmond and 11 others. These regional Federal Reserve Banks are, in a legal sense, private corporations. They have presidents, in this case Al Broaddus, and boards of directors. They even have shareholders. And while these corporations are extremely profitable—to the tune of over $20 billion a year for the 12 of them together—their shareholders do not reap the benefits. Instead, the Fed's prodigious profits are turned over to the United States Treasury—a very friendly gesture. Atop this organization of 12 putatively private corporations, there sits a seven-member Board of Governors in Washington, whose members are not elected by any of the stockholders, but rather are politically appointed. A very, very curious organizational structure.

So the question arises: Who does the Fed serve? Congress and the President? Most certainly not. Although the Fed is a creature of Congress, and its governors are all presidential appointees, the Fed does not exist to do their bidding. After all, that would make a mockery of the doctrine of central bank independence.

What about the banks? Well to some extent, the answer must be yes. The Fed is a bank for banks. It sells to these banks a variety of services, many of them in direct competition with private suppliers. The Fed is also deeply concerned with the health of the banking and payments system and will, when necessary, take strong steps to safeguard it. However, the Federal Reserve is also the supervisor of thousands of banks, either directly or indirectly, through their bank holding companies. (The Fed supervises all the bank holding companies.) It is a very odd arrangement when you think about it: The Fed is regulating its own customers. There are a lot of businesses in America that would like to regulate their own customers, but very few get to do that. In my view, it is a great mistake for the Federal Reserve to see itself as a service organization for the benefit of banks, however. It is a mistake that people in the Federal Reserve System make occasionally, but fortunately not very often.

Does the Fed serve the financial markets? As the nation's central bank, the Fed is naturally and certainly the ultimate guardian and protector of the entire financial system. In times of acute market distress, the Fed

PART IV Central Banking and the Conduct of Monetary Policy

stands ready to play its classic role as lender of last resort. In more normal times, the Fed worries about such things as the integrity of the markets, financial fragility, speculative bubbles, the value of a dollar, and a host of other things. As I used to say when I was Vice Chairman of the Fed, we get paid, though not very much, to worry about *everything*.

But, in my view, none of these choices—not the President, not the Congress, not banks, not the financial markets—adequately describes the Fed's true constituency. In my view, that constituency can only be the entire nation. While I was on the Federal Reserve Board, I often said that I viewed myself as working for 260 million Americans. Given the central bank's broad reach and pervasive influence, no narrower constituency seemed appropriate. So I want to talk this afternoon about what the Federal Reserve does and should do to serve the national interest.

I think it would surprise most of you to learn that a time-and-motion study of the daily lives of Federal Reserve Governors would reveal that most of their efforts are devoted to bank regulatory issues, broadly defined. Most of this business is routine, extremely familiar, and intensely interesting to the banking industry, and totally unknown, deeply obscure, and generally quite boring to everybody else in society. This is the Federal Reserve that nobody knows. So as not to bore you with these matters, I will skip directly to the Federal Reserve that everybody knows, for nowhere is the Federal Reserve's public service role more visible than in the conduct of monetary policy. It is monetary policy that puts the Fed in the news constantly, and occasionally puts it in the middle of a political maelstrom.

If you don't live your life in the financial world, it is almost impossible to imagine how tightly focused the media and the markets are on the Federal Reserve. Fixated is not too strong a word. "Federal Reserve fetish" has not yet come into current use as a term of art, but I think it describes a lot of the behavior of the financial press and people in the financial markets. To the financial press, a Federal Reserve Governor is more engaging than a movie star. (Think about that one for a while!) When I was Vice Chairman of the Federal Reserve Board, I simply came to expect to find 15, 20, or 25 reporters, plus several TV cameras, waiting any time I made a public appearance—no matter how boring my speech was going to be. (This, as you've noticed, doesn't happen to me anymore.)

Things were not always this way. The story is told that the only way President Kennedy could remember the difference between *monetary* policy and *fiscal* policy was that the letter "M" for monetary was also the first letter of the name of the Fed Chairman at that time, William McChesney Martin. Times have sure changed. I can assure you that President Clinton had no such problem, and neither did President Bush.

THE GOALS OF MONETARY POLICY

Just how is the Fed supposed to serve the national interest with this strange instrument called monetary policy? Under the terms of the Federal Reserve Act, as amended, Congress has directed the Fed to promote "maximum employment, stable prices, and moderate long-term interest rates." That sounds like three goals, but the phrase is often called the Fed's "dual mandate" because the interest rate objective is considered redundant. Price stability will almost certainly bring low long-term interest rates in its wake.

At this point, I need your indulgence for a very brief Economics 101 lecture on how monetary policy affects employment and inflation. It all works roughly as follows.

In the short run, employment is largely determined by total spending in the economy. Interest rates are one, though not the only, important determinant of that spending. So the Federal Reserve, via its effect on market rates of interest, exerts considerable indirect influence over employment and unemployment. But the process takes time. As economists put it, monetary policy works with long lags. While the lagged effects of monetary policy on unemployment are distributed through time—a little now, a little more the next quarter, and so on—it won't hurt you to think of them as taking about a year or two.

Changes in inflation, up and down, are largely determined by the balance between total spending, which is heavily influenced by monetary policy, and the economy's capacity to produce, which is not. If spending falls short of the economy's productive capacity, as happens in a recession, inflation will fall. If spending overshoots capacity, as sometimes happens in a boom, inflation will rise. But the lag from monetary policy decisions to inflation is even longer than the lag from monetary policy to employment because monetary policy first has to affect spending, and then spending must affect inflation. Think of the whole process—from a decision of the Federal Reserve on monetary policy to the reaction of inflation—as taking more than two years.

The central dilemma of monetary policy is this: Unless inflation is below the Federal Reserve's long-run target, which hasn't been true in a very long time, there is a short-run trade-off between the two goals—maximum employment and stable prices—that are set forth in the Federal Reserve Act. To push inflation lower, the Fed must make interest rates high enough to hold total spending below the economy's capacity to produce. But if it does that, the Federal Reserve will be reducing employment, contrary to the dictum to pursue "maximum employment." So monetary policy is forced to strike a delicate balance between the two goals. It is an excruciatingly difficult decision, with a great deal at stake. As a former holder of my former office once quipped, "That's why they pay them the big bucks!"

THE TRADE-OFF AND JACKSON HOLE

Early in my term as Vice Chairman of the Fed, I allegedly stirred up a controversy at a Federal Reserve conference in Jackson Hole, Wyoming, by acknowledging this trade-off explicitly. The context is important to an understanding of what happened, because the subject of that conference was *reducing unemployment*. Being a central banker at the time, I thought it was appropriate for me to address the role of central banks in that task. In my brief remarks I noted that monetary policy actions have a profound effect on employment. I also suggested that a central bank could do its part to achieve low unemployment by pushing the nation's total spending up to the level of capacity, but not further. I observed that the Fed's dual mandate could reasonably be interpreted in precisely that way. So I endorsed that mandate as eminently reasonable instructions for the Congress to have given the Fed, rejecting the alternative of concentrating exclusively on price stability and ignoring unemployment.

Nothing I said at Jackson Hole that day was really controversial, and certainly nothing was original. My conceptualizations of monetary policy's role and of the trade-off between inflation and unemployment were totally conventional. My endorsement of the Fed's dual mandate meant that the Vice Chairman of the Federal Reserve was publicly endorsing the Federal Reserve Act. Now there's news for you! Furthermore, my implied "advice" to central bankers was fully consistent with the practices of central banks all over the world, regardless of what they preach. Indeed, I think a very fair academic critique of my little talk that day would have labeled it banal. Had a student in a course submitted that talk to me as a paper I think I would have said, "There is not an original idea here. You have to be able to do better than this."

About a dozen financial journalists were in the audience that day, and all but one of them heard it that way. But Keith Bradsher of *The New York Times* decided that he had just heard "a big story." I had, he was led to believe by some anonymous whispers, violated the sacred trust of central bankers by saying a few obvious things out loud. He told readers of *The Times* that I had publicly clashed with the Fed Chairman. That's funny; Alan Greenspan was sitting right there as I spoke, and he didn't hear it that way at all. I know, because the two of us had breakfast together the next morning, and he never indicated that I had said anything unusual—which I hadn't. No matter. On a slow news day in August Bradsher's story from Jackson Hole wound up on page one of *The New York Times*.

Media firestorms have a life of their own and, until you have been the subject of one, it is hard to imagine what they are like. For more than a month, a seemingly unending barrage of stories appeared in newspapers, magazines, over the financial wires, and even on TV and radio. I was made "controversial," which is one of the ways they try to stick the knife in you in Washington. The Fed, the public was told, had an outspoken new Vice Chairman who had broken several central banking taboos and publicly tangled with his Chairman. The hysteria reached a crescendo with truly a malicious attack published in both *Newsweek* and *The Washington Post* by Robert Samuelson, who decided—without ever bothering to call me up even once to talk about my views—that I was unfit both morally and intellectually to lead the Fed. One would be okay, but *both* morally and intellectually?

READING 18 Central Banking in a Democracy

Whoever said that serving in the government isn't fun?

I recount this episode not to dredge up the ghosts of irresponsible journalists' pasts, but for three reasons that are closely related to today's topic. The first is to give you a little window into what can happen when a Federal Reserve Governor publicly endorses the view that the Federal Reserve should be serving the national interest rather than just the parochial interest of the bond market. But I must insist that serving the national interest is the *only* correct way to conceptualize the Fed's mission; to me, the issue is not open to either compromise or debate.

The second reason is to tell you that I remain totally unrepentant and never retreated one inch from the position that I enunciated that day—not in public, and not inside the Federal Reserve. What I said that day was true then, and it is true now. There is abundant evidence that Keynes was right back in the '30s when he said that modern industrial economies are not sufficiently self-regulating. They need a little help. Total spending sometimes roars ahead of productive capacity, which leads to accelerating inflation. And total spending sometimes lags behind productive capacity, leading to unemployment.

In principle, either fiscal policy—the government's taxing and spending policy—or monetary policy could serve as the balance wheel, propping up demand when it would otherwise sag and restraining it when it threatens to race ahead too rapidly. In practice, however, monetary policy is the only game in town nowadays. And when I say "in town," I don't mean just in Richmond or just in the United States—I mean all over the industrial world. The reason is the same here and in Europe: The need to reduce large fiscal deficits dictates that budget policy remain a drag on total spending for the foreseeable future, regardless of the state of the macroeconomy. With the fiscal arm of stabilization policy thereby paralyzed, a central bank that decides to concentrate exclusively on price stability is, in effect, throwing in the towel on unemployment.

So, to me, the argument for the Fed's dual mandate is both straightforward and convincing. The central bank exists to serve society. The public cares deeply about fluctuations in the pace of economic activity. And well-executed monetary policy has the power to mitigate fluctuations in employment. As the mathematicians say, "QED." Fortunately, almost all central bankers accept this argument nowadays, notwithstanding a great deal of misleading rhetoric to the contrary.

That leads me straight to the third reason for telling you the Jackson Hole story. As a citizen of a democracy, I have always found it intolerable for the government to deceive the governed. As a public servant, I also found it unconscionable. And I see no reason whatsoever why the central bank should have a special exemption from the requirement to level with the public.

CREDIBILITY

It is sometimes argued, to the contrary, that honest acknowledgment of the trade-off between unemployment and inflation, and of the central bank's concern with each, would rattle the financial markets—which want to believe that the central bank cares only about low inflation. This argument is nonsense. Both market participants and the financial press know the score and are far too sophisticated to be taken in by ritualistic rhetoric. I remember very well a conversation I had with a very smart financial reporter shortly after I left the Fed. He said that he has learned over the years to ignore what the Fed *says* and watch what it *does*. I had to concede that he was right, but it troubled me a great deal that the two would be so different. In my view, they should be a matched pair.

There is much talk at the Federal Reserve, as in the central banks all over the world, about the importance of *credibility*, which, according to the dictionary in my office, is "the ability to have one's statements accepted as factual or one's professed motives accepted as the true ones." Let me read the last phrase again: "one's professed motives accepted as the true ones." Precisely the point! Why is credibility considered so important?

The main reason, in my view, is that a central bank is a repository of enormous power over the economy. And if the central bank is independent, as the Federal Reserve is, this power is virtually unchecked. Such power is a public trust, assigned to the bank by the body politic through its elected representatives. In return, the citizens and their elected representatives have a right to expect—indeed to demand—that the bank's actions match its words. And matching deeds to words is, to me and my dictionary, the hallmark of credibility.

CENTRAL BANK INDEPENDENCE

The Fed's role as the macroeconomic balance wheel is terribly important because it palpably affects people's lives. Stabilization policy is not something abstract; it is about how many jobs there will be, how many businesses will succeed. In my view, it is far and away the most important thing a central bank does for or to its society. And I felt that responsibility keenly every day that I served as Vice Chairman of the Fed, as I know Al Broaddus still does in his role as a member of the Federal Open Market Committee. Society, therefore, has a strong interest in seeing to it that the central bank does its job well. Evidence collected in recent years suggests that making the central bank more independent should help.

Before elaborating on this point, however, I need to define what I mean by an independent central bank—because there is no agreed-upon definition. To me, the term connotes two things.

The first is that the central bank is free to decide *how* to pursue its goals. This freedom does not mean that the Bank gets to select the goals on its own. On the contrary, in a democracy it seems not just appropriate, but virtually obligatory, that the political authorities should set the goals and then instruct—and I use that very advisedly—the central bank to pursue them. If it is to be independent, the bank must have a great deal of discretion over how to use its instruments in pursuit of its assigned objectives. But it does not have to have the authority to set the goals by itself. Indeed, I would argue that giving the bank such authority would be an excessive grant of power to a bunch of unelected technocrats. In a democracy, the elected representatives of the people should make decisions like that. The central bank should then serve the public will.

The second critical aspect of independence, in my view, is that the central bank's decisions cannot be countermanded by any other branch of government, except under extreme circumstances. In our system of government, neither the President nor the Supreme Court can reverse a decision of the Federal Open Market Committee. Congress can, in principle, reverse such a decision, but only if it passes a law that the President will sign (or by overriding a presidential veto). This makes the Fed's decisions, for all practical purposes, immune from reversal; and, indeed, they never have been reversed. Without the immunity, the Fed would not really be independent, for its decisions would stand only as long as they did not displease someone more powerful.

In recent years, considerable empirical evidence has accumulated in support of the idea that macroeconomic performance is superior in countries that have more independent central banks. Researchers here and in other countries have developed several creative ways to measure central bank independence. Such measures include the bank's legal status, the rate of turnover of its leaders, the legal mandate in the bank's charter (for example, whether it is directed to pursue price stability), and answers to a questionnaire about its organizational structure. The clear weight of this evidence, and by now there is a lot of it, is that countries with more independent central banks have enjoyed lower average inflation without suffering lower average growth. This finding is, of course, completely consistent with economists' general view that, while there is a short-run trade-off between inflation and unemployment, there is no long-run trade-off.

These research results on the benefits of central bank independence raise a provocative questions: Why is it that central banks possessing greater independence produce superior macroeconomic results on average? I want to suggest three reasons, all closely related.

First, as I emphasized in my brief Economics 101 lecture a couple of minutes ago, the effects of monetary policy come with long lags. So, to conduct monetary policy well, you must look far in the future and then wait patiently for the results. Farsightedness and patience, I dare say, are not the strong suits of the political process in a democracy. But they are absolutely essential to pursuing a successful monetary policy.

Second, and related to the time-horizon questions, inflation-fighting has the characteristic cost-benefit profile of a long-term investment: You pay the costs of disinflation up front, and you reap the benefits—lower inflation—only gradually through time. So, if politicians were to make monetary policy on a day-to-day basis, they would be sorely tempted to reach for short-term gains at the expense of the future—that is, to inflate too much. Aware of this temptation, many governments wisely depoliticize monetary policy by delegating authority to unelected technocrats with long terms of office, thick insulation from the hurly-burly of politics, and explicit instructions to fight inflation.

Third, and related to this point about technocracy, the conduct of monetary policy is at least somewhat technical. It is a bit like shooting a rocket to the moon, though not nearly as exact. Very few elected officials in this or other countries have much understanding of how the monetary transmission mechanism works, of the long lags that I have mentioned, or of a variety of other technical details about monetary policy. So countries can probably get higher-quality monetary policy by turning the task over to trained technicians, subject, of course—and this is important in my view—to political oversight.

CENTRAL BANK INDEPENDENCE AND DEMOCRACY

At this point, a very deep philosophical questions arises: Isn't all this profoundly undemocratic? Doesn't assigning so much power to unelected technocrats contradict some fundamental tenets of democratic theory? It is a legitimate question. My answer is: If you assign this power well, it needn't be antidemocratic. And I want to conclude this lecture with a detailed defense of that answer. The question is: How can an independent central bank be rationalized within the context of democratic government? My recipe comes in six parts.

First, we all know that, even in democracies, certain decisions are reserved to what is sometimes called the "constitutional stage" of government, rather than left to the daily legislative struggle. These are basic decisions that we do not want to revisit often; they should, therefore, be hard to reverse. So, for example, amending the U.S. Constitution requires much more than majority votes of both houses of Congress. The Founding Fathers thereby made it almost, but not quite, impossible to change certain basic provisions of law. And they meant it that way; it wasn't an accident.

Similarly with monetary policy. The Fed's independence, which derives from authority delegated by Congress, makes it very difficult, but not quite impossible, for elected officials to overrule or influence a monetary policy decision. Wise politicians made a once-and-for-all decision years ago to limit their own power in this way just as, for example, the Constitution made it very difficult to change the length of the President's term of office. The reasoning was precisely the same as that which led Ulysses to tie himself to the mast. He knew he would get better long-run results even though he wouldn't feel so good about it in the short run!

Third, the public has a right to demand honesty from its central bankers. This, again, is a point I made earlier in discussing the idea of credibility, which I defined as matching deeds to words. The central bank, in my view, owes this to the body politic in return for the broad grant of power it enjoys.

The fourth ingredient is closely related to this last point. I call it *accountability*, or perhaps just *openness*. Monetary policy actions have profound effects on the lives of ordinary people. In my view, a central bank in a democracy therefore owes these folks an explanation of what it is doing, why it is doing it, and what it expects to accomplish by its actions. As I often said while I was at the Fed, "It's their economy, not ours." By offering a reasonably full and coherent explanation of its actions, the central bank can remove much of the mystery that now surrounds monetary policy, enable interested parties to appraise its decisions contemporaneously, and then—importantly—allow outsiders to judge its success or failure after the fact, for the verdict of history is the only one that ultimately matters.

Let me assure you that greater openness is not a popular cause in central banking circles, where some see mystery as essential to effective monetary policymaking. Making the central bank more open and accountable, it is alleged, may subject it to unwelcome scrutiny that could threaten its independence.

I couldn't disagree with this argument more. In fact, I think it gets matters exactly backward. To me, public accountability is a moral corollary of central bank independence. In a democratic society, the central bank's freedom to act implies an obligation to explain itself to the public. Thus independence and accountability are symbiotic, not conflicting. Accountability legitimizes independence within a democratic political structure.

Nor, by the way, do I accept the claim, heard so much in central banking circles, that more accountability will harm the central bank—as long as the bank is independent. If the central bank makes good decisions, it should have no trouble explaining them to the public. If the Fed cannot articulate a coherent defense of its actions, maybe those decisions are not as good as it thinks. Indeed, being forced to articulate such a defense would probably be a good disciplinary device. Remember—and this is critical—I am talking here only about explaining the decisions after they are made, not putting them to a vote!

The Federal Reserve, tight-lipped as it is, is far from the worst offender in this regard. In fact, the Fed is probably more open and accountable than most central banks in the world. But the competition in this league is not very stiff—I think the New York Jets could win the championship in this particular league—and I believe the Federal Reserve could and should go much further. After all, we live in the most open society on the face of the earth, so just to say that we've beaten the world average is no great achievement for Americans.

The fifth ingredient in my democratic stew is that the leaders of the central bank should be politically appointed by the President, as is the current practice. When I went to the Federal Reserve Board in June 1994 as the first appointee of President Clinton, I joined Alan Greenspan, Mike Kelley, and John LaWare, who were originally sent there by President Reagan, and Larry Lindsey and Susan Phillips, who were appointed by President Bush. None of us was ever elected to anything. But Bill Clinton and George Bush and Ronald Reagan were. We obtained our political legitimacy from the men who appointed us, and they in turn got it the old-fashioned way—directly from the voters. That is as it should be.

Finally, the sixth ingredient—which I would argue should be present, but very rarely used: Central bank decisions should be reversible by the political authorities, but only under extreme circumstances. Reversal should not be routine occurrences. As I've mentioned already, a Federal Reserve decision on monetary policy can, in principle, be overturned by an act of Congress. And Fed governors can be removed from office for good cause. These mechanisms have never been used in the history of the Federal Reserve; but America is wise to have them in place nonetheless. Delegated authority should be retrievable, not absolute.

A SUMMING UP

So, in summary, let us review how the Fed, or any other central bank for that matter, can best serve its nation with monetary policy.

To begin with, the central bank must always remember that it exists as a public institution chartered to serve the broad national interest, not the parochial interests of either the banking industry or the bond market. Often those interests coincide. But when they clash, the central bank should not hesitate before taking sides.

The highest calling of the central bank is to help stabilize the national economy. For if the bank should fail at this task, no one else will be around to pick up the pieces. In its role as macroeconomic steward, the Fed, I believe, should pursue two goals—both low unemployment and low inflation—not just one. That is what the people want and, in my view, the people have got it right.

A central bank can perform its monetary policy role better if it's independent from political manipulation, and that's probably why more and more governments around the world are granting their central banks independence these days.

Even though the Fed's independence looks superficially undemocratic, I believe it is consistent with democratic theory for several reasons: it is based on authority delegated by Congress; the basic goals of monetary policy are set legislatively; the leaders of the Fed are appointed by the President; and Congress retains ultimate control in case of dire emergency. But a central bank in a democracy has a duty to level with the public it serves, not to obfuscate. I used to ask some of my colleagues on the Federal Reserve staff in Washington what they would have thought if their father, every time he spanked them, had only said that he was doing it "to promote sustainable non-inflationary growth"—and nothing more. I don't believe that would have been considered good parenting, and I don't think it's good central banking. More fulsome explanation is appropriate.

A great Virginian, probably the greatest Virginian, once wrote, "Governments are instituted among men" (I'm sorry it was only men in those days) "deriving their just powers from the consent of the governed." It is very hard for the governed to give their consent if they don't have a clue about what is going on. Openness, accountability, and credibility are therefore, in my view, moral corollaries of central bank independence.

READING 18 Central Banking in a Democracy

Furthermore, and finally, I dispute the notion that is so popular in some circles that monetary policy is best done amidst mystery, blue smoke, and mumbo jumbo. Central banks work their will through financial markets, and economists rarely argue that markets function better when they are less well informed. In my view, some small portion of the prodigious uncertainties over the effects of monetary policy exists because the markets have a hard time divining the Fed's intentions. This particular source of uncertainty can, and in my opinion should, be removed by greater openness. But that, I'm afraid, is a story for another lecture and another day.

QUESTIONS

1. What oddities of Fed structure and activities does Blinder note?

2. What are the short-run and long-run effects of monetary policy and what does Blinder identify as monetary policy's "central dilemma?"

3. Why does Blinder assert that "monetary policy is the only game in town nowadays?"

4. How does Blinder define central bank independence and what does he think accounts for the generally superior macroeconomic performance of countries that have independent central banks?

5. How does Blinder believe that central bank independence can be made compatible with political democracy?

READING 19

Why Central Bank Independence Helps to Mitigate Inflationary Bias

Timothy Cogley

The President and Congress are directly responsible for fiscal policy, but Congress has chosen (through the Federal Reserve Act) to delegate authority for monetary policy to the Federal Reserve System. Furthermore, it has granted the Federal Reserve a substantial degree of independence. Decisions about monetary policy are made by the Federal Open Market Committee (FOMC), which consists of 7 Governors, who are appointed by the President and confirmed by Congress, and 12 regional bank Presidents, who are chosen jointly by the Federal Reserve Board and the boards of the regional banks. On a short-term basis, FOMC decisions are largely independent of direct input from the President or Congress. And since members of the FOMC serve long terms and do not stand for election, they are largely insulated from the political process.

Why did the founders of the Federal Reserve choose to insulate the central bank in this manner? One possibility is that they were concerned that there would be an inflationary bias if monetary policy were too strongly influenced by elected officials. The empirical evidence suggests that this concern is warranted: across countries, there appears to be an inverse relation between average inflation and the degree of central bank independence (for example, see Alesina 1988 and Grilli, Masciandaro, and Tabellini 1991). But what is it about the political process that tends to create an inflationary bias? A recent paper by Jon Faust (1996) provides an intriguing answer, and this *Weekly Letter* discusses his arguments.

AN ANALOGY WITH THE SUPREME COURT

In most circumstances, our system of government favors the rule of simple majorities as a way to decentralize political power, but this preference is far from universal. There are any number of examples in which governmental decisions are insulated to a greater or lesser extent from the rule of simple majorities. The best example is the

---

Reprinted from Federal Reserve Bank of San Francisco *Weekly Letter*, No. 96-08, February 23, 1996. The opinions expressed in this article do not necessarily reflect the views of the management of the Federal Reserve Bank of San Francisco, or of the Board of Governors of the Federal Reserve System.

READING 19 Why Central Bank Independence Helps to Mitigate Inflationary Bias

U.S. Supreme Court. Like the Federal Reserve Board, Supreme Court Justices are nominated by the President and confirmed by Congress but do not stand for election. They serve life terms, and they can't be fired for rendering unpopular decisions. Hence, in the short run, the Supreme Court is largely insulated from the will of the electorate.

The rationale for having an independent Supreme Court is a belief that majority rule may sometimes produce undesirable outcomes. For example, in times of crisis, a majority of voters might be persuaded to temporarily suspend certain fundamental rights, such as that of free speech or assembly. While such an action might appear to be expedient, it might prove to be difficult to reverse once the crisis has passed. Once rights are suspended, they may be difficult to restore. There is also a moral hazard problem: some factions in society might provoke a crisis in order to undermine public support for basic rights. An independent Supreme Court limits the power of transient majorities to alter certain fundamental aspects of our political system and thus contributes to its long-term stability.

In the language of Alexis de Tocqueville (1969), an independent Supreme Court helps to protect against the "tyranny of the majority." Can the same be said for an independent central bank? Faust argues that it can.

UNEXPECTED INFLATION TRANSFERS WEALTH FROM CREDITORS TO DEBTORS

The first step in his argument concerns the effects of unexpected inflation on the distribution of wealth. In the United States, most debt contracts are written in nominal terms. A creditor agrees to lend a sum of money at a given nominal interest rate for a given period of time, and the borrower agrees to repay the principal plus interest at maturity. The interest payment consists of two components. First, borrowers must pay something in order to persuade lenders to part with their capital for the term of the loan. Second, inflation erodes the real value of the principal during the term of the loan, and borrowers must compensate lenders for this loss. Since the nominal interest rate is typically set at the beginning of the loan, the compensation for the erosion of purchasing power must reflect expected inflation, rather than actual inflation.

These two components are reflected in the Fisher equation, which states that the nominal interest rate is equal to the real interest rate (payment for use of capital) plus the expected inflation rate (compensation for the erosion of purchasing power).

If expectations turn out to be correct, then the inflation compensation that was agreed upon at the beginning of the loan exactly makes up for the erosion in purchasing power during the life of the contract. If actual inflation turns out to be higher than expected, the inflation compensation turns out too small. Since the creditor is only partially compensated for the erosion of purchasing power, the debtor gains at his expense. On the other hand, if actual inflation turns out to be lower than expected, the inflation compensation more than offsets the erosion of purchasing power, and the lender gains at the expense of the borrower. Thus, unexpected inflation transfers wealth between creditors and debtors. Debtors gain when inflation is unexpectedly high, and creditors gain when it is unexpectedly low.

SETTING MONETARY POLICY BY MAJORITY RULE

Now imagine what would happen if monetary policy were set by majority vote. Once loans are made, creditors would have a short-term incentive to vote for policies which would deliver an inflation rate that is lower than the one implicit in the debt contract, because this would redistribute wealth in their favor. Similarly, debtors would have a short-term incentive to vote for policies which would generate an inflation rate that is higher than the one implicit in the debt contract, because this would redistribute wealth in their favor. If monetary policy were set by majority vote, the more numerous faction would prevail.

This raises the question, "are debtors or creditors more numerous?" Direct evidence on this question is hard to come by, but two observations suggest that debtors may be more numerous. One follows from typical life-cycle spending patterns and the fact that the population grows over time. Early in life, people tend to borrow to invest in education, to smooth consumption between low income periods in their youth and higher income periods later in life, and to buy houses and other durable consumption goods. As people age, they pay off these debts and accumulate wealth for retirement. Thus, younger people are more likely to be debtors and older people more likely to be creditors. With population growth, there are more young people than old, and this suggests that debtors may be more numerous.

This life-cycle consideration is reinforced by the form in which many people finance their housing purchases. When people take out a mortgage, they acquire a real asset (land and a house) and a nominal debt (the mortgage). Like other fixed income securities, a fixed-rate mortgage incorporates a premium for expected inflation. Since this debt is nominal, its real value falls if inflation turns out to be higher than expected. Adjustable rate mortgages also tend to fall in real value when there is an unexpected increase in inflation, because they usually contain annual and lifetime caps on the nominal mortgage rate. These caps become especially important when there are big changes in inflation. On the other side of the balance sheet, households hold land and houses. Since these are real assets, their real (or inflation-adjusted) value is much less sensitive to unexpected changes in inflation. Thus, households who hold nominal debts and real assets would also benefit from monetary policies which generate surprisingly high inflation.

If debtors are more numerous than creditors, a majority of voters would have a short-term incentive to vote for policies which generate an unexpected increase in inflation. But over a long period of time, inflation cannot be higher than expected on average. Creditors are not fools. They would build this knowledge of voting patterns into their inflation forecasts and mark up the Fisher premium accordingly. Inflation would sometimes turn out to be higher than expected and sometimes lower, but on average the majority faction would not be able to use monetary policy to redistribute wealth. Systematic attempts to do so would just raise the average rate of inflation.

Moreover, although the majority would prefer low average inflation, they would not be able to achieve it. When seeking new loans, borrowers would like to promise to vote for low inflation, but once the contract is signed they would be free to vote as they please and would again have a short-term incentive to vote for high inflation. Creditors would see through this and give their promise little weight. They would insist upon a big Fisher premium to compensate for high expected inflation, and borrowers would support a high inflation policy in order to reduce the real value of the nominal interest rate, thus confirming creditors' expectations of high inflations. Setting monetary policy by majority vote generates an inflationary bias which makes everyone worse off. In particular, the majority is worse off because they suffer the costs of higher inflation without achieving any redistribution.

If everyone prefers low average inflation, why can't the electorate or the legislature solve the problem by giving the central bank explicit instructions in the form of official low-inflation targets? Creditors and debtors both have a long-term incentive to support low inflation, so both groups would presumably support such a plan. But how would these targets be enforced? Once debt contracts are signed, borrowers would have a short-term incentive to support an "exception" to the low inflation target in order to redistribute wealth in their favor. Hence the majority's support for low inflation would not be consistent over time. Their short-term interests for redistribution would undermine their long-term interests for low average inflation.

DELEGATING MONETARY POLICY TO AN INDEPENDENT COMMITTEE

The majority needs to find a way to commit to a low-inflation policy. One way to do so is to delegate authority to an independent committee and then let them make decisions about monetary policy. In effect, this makes it more difficult for the majority to change its mind. To achieve this independence, it may be important to insulate the central bank from the electorate and their representatives, so that they cannot easily punish central bankers for rendering decisions that are unpopular in the short run.

While central bank independence is important, it is not sufficient to solve this inflationary bias. The composition of the committee is also important. For example, if this committee were simply a microcosm of the general population, then majority voting within the committee would just replicate the inflationary bias in the general population. Thus, it may also be important to choose committee members so as to balance the forces for and against inflation. To achieve this balance, it may be necessary for the anti-inflation forces to be overly represented relative to their proportion in the general population.

CONCLUSION

Unexpected inflation redistributes wealth from nominal creditors to nominal debtors. If debtors are more numerous than creditors, majorities may often favor monetary policy actions that generate unexpected inflation. But since monetary policy can't systematically generate surprisingly high rates of inflation, attempts to use it to redistribute wealth would just raise the average inflation rate without achieving the intended redistribution. In the end, policy by majority may lead to outcomes that are inferior even for the majority, and insulating monetary policy makers from the electorate may produce superior outcomes.

REFERENCES

Alesina, Alberto. 1988. "Macroeconomics and Politics." In *NBER Macroeconomics Annual*, Stanley Fischer, ed. Cambridge, MA: MIT Press.

Faust, Jon. 1996. "Whom Can We Trust to Run the Fed? Theoretical Support for the Founders' Views." *Journal of Monetary Economics* (forthcoming).

Grilli, Vittorio, Donato Masciandaro, and Guido Tabellini. 1991. "Political and Monetary Institutions and Public Financial Policies in the Industrial Countries." *Economic Policy* 13, pp. 341-392.

Tocqueville, Alexis de. 1969. *Democracy in America*. Garden City, NY: Doubleday.

READING 19 Why Central Bank Independence Helps to Mitigate Inflationary Bias

QUESTIONS

1. Is the independence of the Supreme Court desirable? Why? Is it equally desirable to have an independent Federal Reserve? Why?

2. What is the Fisher equation?

3. What evidence does Cogley present that debtors may outnumber creditors? Which of these groups prefers unexpectedly low inflation? Why?

4. According to Cogley, why does the U.S. have an independent central bank?

READING 20

Fed's Huge Empire, Set Up Years Ago, Is Costly and Inefficient

John R. Wilke

MINNEAPOLIS—Construction cranes rising above the Mississippi River hoist the final stone blocks for the elegant new Federal Reserve Bank headquarters here, the latest monument to the U.S. central bank's immense wealth and power.

The $100 million building sits on nine acres of prime riverfront, with a 10-story stone clock tower overlooking terraces and gardens. It will offer fortress-like security and robot-attended, automated vaults, plus an indoor pistol range, a fitness center and subsidized dining. The Fed's construction boom also includes the lavish new $168 million Dallas Fed and a planned $178 million Atlanta Fed.

Located in a dozen cities—with branches in another 25—The Fed's palatial banks suggest permanence and importance. They operate with great independence far from the Fed's power center in Washington and, with $451 billion of assets, are staggeringly wealthy. Their job is to run the basic plumbing of the nation's economy by monitoring local banks, distributing currency, processing checks and settling interbank payments.

COSTLY RELICS

But the plumbing at the Fed banks seems to be getting rusty, despite their heavy spending. Rapid changes in technology, consolidation in banking and rising competition in some of their basic services threaten to make Fed banks costly relics. Except for the New York Fed, the system's link to world markets, many Fed functions could be centralized at far less cost and some Fed banks could be closed, federal auditors say.

"It's not about saving nickels and dimes," says James Bothwell, a General Accounting Office auditor who recently completed a two-year study of the Fed's books. "There are serious, long-term questions about their mission and structure."

The Fed's best-known mission—steering U.S. monetary policy and thus charting the course of the economy—isn't at issue. Even its critics hail the Fed's success in holding down inflation.

Wall Street Journal, September 12, 1996, A1, A8. Reprinted by permission of The Wall Street Journal, © 1996 Dow Jones & Company, Inc. All Rights Reserved Worldwide.

READING 20 Fed's Huge Empire, Set Up Years Ago, Is Costly and Inefficient

VAST OPERATION

What concerns some in Congress and its GAO watchdog agency is the sprawling Fed empire, which reaches far beyond its marble headquarters in Washington to maintain a presence in most major American cities. The Fed has 25,000 employees, runs its own air force of 47 Learjets and small cargo planes, and has fleets of vehicles, including personal cars for 59 Fed bank managers. It publishes hundreds of reports on itself each year—even Fed comic books on monetary policy for kids. A full-time curator oversees its collection of paintings and sculptures.

Yet Fed spending gets little public scrutiny, even as the rest of the federal government struggles to tighten its belt. That's because the Fed funds itself from the interest on its vast trove of government securities acquired in its conduct of monetary policy. Last year, it kept $2 billion of those interest earnings for itself and returned the rest, $20 billion, to the Treasury. Thus, every dollar spent on a new building in Minneapolis—or anything else—is a dollar that could have been used to cut the federal deficit. Unlike every other part of government, the Fed doesn't have to ask Congress for money, and that's the key to its independence from political interference on monetary-policy issues.

The Minneapolis Fed would seem a prime candidate for downsizing. Its spending is in striking contrast to the cutbacks and consolidations at many of the commercial banks it serves; only two major banks are left in its six-state district. And its biggest job, processing and clearing checks for local banks, is under increasing pressure from private competitors and new electronic-payment technologies.

POSSIBLE SAVINGS

Without check-clearing, the Minneapolis Fed might not need its costly new building and the hundreds of employees who work three shifts shuffling checks. It could eliminate huge overhead costs and focus on distributing U.S. currency and monitoring the local economy.

The basic structure of the Federal Reserve System has changed little since it was created in 1913, despite huge shifts in the nation's population and economy. Back then, Fed banks were sited according to the politics of the day and the quaint principle that a commercial banker should be able to reach a Fed branch within one-day train ride, in case he needed cash for unexpected withdrawals.

Today, these locations make little sense. Missouri, once an economic and political power because of its riverboat economy, has two Fed banks; booming Florida has none. California and its vast economy have only one Fed bank—which also serves eight other states and covers 20% of the U.S. population. Yet when Fed policy makers meet in Washington, the San Francisco Fed president can vote only one year of three, less often than the presidents from Cleveland or Chicago.

"It reflects the economy and politics of a long time ago," says Robert Parry, the San Francisco Fed's president. "If you were doing it today, you'd do it differently." Michael Belongia, a University of Mississippi professor and former Fed economist, says that three Fed banks and 16 branches could be closed and that four other banks could be downsized to branches. He calculates the savings at $500 million a year, even without trimming back the check-clearing business.

"The taxpayers pays billions of dollars for this monolithic system that isn't efficient anymore," he says.

Fed Chairman Alan Greenspan rejects many GAO findings, especially the idea of closing some Fed banks. He says it would take years to recoup the cost of closing one. "We're strongly committed to ensuring that the Federal Reserve System is managed efficiently and effectively," he said in recent congressional testimony. Most important, he defends the Fed banks' independence as crucial to keeping the Fed free of political interference and aware of regional economic conditions.

Yet he has expressed some misgivings about Fed spending. With the new Dallas building, for example, he said, "My first reaction was, 'For God's sake, why do you have to have a new building'? Dallas is in a state of commercial real-estate recession. You should be able to pick and choose at zero cost." But he added that he was ultimately persuaded that no existing building met the bank's special needs.

MARCHING TO THEIR OWN DRUMMER

The Fed banks are even less accountable to Congress than the Fed Board of Governors in Washington, whose seven members are appointed by the president and confirmed by the Senate. The 12 Fed bank presidents, by contrast, are chosen by their private-sector boards, though their annual budgets and building plans are subject to review by the governors in Washington. Congress has no say over who runs the regional banks, despite their important role in running the nation's monetary system.

Congress doesn't even set the regional presidents' salaries. The Minneapolis president gets $195,000 a year, and others range as high as $229,000, far exceeding Chairman Greenspan's $133,100.

Even so, only 1,600 Fed employees, including a stable of economists and statisticians, work on monetary policy. Most of the rest, and the lion's share of the Fed's $2 billion budget, go to the Fed banks' check-clearing and other services—the jobs under the most pressure from competitors and changes in banking. The Fed banks also process Treasury checks, but a new law mandating electronic distribution will eliminate 400 million Treasury checks annually in three years.

As their workload dwindles, Fed banks could be left with what insiders delicately term "the Post Office problem": They will be handling checks for mostly small, high-cost customers such as rural banks. Already, less than 25% of Fed customers create 95% of check volume. So, the Fed is vulnerable as major banks begin processing more checks through private clearinghouses or other cheaper alternatives, such as Visa International.

READING 20 Fed's Huge Empire, Set Up Years Ago, Is Costly and Inefficient

A DELUGE OF CHECKS

At the Minneapolis Fed, check-clearing already resembles the work inside the city's main Post Office nearby. Every day, trucks back up to the Fed's loading dock and drop off pallets of checks. Workers feed them into 25-foot-long automated sorters, and the checks, guided by codes identifying the paying bank, cascade into pouches. Lately, many of the tens of thousands of checks have been small—$2 razor-blade rebates and $4.69 drafts cashed by Huggies diaper customers. Minneapolis handles three million checks a day—a low-margin, labor-intensive business, not unlike delivering the mail.

In most countries, private companies or banks handle check-processing, with central banks playing a supervisory role to ensure the payment system is sound. In the U.S., new players ranging from Microsoft Corp. to Merrill Lynch & Co. are racing to offer electronic alternatives to bank-based payment systems, and some bankers fear the Fed's dominance will impede innovation and leave them behind.

Lee Hoskins, who once ran the Cleveland Fed and now heads Ohio's Huntington National Bank, says the Fed should get out of check-clearing. "The central bank no longer has a legitimate role as a provider of payment services," he says.

Huntington helped start the National Clearinghouse Association, which includes most large U.S. banks and has begun competing head-on with the Fed at lower prices. The Fed is fighting back with a new, lower-priced national check-sorting service and has cut prices in some cities where it is losing market share. As the Fed's volumes have declined, Fed officials concede, its check-clearing failed to cover costs two years ago and fell short again last year. But they say it turned the corner in the first half of 1996.

TOUGH COMPETITOR

Despite its problems, the Fed is a tough competitor and has continued investing in check-clearing and other services. It changed the formula used to figure whether or not it is making a profit and made unusual transfers, including some $36 million a year from an overfunded pension plan, into the check business, federal auditors say. It also let at least one Fed bank defer the huge cost of a new computer system so the outlay wouldn't be included in profit calculations, effectively understating the cost of clearing checks.

The Fed has also squeezed smaller firms that haul bank checks in competition with the Fed's own transport service, which flies pouches of checks overnight from bank and bank. It tried to force an aggressive rival, the U.S. Check unit of AirNet Systems Inc., of Columbus, Ohio, from the Florida market by providing its own contractor with subsidized jet fuel, according to documents and depositions collected by Rep. Henry Gonzalez. The Texas Democrat, a longtime Fed critic, says the Fed also subsidizes its higher costs by putting other cargo, such as its own interoffice mail, on its planes, and charging Fed banks for the service.

"I'm not saying they are competing unfairly, but I'd like to know how they cut prices when they're losing money," says Andy Linck, administrator at the National Clearinghouse. Under a 1980 law, the Fed is supposed to price services by commercial standards, but its rivals are reluctant to complain. "We're forced to compete with our own regulator," says an executive of a major Western bank with a big check business. "They can make life pretty difficult for us if we make trouble."

Fed officials say they play by the rules and use appropriate bookkeeping.

"We're competing fairly—and we're doing it with one arm tied behind our backs," says Ted Umhoefer, a check-clearing manager at the Minneapolis Fed. "I have to charge the same price to the Citizen's Sate Bank of Pembina, North Dakota, that I charge to them," he says, waving toward a big commercial bank in a nearby skyscraper. "Yet my counterparts in the private sector can cut volume deals with other big banks, leaving us with all the junk they can't make money on."

DEFENDING THE BUSINESS

In Washington, Fed officials reject the suggestion they should leave check-clearing to private companies. "That's how the Fed banks make their living," says Edward Kelley, the Fed governor who oversees many Fed bank activities and is leading an effort to improve planning and efficiency. "We'll be in that business until checks disappear or the Congress takes us out of it." The Fed grosses nearly $800 million a year from check-clearing and bank services.

Until recently, Chairman Greenspan spent almost all his time on monetary policy and rarely focused on Fed operations. But in recent testimony before Congress, he said he is now "actively reviewing the appropriate infrastructure for providing certain financial services, taking into consideration both cost efficiency and service quality." He said that although he believes the Fed should have a continuing role in the payments system to ensure its integrity—particularly the wholesale cash-transfer system known as Fedwire, which handles $1.5 trillion a day—he hinted for the first time that the Fed might privatize or downsize its retail check business.

"It is quite possible, if not likely, that as changes occur in the financial-services marketplace . . . our role in providing other services such as check collection may change." But he said something will have to be done to ensure that small banks have access to check services "because I don't think that they believe they're going to be able to pay the prices [they] will be forced to pay by the market." He said Congress may be asked to subsidize these small-bank services so that bank customers in small towns don't have to pay higher check fees.

Officials say the Fed banks already are taking steps to scale back check-clearing and have cut 600 jobs at various locations. But Fed critics content that the institution is unlikely to undertake the fundamental reform they say is needed because it could require thousands of layoffs—and the loss of substantial prestige.

READING 20 Fed's Huge Empire, Set Up Years Ago, Is Costly and Inefficient

A MATTER OF PRESTIGE

Prestige seemed important in Minneapolis when Fed officials decided to abandon their grand looking but poorly designed downtown tower. They considered moving to a cheaper, more convenient site by the airport, but that idea was dropped after it raised eyebrows at the Fed in Washington. "What would we have called it, the Federal Reserve Bank of Eagan, Minnesota?" one official asks. "The location is written into the law, and changing it would have required an act of Congress."

Indeed, that may be what the Fed fears most. "Do we really want to have 435 congressmen tinkering with what is supposed to be an independent institution?" asks Ernest Patrikis, first vice president of the New York Fed. Arthur Rolnick, research director at the Minneapolis Fed, says Congress "didn't have economic efficiency in mind when it created the Fed." Above all, he says they wanted a decentralized institution, independent of both big banks and politicians.

"I wouldn't be surprised if a hard look at the system shows that some of Fed branches should be closed," Mr. Rolnick adds. "The market has changed, and the technology has changed . . . . [But] do we really want to fool around with the Fed's independence just to save a few hundred million dollars a year?"

QUESTIONS

1. What are the arguments in favor of downsizing or even eliminating at least some of the Federal Reserve banks and branches? What are the arguments against such moves?

2. Which position on the downsizing issue is a proponent of Fed independence likely to take? Why? Which position is a proponent of the theory of bureaucratic behavior likely to take? Why?

3. Are the steps the Fed has taken to remain competitive in check-clearing consistent with the theory of bureaucratic behavior? Explain.

4. Is there a conflict between Fed efficiency and Fed independence? If so, which ideal should have highest priority?

READING 21

Where Is All the U.S. Currency Hiding?

John B. Carlson and Benjamin D. Keen

The total amount of U.S. currency held by the nonbank public equals about $375 billion, or nearly $1,400 for every man, woman, and child in the country. Clearly, few individuals ever hold this much cash at any point in time. On the surface, the sheer volume of currency outstanding seems inconsistent with common sense. Even if one considers currency balances held by businesses involved largely in cash transactions—like retailers—and by participants in the underground economy—like drug dealers—it is hard to reconcile the difference between households' holdings and total currency outstanding. So where is this currency hiding?

Recent evidence suggests that a growing proportion of U.S. currency is held outside the country by individuals who are uncertain about their own currency's future value. To these people, the dollar is a refuge during times of political and economic uncertainty. Knowing precisely how much currency is held outside the United States, however, is no simple matter. Unlike checking accounts, currency flows do not leave a paper trail. However, informal reports to the Federal Reserve and the U.S. Customs Department regarding currency flows abroad do provide a rough indication of foreign demand.

Having some idea about the magnitude of overseas holdings is important for several reasons. First, if the demand for currency is becoming driven largely by foreign portfolio decisions, then fluctuations in the level of currency outstanding may have little to do with domestic economic activity. Second, movements in the narrow monetary aggregates—of which currency is a sizable component—will not provide the same information as they have historically. Third, to the extent that foreigners demand currency, which is non-interest-bearing debt, the U.S. Treasury's need to issue an interest-bearing alternative is reduced.

To address these issues, we will examine why individuals hold currency and why the U.S. dollar is so popular abroad. We will also discuss some recent research on the share of currency held abroad and look at the implications for policy.

WHY DO PEOPLE HOLD CURRENCY?

For most Americans, the answer to this question is simple: to make payments when

Reprinted from Federal Reserve Bank of Cleveland, *Economic Commentary*, April 15, 1996.

neither checks nor credit cards are convenient or accepted. The U.S. dollar has the textbook qualities often used to define money. That is, it is both a unit of account and a medium of exchange. Although stories about currency stashed under the mattress occasionally come to light, most Americans choose to hold cash only for transaction purposes. Since it bears no interest, there is little incentive to hold currency when no transactions are anticipated.

Textbooks also identify "store of value" as a quality of money. This characteristic, however, applies to many nonmonetary assets as well. During inflationary periods, houses are often considered good stores of value. Gold, rare art, coins, and stamps can also serve this purpose.

The dollar, on the other hand, has some characteristics that make it preferable to other stores of value. First, it is both compact and portable. One can barely move a house across town, let alone abroad. Even carrying gold can be cumbersome. Second, currency affords anonymity not offered by, say, ownership of a Van Gogh. Third, the U.S. dollar is liquid in many parts of the world. That is, it is easily converted to spendable forms with no (or minimal) transactions costs and little risk of capital loss. And finally, unlike most real property, currency is divisible. If the denomination of a bill is larger than the price of an exchange, then change can be made.

WHY DO FOREIGNERS HOLD U.S. CURRENCY?

In contrast to domestic demand, foreign demand for the U.S. dollar owes more to the store-of-value quality of money. The dollar is preferred to many other currencies because it is a relatively stable source of purchasing power, widely accepted, and reasonably secure from counterfeiting. Another appealing feature is that unlike some other currencies, which may be recalled with little notice or limited opportunities for exchange, Federal Reserve Notes are ultimately exchangeable at full face value, regardless of when they were issued. Moreover, because shipments of less than $10,000 do not have to be reported, U.S. currency maintains a degree of anonymity for its holder.

These favorable features of the U.S. dollar ultimately reflect the political and economic stability we enjoy. For countries whose political situation is uncertain, the dollar offers a form of wealth that may be put in a suitcase and carried should a resident need to flee. Political instability is often associated with economic turmoil and a debasing of a country's currency. Despite the episodes of double-digit inflation in the 1970s and early 1980s, the United States has never experienced a hyperinflation.

TRENDS IN FOREIGN HOLDINGS OF U.S. CURRENCY

Foreign demand for the U.S. dollar is particularly strong in certain parts of the world. In Liberia and Panama, the dollar is the official currency. Large amounts of currency are known to be circulating in Central and South America, especially in Argentina, where it is often used to settle real estate and auto transactions. The dollar is also very popular in Eastern Europe, especially in the former Soviet Union, where inflation, declining exchange rates, and currency recalls have made the ruble a poor store of value. U.S. military personnel stationed overseas and many international travelers likewise rely on the dollar.

Measuring the *flow* of U.S. currency abroad is extremely difficult. Cash is often sent in the mail, and, as mentioned above, individual shipments of up to $10,000 do not have to be reported to the Customs Department. Customs does keep records of shipments above $10,000, however, and these provide some information on currency flows abroad. Another major source of data is found in the informal reports that commercial banks submit to the Federal Reserve regarding their overseas currency shipments. These reports suggest that sine 1988, about half of all U.S. currency sent overseas has gone to Europe (Russia is the most likely destination), 30 percent has gone to the Middle East and Far East, and around 20 percent has gone to Central and South America, with a fair amount of that ending up in Argentina.[1]

Determining the total *stock* of currency held abroad is even more difficult. In fact, the only available data are shipment numbers from informal reports to the Customs Department and the Federal Reserve. Currently, many analysts believe that a substantial portion of all U.S. currency is held overseas.

Researchers at the Federal Reserve Board have examined this issue in depth. A preliminary study conducted in 1993 estimated that more than 70 percent of all U.S. currency is held outside our borders, with most of the outflows occurring since 1970.[2] Recently, a broader examination set that figure at between 50 and 70 percent, with about 80 percent of all currency growth since 1980 tied to increased foreign demand.[3]

Figure 1 illustrates two estimates of the level of currency held abroad. Both are based on statistical approaches that exploit the similarity between seasonal fluctuations in the domestic demands for U.S. and Canadian currency.[4] Because the seasonal factor in currency for both countries is largely driven by similar season fluctuations in retail sales, one approach adjusts for differences in the seasonality of retail sales between the two countries.

SOME RECENT ISSUES

The strong international demand for the dollar inevitably makes it a target for would-be counterfeiters. Although the current design of U.S. currency is sufficient to prevent mass counterfeiting, photocopying technology may soon reach the point where nearly perfect copies can be easily produced. The Treasury anticipated this potential problem in 1983 and began working on a plan to redesign the currency. Even though Treasury officials believe that the amount of counterfeit currency in circulation is minimal, recent rumors of an

READING 21 Where Is All the U.S. Currency Hiding?

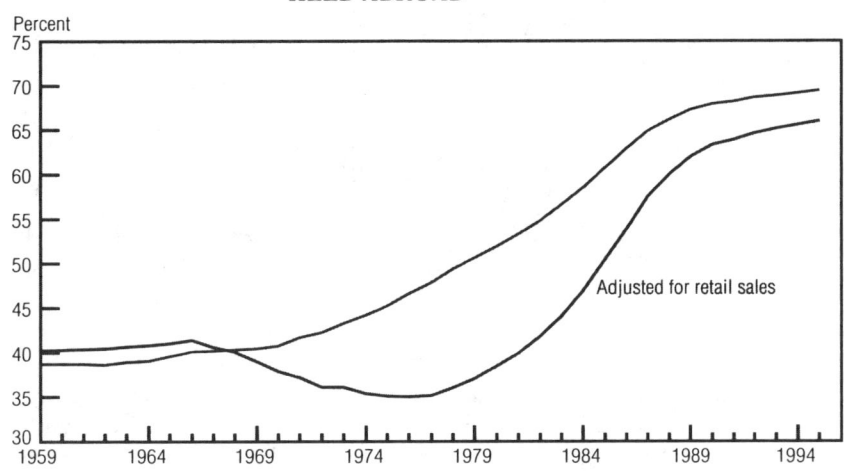

FIGURE 1   ESTIMATED SHARE OF U.S. CURRENCY HELD ABROAD

SOURCE: Richard D. Porter and Ruth A. Judson, "The Location of U.S. Currency" (footnote 1).

almost-perfect counterfeit produced in the Middle East—the so-called *supernote*—gave added incentive to the redesign effort.[5]

Because most foreigners prefer to hold $100 bills and most counterfeits are found overseas, the Treasury decided to redesign that note first and set a release date of March 1996. To avoid disturbing foreign economies and to protect the special anonymity feature of the dollar, officials announced that the old currency would not be recalled and would always be accepted at 100 percent of face value. To spread the word, the department is spending millions of dollars on advertising and on setting up toll-free hot lines around the world. Nevertheless, promises about cash are often viewed with deep suspicion by foreigners who have watched their own currencies become virtually worthless.

In early 1995, as news of the soon-to-be released $100 bill spread abroad, currency growth plummeted, from about 8.5 percent over the last two decades to about 3 percent in 1995. (see figure 2). Many analysts believe that this slowdown largely reflected foreign holders' concerns about the new currency. Moreover, now that the redesigned note has been released, currency growth is expected to accelerate to near previous levels. Preliminary data since the March introduction reveal no sharp rise in the currency numbers, but it must be stressed that this information is very limited (see figure 3). Only time will tell if the currency growth rate will return to a level more consistent with its previous trend.

PART IV Central Banking and the Conduct of Monetary Policy

FIGURE 2   U.S. CURRENCY GROWTH

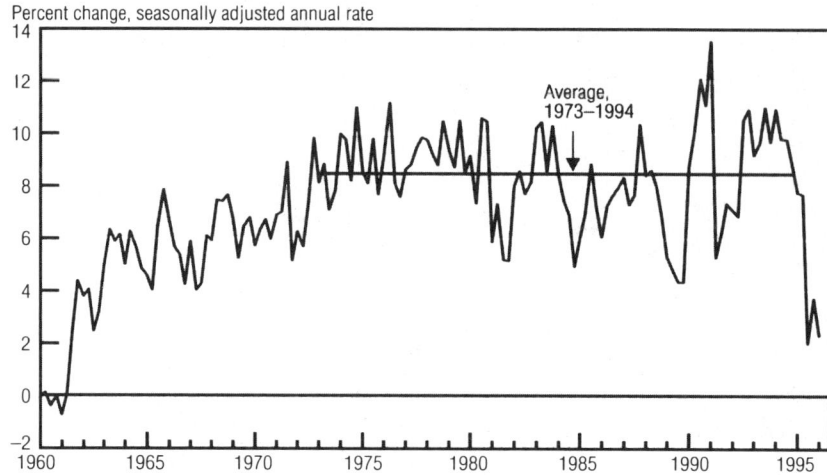

SOURCE: Board of Governors of the Federal Reserve System.

FIGURE 3   U.S. CURRENCY LEVELS

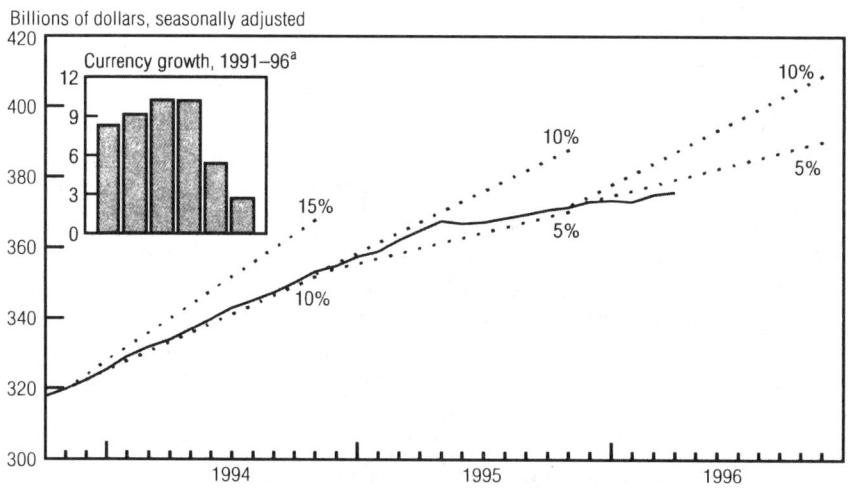

a. Growth rates are percentage rates calculated on a fourth-quarter over fourth-quarter basis. Annualized growth rate for 1996 is calculated on an April over 1995:IVQ basis.
NOTE: Dotted lines represent growth ranges and are for reference only.
SOURCE: Board of Governors of the Federal Reserve System.

POLICY IMPLICATIONS

Large swings in overseas holdings of U.S. currency typically have little impact on the current level of domestic economic activity. Rather, such movements distort the historical relationship between currency and the economy, making currency a less reliable indicator. Although the level of currency has never received much attention in policy analysis, it is a substantial component of the monetary base (about seven-eights currency) and of M1 (about one-third currency), which are watched closely by some analysts.

Events such as the introduction of the new $100 bill can thus create misleading signals in the narrow money measures, making them less reliable for policy purposes. For example, the slowdown in currency growth in early 1995 accentuated the decline in both the monetary base and M1.[6] Because the currency slowdown most likely reflects reduced foreign demand, it seems doubtful that deceleration in the narrow money measures portends a weakening economy, as it might have in years past. Moreover, foreign demand tends to be induced by unpredictable events. To the extent that U.S. currency is becoming increasingly subject to the vagaries of foreign demand, the use of narrow money measures as guides for policy will prove problematic.

Another important implication concerns the federal budget, U.S. currency pays no interest, yet is ultimately a debt of the federal government. Essentially, it is an interest-free loan. The greater the level of currency outstanding, the less the level of interest-bearing debt outstanding and hence the smaller the interest bill of the U.S. Treasury. This implicit yield of currency—known as seigniorage—reduces the annual tax bill by between $15 and $20 billion. To the extent that foreign demand for the dollar increases, the tax burden of U.S. citizens is further lightened.

ENDNOTES

1. See Richard D. Porter and Ruth A. Judson, "The Location of U.S. Currency: How Much Is Abroad?" Board of Governors of the Federal Reserve System, manuscript, June 1995.
2. See Richard D. Porter, "Estimates of Foreign Holdings of Currency—An Approach Based on Relative Cross-Country Seasonal Variations," Board of Governors of the Federal Reserve System, manuscript, September 1993.
3. See Porter and Judson, "The Location of U.S. Currency" (footnote 1).
4. Essentially, both approaches assume that foreign demand for Canadian currency is negligible and that the foreign-held component of U.S. currency has no seasonal pattern. Hence, the difference between the seasonal factors in total demand for U.S. currency and Canadian currency largely reflects foreign demand for U.S. currency.
5. According to the U.S. General Accounting Office, "the total level of counterfeit-currency detections—$208.7 million in fiscal year 1994—represented less than one one-thousandth of U.S. currency in circulation." See *Counterfeit U.S. Currency Abroad: Issues and U.S. Deterrence Efforts*, Washington, D.C.: GAO, February 1996, p. 2.
6. The implementation of sweep accounts has also tended to dampen the growth of both of these aggregates relative to economic activity.

PART IV Central Banking and the Conduct of Monetary Policy

> **QUESTIONS**
>
> 1. How does currency perform the classic textbook functions of money? What advantages does currency have over other assets in performing these functions?
>
> 2. Why do foreigners hold U.S. dollars rather than other currencies?
>
> 3. How does an increase in the currency to checkable deposit ratio affect the U.S. money multiplier and money supply? Given this, how is the U.S. money supply affected by foreign holdings of U.S. dollars?

READING 22

Falling Reserve Balances and the Federal Funds Rate

Paul Bennett and Spence Hilton

During the past year, required balances held by commercial banks and other depository institutions in their accounts at the Federal Reserve have fallen sharply. This development primarily reflects the spread of "sweep" arrangements, a banking innovation that allows depository institutions to shift customers' funds out of accounts subject to reserve requirements. Recently, questions have arisen about the potential effects of the decline in required balances on the interbank federal funds market in which these balances are borrowed and lent. At issue is whether the interest rate on transactions in this market—the federal funds rate—is becoming more volatile as banks try to manage their accounts with very low balances. Since the Federal Reserve implements monetary policy by influencing the federal funds rate, and the funds rate affects other short-term interest rates, a large increase in its volatility could have broader implications.

This edition of *Current Issues* investigates the drop in reserve balances and its effects on interest rate volatility. After describing the mechanism through which reserve balances influence the behavior of the federal funds rate, we assess the evidence suggesting that lower reserve requirements are leading to larger fluctuations in this rate. Our investigation prompts us to conclude that slightly higher short-term volatility in the federal funds rate may be resulting from the decline in reserve balances to date. Nevertheless, market participants have been adapting well to the drop in reserves and, as Federal Reserve Chairman Alan Greenspan (1997) noted in recent congressional testimony, the Federal Reserve has "not . . . experienced any specific problem in implementing monetary policy."

A LOOK AT BANK BALANCES AT THE FED

Banks and other depository institutions typically hold accounts at their district Federal Reserve Bank for two reasons: to conduct payments activities (sending funds to, and receiving funds from, other banks) and to meet balance requirements.[1] Balance requirements consist of required reserve balances and required clearing balances. (The box describes how these balances are calculated.)

Reprinted from Federal Reserve Bank of New York *Current Issues in Economics and Finance* 3, no. 5, April 1997.

PART IV   Central Banking and the Conduct of Monetary Policy

How Required Balances Are Calculated

Suppose that a bank has $200 million in transaction deposits and $15 million in vault cash. In March 1997, the bank faces a total reserve requirement equal to 3 percent of the first $49.3 million in transaction deposits, plus 10 percent of amounts over that, coming to $16.549 million. Less the vault cash, the bank's required reserve balance is $1.549 million. Suppose in addition that the bank purchases $1,000 worth of priced services from the Fed during each two-week maintenance period. Given a federal funds rate of, say, 5 percent, if the bank contracted to hold a required clearing balance of $0.514 million for two weeks, it would earn credits just covering its priced services charges.* Thus, during the two-week maintenance period, the bank would have to maintain end-of-day balances averaging no less than $2.063 million, or $1.549 million plus $0.514 million. If the balances averaged more, then the excess amount would earn neither interest nor credits.

*More exactly, $514,286 in clearing balance principal times .05 annualized rate of interest times (14 days/360 days per year) = $1,000 interest. (The 360-day year is an idiosyncracy of interest rate calculation in this market.)

Banks maintain required reserve balances in partial fulfillment of the total reserve requirement set by the Board of Governors of the Federal Reserve System. Currently, the reserve requirement equals 3 percent of the first $49.3 million of a bank's "transaction deposits" (demand deposits and other checkable accounts) plus 10 percent of amounts beyond that.[2] Banks satisfy most of this requirement through their holdings of vault cash; to calculate the amount that they must meet with balances in their Fed accounts, they subtract cash holdings from the total reserve requirement. The reserve balance requirement applies to the *average* level of a bank's end-of-day balances during a two-week "maintenance period"; end-of-day balances on given days within a period may vary, although end-of-day overdrafts are penalized.

Clearing balances, the second component of required balances, are "required" only in the sense that banks contract to maintain these balances at a particular level. Banks decide whether or not they will hold a clearing balance; those that undertake this commitment typically do so to earn credits that they can use to pay for Federal Reserve priced services such as check clearing or funds transfers over the Fedwire system. Although the Federal Reserve is not allowed to pay actual interest on any balances in its accounts, these credits—the near-equivalent of interest—make clearing balances more attractive to banks. Nevertheless, because earned credits in excess of those needed to pay for Fed services are worthless, the amount of funds that it is advantageous for banks to hold in their clearing balances is limited.

Clearing balances are structured to work like reserve balances in that banks must meet average end-of-day balance amounts for the same two-week maintenance periods.[3] Shortfalls are penalized, and amounts beyond the sum of required reserve balances and required clearing balances are "excess reserves" and earn no interest.

FALLING RESERVE BALANCES AND THE SPREAD OF SWEEP ACCOUNTS

In recent years, required balances have trended downward, reflecting a decline in required reserve balances (Chart 1). The decline in required reserve balances stems from several developments: In 1990-91, the Federal Reserve eliminated reserve requirements on time and Eurodollar deposits and, in 1992, reduced the ratio used to compute total reserve requirements on transaction deposits from 12 to 10 percent. During the same period when these cuts were being made, the vault cash available to fulfill total reserve requirements increased, further reducing required reserve balances. Partly in response, a number of banks opted to increase their required clearing balances in the early 1990s, but many have apparently reached the maximum balances warranted by their use of Federal Reserve payments services.

While regulatory changes largely drove the decline in required reserves in the past, the most influential factor lowering required balances recently has been the growth of sweep account arrangements. Under most sweep arrangements, funds in bank customers' retail checking accounts are swept overnight into savings accounts not subject to reserve requirements and then returned to customers' checking accounts the next business day.[4] In this manner, a bank reduces its reserve requirement while depositors retain the ability to utilize their transaction accounts to make payments or withdrawals.

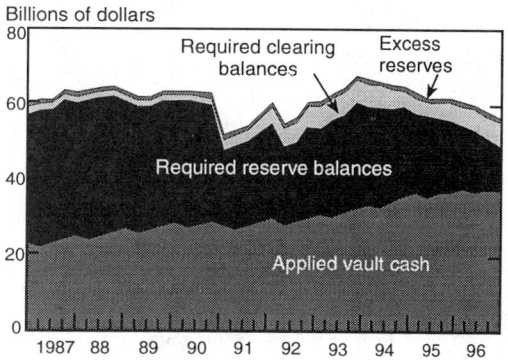

Chart 1

Components of Reserves and Account Balances at the Fed
Quarterly Averages

Source: Board of Governors of the Federal Reserve System.

Sweeps have been implemented by banks in various forms for a number of years, but since 1995 their use has escalated rapidly. In lieu of collecting regular reports on such arrangements, the Federal Reserve in early 1994 began to track the amount of deposits affected at the start of each bank's sweep program or any major subsequent expansion. Summing these initial amounts gives a rough

PART IV   Central Banking and the Conduct of Monetary Policy

Chart 2
Sweeps of Retail Transaction Deposits into Savings Deposits

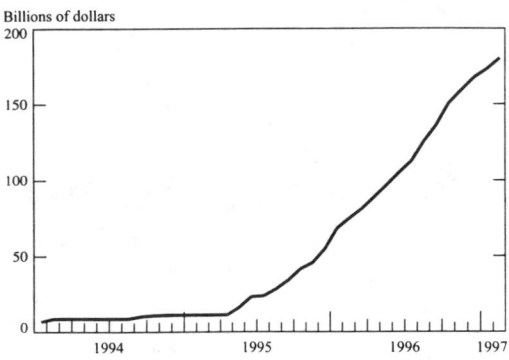

Source: Board of Governors of the Federal Reserve System.

Notes: The chart shows the cumulative total of transaction account balances swept into money market deposit accounts at the introduction of new sweep programs. The values plotted are based on monthly averages of daily data.

but useful indication of the size and growth of sweep accounts (Chart 2).

Using this information, we can estimate the extent of the sweeps' impact on required reserves. By February 1997, the initial values of all transaction balances subject to retail sweep arrangements had accumulated to about $184 billion. At current reserve requirement ratios, this development implies that the spread of sweeps has reduced total required reserves by roughly $18 billion since the end of 1993. We know that required reserve balances actually fell from $29.4 billion in December 1993 to $11.5 billion in February 1997, a drop of $17.9 billion. Most of this decline can be attributed to the spread of sweeps. In recent months, transaction balances subject to sweeps have continued to rise rapidly (Chart 2), suggesting that the trend toward lower required reserve balances is likely to continue.

How will the growth of sweep accounts and the corresponding fall in required reserves affect the market in which these balances are borrowed and lent? In the next two sections, we look at the mechanism through which such developments could affect rates in the federal funds market.

BANK RESERVE MANAGEMENT AND FED OPERATIONS

One way that a bank can obtain the funds it needs to meet balance requirements or to cover an overdraft is to borrow directly from another bank in the federal funds market, the interbank market for unsecured borrowing and lending of the balances in Fed accounts. Most of the borrowings in the federal funds market are on an overnight basis, and funds are delivered on the same day that a deal is struck. Indeed, because the market for federal funds remains active after most other financial markets have closed, it provides virtually the only opportunity for a bank to borrow funds in the market late in the day. Lenders in this market typically are banks seeking to reduce their holdings of excess reserves, which earn no interest.

The Federal Reserve Bank of New York can influence the rate on federal funds transactions by adjusting the aggregate supply of account balances through open market purchases and sales of government securities. A key objective of those open market operations is to keep the federal funds rate

READING 22 Falling Reserve Balances and the Federal Funds Rate

near the level that the Federal Open Market Committee (FOMC) indicates is consistent with its monetary policy stance. By keeping the aggregate supply of reserves in line with the demand, the Federal Reserve has been able to maintain the federal funds rate close to its desired level.

Banks' reserve management practices also play a role in keeping the federal funds rate stabilized around its target. Because balance requirements are met on a two-week daily average basis, banks can substitute balances across days. For example, if on a given day a bank finds itself with balances above the average amount it will need to meet its requirements for the overall two-week period, it can offset the surplus by holding lower end-of-day balances on subsequent days in the maintenance period. Analogously, a bank with an unexpectedly low balance one day can make it up the next, so long as the bank does not end any given day overdrawn. This ability to adjust reserve holdings across a maintenance period eases the pressure on banks to borrow or lend on any one day, reducing the likelihood that supply and demand forces will cause the federal funds rate to fluctuate very sharply.

The banks' awareness of the funds rate targeted by the Federal Reserve can further dampen volatility. Because the Fed now makes its target rate public, banks will know if the rate on a given day deviates significantly. In that event, banks can postpone or accelerate transactions in the expectation that the Fed will use its control over the supply of reserves to return the rate to the intended level on subsequent days in the maintenance period. Thus, the flexibility that banks have in timing their transactions helps ensure that deviations from the target federal funds rate do not become unduly large. Note, however, that as a maintenance period draws toward its end and banks must meet their balance requirements, this flexibility diminishes and volatility often increases.

POTENTIAL FOR HIGHER FEDERAL FUNDS RATE VOLATILITY

Our look at bank reserve management and Fed operating practices has revealed how volatility in the federal funds rate is normally kept in check. We now consider how the decline in required reserves brought about by sweep accounts and other developments in the 1990s could cause volatility to rise.

With very low levels of required balances, banks will try to keep actual balances correspondingly low while avoiding end-of-day overdrafts. A bank might guard against overdrafts by holding more excess reserves, but most institutions will want to economize on their holdings of balances that bear no interest. Given the normal size and frequency of payments-related debits and credits to Fed accounts, when average balances are lower, the probability that a bank will end the day in overdraft will be higher. A bank facing a high likelihood of ending the day in a negative position must find and purchase funds in the market. Its demand for funds will be quite inelastic, particularly as the close of the day approaches. In contrast, if the bank were targeting a significantly higher balance requirement, it would face less risk of end-of-day overdraft and have more flexibility to postpone purchases of funds until later within the maintenance period.

If enough banks are in negative positions or if the overdrafts are unexpectedly large on a given day, the increased demand for funds can lead to upswings in the federal funds rate. If, in addition, the overall supply of funds in the market is insufficient to meet the demand, the upward movement in the rate may be correspondingly larger. But even when aggregate supplies of balances appear adequate, balances may become distributed in such a way that banks with an excess supply of funds cannot be quickly matched with banks that have an excess demand. Such distributional pressures typically arise, for example, when payment flows in the banking system are heavy, such as at the end of a calendar year or on days when large numbers of securities transactions are being settled. Under such conditions, low balance requirements are likely to heighten the volatility in the funds rate by making it more difficult to relieve distributional pressures. Individual banks will be less willing to supply funds if that raises their overdraft risk, or to agree to borrow funds that are likely to push their balances substantially above the low required levels.

EVIDENCE ABOUT VOLATILITY

We have seen that reductions in required balances could, in principle, lead to a more volatile federal funds rate. But is there empirical support for such a link? While direct evidence on this issue is extremely limited, a look at the record suggests that a relationship, though modest, does exist.

First, bank behavior on the last day of a two-week maintenance period provides a model of how a low-balance environment can give rise to volatility. On this day, banks with excess positions are particularly motivated to sell federal funds, which will otherwise lose economic value.[5] Banks with positions in overdraft or below required maintenance period levels will need to cover them that day. The consequent inelastic buying or selling pressures experienced by these institutions have tended to create volatility in the price of funds. Indeed, the range of interest rates on federal funds transactions is typically much wider on the final days of maintenance periods.

Evidence that lower reserve balances can trigger higher volatility is also provided by the behavior of the federal funds rate at the end of 1990, when reserve requirements on wholesale deposits were eliminated. The cut in requirements coincided with a seasonal decline in required reserves and a rise in vault cash associated with year-end holidays—two events that together bring required reserve balances to their annual low point at the beginning of each new year. The consequent large drop in required balances was accompanied by an unusual rise in excess reserves and a dramatic increase in the intraday volatility of the federal funds rate. Rates on transactions ranged from near zero at times to as high as 100 percent, with some days seeing extremes in both directions. The extreme rate movements persisted for several weeks in 1991 until required reserve balances rose above their

READING 22 Falling Reserve Balances and the Federal Funds Rate

early-year low point and banks increased required clearing balances.

Further evidence of a linkage between balance requirements and volatility is offered by an apparent upward tilt in federal funds rate volatility during the past year. Using the available measure of intraday volatility—the difference between the highest and the lowest rates observed on transactions—we can put this most recent trend in some historical perspective. Over the last two decades, monthly averages of these high-low spreads have been extremely variable, and in some periods have exhibited persistently high levels (Chart 3). Volatility was particularly marked in the early 1980s, when the FOMC was targeting reserve aggregates rather than particular levels of the federal funds rate, and transactions consequently took place over a wide range of rates. In late 1990 and the first quarter of 1991, as noted earlier, volatility rose sharply after reserve requirements on wholesale deposits were dropped. Following that episode, however, volatility trended downward for several years, in part because banks were improving their account monitoring and management capabilities.[6]

Since 1995, as the increased use of sweeps has lowered required balances, intraday volatility has again moved upward. During the second half of 1996, this measure frequently reached 200 basis points (excluding settlement Wednesdays) on a monthly average basis, a relatively high level by recent historical standards.

Chart 3
Intraday Range of Federal Funds Rate
Nonsettlement Days

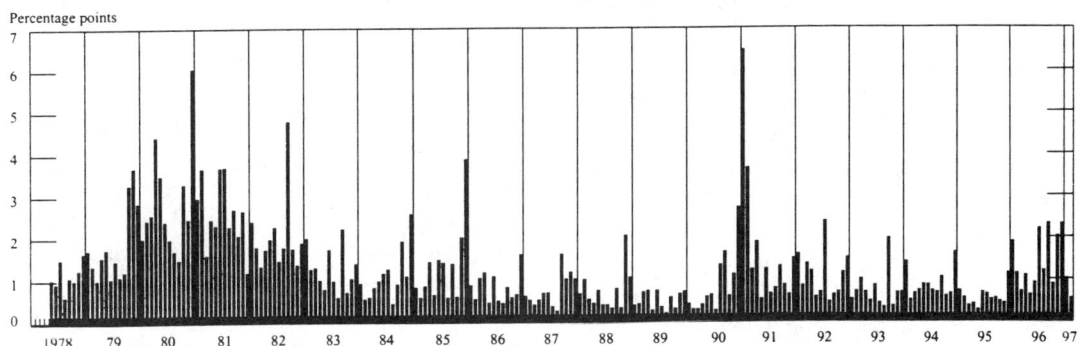

Source: Federal Reserve Bank of New York.

WHY CONCERNS ABOUT VOLATILITY MAY BE EXAGGERATED

The empirical evidence suggests that low balance requirements do contribute to higher federal funds rate volatility. But even if we should expect the current rise in volatility to continue as sweeps depress banks' reserve balances further, the increase is likely to be limited in scope and effect.

The 1990-91 episode reveals that the conditions accompanying a drop in required reserves will significantly influence the degree of ensuing volatility. In 1990, reserve requirements were reduced at the same time that year-end pressures from balance sheet adjustments and large payment flows were building in the federal funds market. Moreover, because the reduction resulted from changed regulatory mandates, the effects were concentrated within a very short time span. These factors go far toward explaining the unusually severe fluctuations in the federal funds rate in this period.

By contrast, the current decline in required balances has taken place at the initiative of the banks and has been distributed over a number of quarters. Banks expanding sweep arrangements have been making their own judgements about their abilities to manage their Fed accounts with lower balances and have been able to adjust gradually to the changing conditions in the federal funds market.

Also reassuring is that the current rise in volatility has to date been rather modest and its effects contained. Greater fluctuation in the intraday federal funds rate has not led to increased volatility in other interest rates. Moreover, because the FOMC promptly publicizes changes in the targeted federal funds rate, moderately greater volatility in the funds rate is unlikely to confuse market participants about the intended stance of monetary policy.[7]

CONCLUSION

There are valid reasons to believe that very low required balance levels induce higher federal funds rate volatility. With banks seeking to end the business day with low balances while avoiding end-of-day overdrafts, a distributional imbalance of funds among banks or an aggregate surplus or shortage of funds is more likely to trigger fluctuations in the funds rate. The historical record confirms the relationship between reserve levels and volatility: in 1990-91 and again in the years since 1994, reduced reserves have been associated with a widening of the intraday range of the federal funds rate.

To date, however, significantly lower balance requirements have not interfered with the smooth functioning of the federal funds market. The drop in balances has been gradual, and the sweep programs that are responsible for the drop have been carried out at the discretion of the banks. As a result, the observed increase in volatility has not reduced the effectiveness of banks' money market operations nor affected the implementation of monetary policy. To be sure, sweep accounts are still growing, and a continuing decline in balance requirements could over time increase federal funds rate volatility more dramatically. Nevertheless, it appears that market participants are currently adjusting well to the changing environment.

ENDNOTES

1. All depository institutions will be referred to as "banks" for the remainder of this article.
2. For more details, see Board of Governors of the Federal Reserve System (1997).
3. For more information on required clearing balances, see Stevens (1993).
4. For a more detailed description of the mechanics of different types of sweep arrangements, see Federal Reserve Bank of New York (1996).
5. Federal Reserve Board Regulation D restricts the amount of reserves a bank can carry over into the next maintenance period to 4 percent or less of its required reserves.
6. For example, since the middle of the 1980s, the Federal Reserve has made available computer screens that allow banks to track large-dollar payments systems debits and credits to their Fed accounts. The usefulness of this information system to bank money managers increased markedly in the early 1990s, when the Fed began to enter virtually all debits and credits on the real-time intraday totals transmitted to banks, essentially giving them very timely account balance estimates to compare with their internal information flows and projections.
7. One final consideration that should temper concerns about increasing volatility is related to our measure of volatility, the difference between the high and low rates on federal funds transactions in any one day. This measure may exaggerate the degree of volatility that actually exists because it captures extreme values and does not distinguish between transactions in which the dollar amount borrowed is small and transactions in which large sums change hands. Indeed, much of the recent moderate widening in the trading range appears due to smaller transactions.

REFERENCES

Board of Governors of the Federal Reserve System. 1997. *Federal Reserve Bulletin*, February.
Federal Reserve Bank of New York. 1996. "Open Market Operations during 1995." Federal Reserve Bank of New York *Annual Report, 1995*.
Greenspan, Alan. 1997. Remarks before the U.S. Senate Committee on Banking, Housing and Urban Affairs. Hearing on the Federal Reserve's Semiannual Report on Monetary Policy. 105th Cong., 1st sess., February 26. Federal Document Clearing House. *FDCH Political Transcripts*. Washington, D.C.
Stevens, E.J. 1993. "Required Clearing Balances." Federal Reserve Bank of Cleveland *Economics Review* 29, no. 4.

PART IV   Central Banking and the Conduct of Monetary Policy

> **QUESTIONS**
>
> 1. Describe how banks' required reserve balances are determined and how they meet these required amounts.
>
> 2. What are clearing balances and why do banks hold them?
>
> 3. Why have banks' required balances trended downward in recent years?
>
> 4. Describe the purpose and operation of the federal funds market, including the roles of the Fed and banks.
>
> 5. Why might the downward trend in required balances lead to greater volatility of the federal funds rate? What concequences would this engender? Is increased volatility becoming a problem? Why?

READING 23

Never Mind Those Ms

Europe's road to monetary union is a rocky one. In some countries, notably Britain, public opinion runs heavily against adopting a single European currency. There is a deep rift between prospective members with solid economic fundamentals and those using creative accounting to make their budget deficits appear smaller. And then there is the burning debate between France and Germany over the role of politicians in managing the new currency.

Another controversy, which is only now starting to heat up, is over how Europe's future monetary policy will be conducted. If monetary union does go ahead, a new European central bank will be charged with managing Europe's money. Exactly how it handles that task will have much to do with whether the new Euro proves a success or a failure.

At present, national central banks follow diverse approaches when it comes to doing their jobs. The Bank of England uses an inflation target to decide whether monetary policy should be loosened or tightened. In contrast, Germany's Bundesbank keeps its eye on various measures of the money supply—known as monetary aggregates—and it wants the European central bank to work in a similar way. A third approach favoured by some other central banks is to base monetary policy largely on the economy's nominal rate of growth, without regard to how much of that figure represents inflation and how much is real economic gain.

Which approach will work best for Europe's new money? A recent paper[1] by Arturo Estrella and Frederic Mishkin, both of the Federal Reserve Bank of New York, suggests that heavy reliance on money-supply measures is a bad idea.

Messrs Estrella and Mishkin examine the relationships between various measures of money-supply growth, inflation and nominal income. In theory, all other things being equal, faster money growth should lead to faster growth in both prices and nominal income. But in practice, they find, the relationship is almost non-existent. Changes in the growth rate of America's M2, the most widely watched money-supply measure, have no strong correlation with either future inflation or future nominal income. What limited predictive power M2 once had has all but disappeared since 1979, they find.

It is not just M2 that has lost its usefulness. When they look at America's monetary base, a narrow measure of money that includes mainly bank reserves and cash, the authors find it to be an even less useful

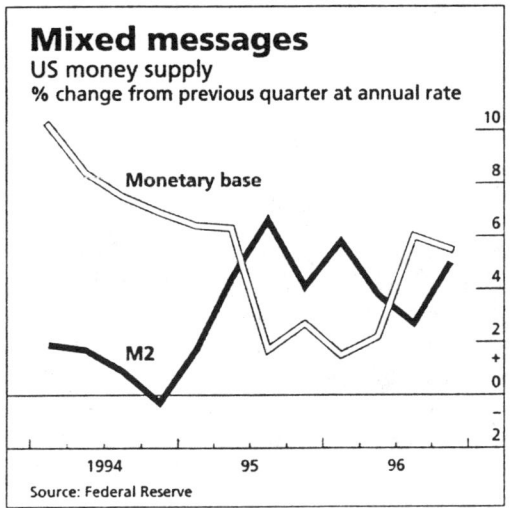

Mixed messages
US money supply
% change from previous quarter at annual rate
Source: Federal Reserve

predictor of future inflation or output than M2. And much the same story seems to hold in Germany. Changes in the Bundesbank's favourite money supply gauge, M3, are only weakly related to changes in German inflation and nominal income. As a result, the economists conclude that monetary aggregates cannot be used in a straightforward way for monetary policy.

Why are the monetary measures no longer useful? The main reason seems to be financial innovation. Before the late 1970s, each money-supply measure rested on assumptions about how easily that form of "money" could be converted into goods and services. M1, which consists mostly of cash and cheque-like deposits, was thought to be easily spendable. Changes in M2, which takes in small time-deposits and money-market fund balances along with cash and cheque accounts, were thought to have a less immediate impact, while M3, which incorporates M2 plus large, longer-term deposits, was felt to have an even weaker influence on spending.

New types of financial instruments have blurred those boundaries. Many money-market funds offer cheque-writing privileges, for example, so money that is being counted in M2 can be spent just as readily as money in the bank cheque-writing accounts included in M1. As a result, the relationship between any of the monetary aggregates and economic variables, such as output and inflation, is much more unstable than it once was. This means that a central bank cannot assure a stable inflation rate simply by targeting a particular growth rate of some monetary aggregate.

A TARGET FOR EUROPE

These findings from researchers at America's central bank should be closely studied by European central bankers. Earlier this month, the European Monetary Institute (the EMI)—the forerunner of the central bank—released a report about how the European central bank should manage future monetary policy. However, the EMI's experts ducked the question of whether a target for inflation or money-supply growth would be the best way to achieve the central bank's goal of price stability. The final decision about how to manage monetary policy will be taken by the governing body of the European central bank.

The new central bank would be foolish to adopt a strict money-supply target, since monetary aggregates could well prove to be even more misleading in a Europe-wide setting than they have been at the national level. With no history to rely on, no one can know what the relationship will be between the supply of Europe's new money and the performance of Europe's economy. In the Euro's first few years, the Ms may be especially volatile as people and businesses adjust to the many changes in the financial system that will accompany the single currency.

In such circumstances, a monetary target could well damage the credibility of the European central bank. In its early years, the bank will be keen to show that its anti-inflationary credentials are as tough as the Bundesbank's. Experience from Canada to New Zealand shows that an inflation target, by making a central bank more publicly accountable, helps to strengthen the credibility of its monetary policy.

This does not mean that the European central bank should ignore the money supply completely. From time to time, changes in the monetary aggregates may offer up vital clues about future inflation. But tracking the money supply alone is more likely to lead policymakers down the wrong path.

ENDNOTE

1. "Is there a Role for Monetary Aggregates in the Conduct of Monetary Policy?" NBER working paper no. 5845. November 1996.

QUESTIONS

1. What various approaches to the conduct of monetary policy are used currently by national central banks in Europe?

2. What evidence and arguments support the claim that money-supply measures have lost their usefulness and should not be used as policy targets by a European central bank?

READING 24

Inflation Targeting: A New Framework for Monetary Policy?

Ben S. Bernanke and Frederic S. Mishkin

The world's central bankers and their staffs meet regularly, in venues from Basle to Washington, to share ideas and discuss common problems. Perhaps these frequent meetings help explain why changes in the tactics and strategy of monetary policymaking—such as the adoption of money growth targets in the 1970s, the intensification of efforts to reduce inflation in the 1980s, and the recent push for increased institutional independence for central banks—tend to occur in many countries more or less simultaneously. Whatever their source, major changes in the theory and practice of central banking are of great importance, for both individual countries and the international economy. In this article, we discuss a new strategy for monetary policy known as "inflation targeting," which has sparked much interest and debate among central bankers and monetary economists in recent years. This approach is characterized, as the name suggests, by the announcement of official target ranges for the inflation rate at one or more horizons, and by explicit acknowledgement that low and stable inflation is the overriding goal of monetary policy. Other important features of inflation targeting include increased communication with the public about the plans and objectives of the monetary policymakers, and, in many cases, increased accountability of the central bank for attaining those objectives.

Inflation targeting in various forms has been adopted in recent years by a number of industrialized countries, including Canada, the United Kingdom, New Zealand, Sweden, Australia, Finland, Spain and Israel.[1] Table 1 offers some details about the specific plans in each country. There are also important elements of inflation targeting, as we discuss below, in the long-standing and well-regarded monetary policy approaches of Germany and Switzerland. In the United States, inflation targeting has been advocated by some influential policymakers, and Senator Connie Mack (R-Fla.) has introduced a bill that, if passed, would establish price stability as the primary goal of monetary policy [S.R. 1266, 104th Cong. 1st sess.]. Finally, the Maastricht treaty mandates price stability as the primary objective of the European Central Bank, and it seems likely—if European monetary union in fact occurs—that the ECB would incorporate major elements of the inflation targeting approach in its procedures (Issing, 1996).

Journal of Economic Perspectives, 11, 2 (Spring 1997): 97-116. Reprinted by permission.

READING 24 Inflation Targeting: A New Framework for Monetary Policy?

Table 1
Operational Aspects of Inflation Targets

Country (date of adoption)	Target Series Definition	Target Level (percentage annual inflation)	Time Horizon
Australia (1993)	Underlying CPI (excluding fruit and vegetables, petrol, interest costs, public sector prices and other volatile prices)	2-3	Ongoing
Canada (February 1991)	Core CPI (excluding food, energy and first-round effects of indirect taxes)	1-3	18 months
Finland (February 1993)	Underlying CPI (excluding government subsidies, indirect taxes, housing prices and mortgage interest payments)	about 2	Ongoing
Israel (December 1991)	CPI	8-11	1 year
New Zealand (March 1990)	Underlying CPI (excluding changes in indirect taxes or government changes, significant changes in import or export prices, interest costs and natural disasters)	0-2 (until November 1996; 0-3 thereafter)	1 year
Spain (January 1995)	CPI (excluding first-round effects of indirect tax changes)	below 3	Through 1997
Sweden (January 1993)	CPI	2±1	Ongoing
United Kingdom (October 1992)	RPIX (RPI excluding mortgage interest payments)	lower half of 1-4 until spring 1997; 2.5 or less thereafter	Until the end of this Parliament

We begin our discussion of inflation targeting with some details of how this approach has been implemented in practice. We focus on the practice of inflation targeting, rather than the theory, because we believe that the rhetoric associated with inflation targeting is often misleading. In particular, we will argue that actual experience with this approach shows that inflation targeting does not represent an ironclad policy *rule*, as some writers on the subject and even some advocates of this approach seem to assume. Instead, inflation targeting is better understood as a policy *framework*, whose major advantage is increased transparency and coherence of policy, and in which fairly flexible, even "discretionary" monetary policy actions can be accommodated.[2] We next discuss in more detail why viewing inflation targeting as a framework, rather than a rule, blunts some of the arguments that have been made against it and in general enhances the appeal of this approach. This is not to say that valid questions do not remain about this strategy for monetary policy; in the final portion of the paper we discuss some important additional issues and draw conclusions about the usefulness of the inflation targeting framework.

INFLATION TARGETING IN PRACTICE

Although every country that has adopted inflation targeting has customized the approach in various ways, certain empirical generalizations about this strategy can be made.

The hallmark of inflation targeting is the announcement by the government, the central bank, or some combination of the two that in the future the central bank will strive to hold inflation at or near some numerically specified level. As can be seen in Table 1, inflation targets are more often than not specified as ranges—for example, 1-3 percent—rather than single numbers, and they are typically established for multiple horizons ranging from one to four years. However, there are exceptions to both observations; indeed, Germany, with the longest experience with inflation-focused monetary policy, specifies its implicit inflation target as a point and only for a one-year horizon. Initial announcements of inflation targeting generally allow for a gradual transition from the current level of inflation to a desired steady-state level, usually the level deemed consistent with price stability. "Price stability" never in practice means literally zero inflation, however, but usually something closer to a 2 percent annual rate of price change, for reasons we discuss later.

There is a lively debate over whether targeting should be of the inflation rate per se or of the price level. Of course, a targeted price level need not remain constant indefinitely, but could be allowed to drift upward in a predetermined way over time (Goodhart and Vinals, 1994; Svensson, 1996). The relative disadvantage of targeting the inflation rate is that unanticipated shocks to the price level may be treated as bygones and never offset; as a result, forecasts of the price level at long horizons might have a large variance under inflation targeting, which presumably impedes private-sector planning.[3] On the other hand, strict price-level targeting requires that overshoots or undershoots of the target be fully made up, which reduces the variance of long-run forecasts of prices but could impart significantly more volatility into

READING 24 Inflation Targeting: A New Framework for Monetary Policy?

monetary policy in the short run.[4] In practice, central banks tend to compensate partially for target misses, particularly at shorter horizons.

Associated with the announcement of inflation targets there is usually some statement to the effect that control of inflation is the "primary" or "overriding" goal of monetary policy and that the central bank will be held accountable for meeting the inflation targets. For example, Section 8 of the Reserve Bank of New Zealand Act of 1989 assigns the central bank the statutory responsibility "to formulate and implement monetary policy directed to the economic objective of achieving and maintaining stability in the general level of prices," with no mention of competing goals. Section 9 of the act requires the Minister of Finance and the Governor of the Reserve Bank to negotiate and make public a Policy Targets Agreement (PTA), setting out specific inflation targets. In other countries, such as Switzerland, Canada and the United Kingdom, the inflation goal is embodied in public statements by the central bank rather than mandated by law.

The rationale for treating inflation as the primary goal of monetary policy is clearly strongest when medium- to long-term horizons are considered, as most economists agree that monetary policy can affect real quantities, such as output and employment, only in the short run. Of course, some economists of new classical or monetarist persuasions might claim that inflation should be the sole concern of monetary policy in the short run as well, arguing that using monetary policy for short-run stabilization of the real economy is undesirable, infeasible, or both. However, in practice no central bank has of yet completely forsworn the use of monetary policy for short-run stabilization, and so the phraseology "primary" or "overriding" must be taken to refer to the longer term.

The degree to which the central bank is held formally accountable for inflation outcomes varies considerably. The New Zealand law links the tenure of the governor of the Reserve Bank to the achieving of the inflation targets, and thus comes closest to providing an explicit "incentive contract," as proposed by Persson and Tabellini (1993) and Walsh (1995).[5] In other countries, no explicit sanctions on the central bank for missing the target are given; presumably, however, missing the target badly would impose implicit institutional or personal costs in terms of lost reputation or prestige. It is rather early in many of the inflation-targeting experiments to judge the extent to which the prospective penalties for missing announced targets will constrain central bank behavior.

Despite the language referring to inflation control as the primary objective of monetary policy, as we have said, inflation-targeting central banks always make room for short-run stabilization objectives, particularly with respect to output and exchange rates.[6] This accommodation of short-run stabilization goals is accomplished through several means. First, the price index on which the official inflation targets are based is often defined to exclude or down-weight the effects of "supply shocks;" for example, the officially targeted price index may exclude some combination of food and energy prices, indirect tax changes, terms-of-trade shocks, and the direct effects of interest rate changes on the index (for example, through imputed rental costs). Second, as already noted, inflation targets are typically specified as a range; the use of ranges generally reflect not only uncertainty about the link between policy levers and inflation outcomes but is also intended to allow the central bank some flexibility in the short run. Third, short-term inflation targets can and have been adjusted to accommodate supply shocks or other exogenous changes in the inflation rate outside the central bank's control. A model here is the Deutsche Bundesbank's practice of stating its short-term (one-year) inflation projection as the level of "unavoidable inflation." In the aftermath of the 1979 oil shock, for example, the Bundesbank announced the "unavoidable" inflation rate to be 4 percent, then moved its target gradually down to 2 percent over a six-year period. In other cases, the central bank or government makes explicit an "escape clause," which permits the inflation target to be suspended or modified in the face of certain adverse economic developments.

In making inflation, a goal variable, the focus of monetary policy, the inflation-targeting strategy in most cases significantly reduces the role of formal intermediate targets, such as the exchange rate or money growth. To the extent that intermediate targets are used, it is emphasized that the inflation goal takes precedence in case of conflict. Unconditional commitment to an intermediate target is of course inconsistent with inflation targeting (except in the unusual case that the intermediate target effectively summarizes all current information about inflation at the forecast horizon). The fact that in most countries the relation between intermediate targets, such as money growth, and the central bank's goal variables has proven to be relatively unreliable—the so-called "velocity instability" problem—is a major motivation for dropping formal intermediate targets and instead attempting to target the goal variable directly.

On the other hand, since targeting inflation directly requires that the central bank form forecasts of the likely path of prices, close attention is typically paid to a variety of indicators that have shown predictive power for inflation in the past. For example, as an aid to inflation forecasting, monetary policymakers in Canada and Sweden make use of a "monetary conditions index," a weighted combination of the exchange rate and the short-term interest rate, in conjunction with other standard indicators such as money and credit aggregates, commodity prices, capacity utilization and wage developments.[7]

In most inflation-targeting regimes, the central bank publishes regular, detailed assessments of the inflation situation, including current forecasts of inflation and discussions of the policy response that is needed to keep inflation on track. A good example is in the Bank of England's *Inflation Report*, published quarterly, which contains detailed analyses of factors likely to affect the inflation rate as well as probabilistic forecasts of inflation, assuming no change in interest rates. The central banks of Canada and Sweden release similar documents, and the Reserve Bank of New Zealand is required to issue a policy statement at least every six months. As we discuss further below, the use of such reports reflects a key objective of inflation targeting, which is improved communication with the public about monetary

READING 24 Inflation Targeting: A New Framework for Monetary Policy?

policy, its goals and, in particular, the long-run implications of current policy actions.

The adoption of inflation targeting is often linked with changes in the laws or administrative arrangements associated with the central bank. Typically, reforms are in the direction of increased independence for the central bank, particularly in respect to its choice of instrument settings.[8] This seems to be a logical consequence of making price stability the overriding goal of policy, since the central bank is the best place to make the technical decisions necessary to achieve price stability and to make judgments about whether the pursuit of other objectives is consistent with this goal. Exceptions to this observation are the United Kingdom and, to a lesser extent, Canada, where despite the commitment to inflation targeting, the government, rather than the central bank, retains the final control over monetary policy. However, even in the British case the adoption of inflation targeting seems to have increased the relative influence of the central bank, as the *Inflation Report* and the timely publication of the minutes of the monthly meeting between the Governor and the Chancellor of the Exchequer provide an independent forum for the bank to express its views; in effect, the government must rationalize for the public any deviations of its policies from those recommended by the bank.

Most or all of the characteristics of inflation targeting described in this section apply to countries adopting this approach within the last eight years or so; as noted in the introduction, these include Canada, the United Kingdom, New Zealand, Sweden, Australia, Finland, Spain and Israel. Germany and Switzerland, which have conducted inflation-focused monetary policies since the mid-1970s, are better viewed as "hybrid" cases, which meet some but not all of the above criteria. These two countries differ from the "pure" inflation targeters primarily in their greater focus on money growth as an intermediate target, and indeed, the Bundesbank has emphasized the superiority (in their view) of money targeting as a means of insuring monetary discipline and transparency (for example, Deutsche Bundesbank, 1995, pp. 67-8). In fact, many observers (including ourselves) would argue that the distinction between inflation and money targeting is overstated and that monetary policies in both countries are driven in the medium and long term primarily by inflation goals. For example, the Bundesbank's money growth targets are derived, using the quantity equation, to be consistent with an annual inflation target, given projections of the growth of potential output and of possible changes in the velocity of money. This inflation target, in turn, has been brought down steadily over time and has remained at 2 percent—the level deemed consistent by the Bundesbank with price stability—since 1986. Further, the Bundesbank has shown itself quite willing to miss its money targets when pursuing these targets threatens to conflict with the control of inflation (von Hagen, 1995; Bernanke and Mihov, 1997).

All in all, the philosophy guiding German and Swiss monetary policies seems relatively consistent with the one motivating the self-declared inflation targeters. The main practical difference between the two sets of countries is that the Germans and Swiss believe that the velocity of money has been relatively more stable in their countries, and so they view money-growth targeting as a useful tool for implementing their inflation objectives. It is also true that Germany and Switzerland have been less explicit in stating their inflation targets; neither central bank publishes a regular inflation report per se. But this distinction seems relatively unimportant; inflation developments receive prominent attention in the regular publications of both banks. Moreover, there may be less need for public declarations given the long-standing commitment of the Bundesbank and Swiss National Bank—and the popular support for that commitment—to price stability. The examples of Germany and Switzerland are important because, unlike the other countries mentioned, these two countries have been following their monetary policy strategies fairly consistently for more than two decades, rather than for only a few years; thus, their experiences may provide researchers attempting to assess the value of inflation-focused monetary policy with useful information.

A FRAMEWORK, NOT A RULE

The motivations for an inflation-targeting approach have been varied. In a number of cases, such as those of the United Kingdom and Sweden, the collapse of an exchange rate peg led the monetary authorities to search for an alternative "nominal anchor" for monetary policy, a way of reassuring the public that monetary policy would remain disciplined. The demise of a fixed-exchange-rate regime similarly motivated the adoption of a money-focused approach by Germany in the mid-1970s. Some countries, such as Canada, came to inflation targeting after unsuccessful attempts to use a money-targeting approach. For example, in the case of Canada, by 1980 inflation was as high as it was in 1975 (10 percent per year) despite adherence to monetary targets that led to lower money growth rates (Howitt, 1993). In other cases, countries that by tight monetary policies had succeeded in reducing their core rate of inflation adopted inflation targeting as an institutional means of locking in their inflation gains.

Developments in macroeconomic theory also played some role in the growing popularity of the inflation targeting approach. These familiar developments included reduced confidence in activist, countercyclical monetary policy; the widespread acceptance of the view that there is no long-run tradeoff between output (or unemployment) and inflation, so that monetary policy affects only prices in the long run; theoretical arguments for the value of precommitment and credibility in monetary policy (Kydland and Prescott, 1977; Calvo, 1978; Barro and Gordon, 1983); and an increasing acceptance of the proposition that low inflation promotes long-run economic growth and efficiency.

Unfortunately, the interpretation of inflation targeting in terms of some long-standing debates in monetary economics has also been the source of confusion. For many years the principal debate about the best approach for monetary policy was framed as an opposition between two polar strategies, termed "rules" and "discretion." Advocates

READING 24 Inflation Targeting: A New Framework for Monetary Policy?

of rules—such as the fixed rule for money growth proposed by Milton Friedman, or a gold standard—argued that "tying the hands" of policymakers will prevent the monetary authorities from implementing counter-productive attempts at short-run stabilization and will thus eliminate the inflationary bias inherent in discretionary monetary policy. Supporters of discretionary policymaking—under which the central bank is left free to "do the right thing" as economic conditions evolve—stress the inability of ironclad rules to deal with unforeseen shocks or changes in the structure of the economy.

For various reasons, including the rhetoric of some of its proponents, inflation targeting is sometimes interpreted as falling on the "rule" side of this traditional dichotomy (for example, Friedman and Kuttner, 1996). We view this characterization of inflation targeting as a mistake; indeed, we would go farther and say that the traditional dichotomy of monetary policy strategies into rules and discretion is itself misleading. In particular, some useful policy strategies are "rule-like," in that by their forward-looking nature they constrain central banks from systematically engaging in policies with undesirable long-run consequences; but which also allow some discretion for dealing with unforeseen or unusual circumstances. These hybrid or intermediate approaches may be said to subject the central bank to "constrained discretion." We argue below that inflation targeting should be viewed in this way, rather than as a rigid policy rule.

If inflation targeting is interpreted as a rule in the classic Friedman sense, then it would have to be conceded that this approach is vulnerable to some important criticisms. First, the idea that monetary policy has (essentially) no legitimate goals besides inflation would find little support among central bankers, the public and most monetary economists. Second, given that central banks do care about output, employment, exchange rates and other variables besides inflation, treating inflation targeting as a literal rule could lead to very poor economic outcomes. As Friedman and Kuttner (1996) emphasize, much in the same way that money-growth targeting in the United States was done in by unpredicted shocks to the velocity of money, so an exclusive emphasis on inflation goals could lead to a highly unstable real economy should there be significant supply shocks, such as large changes in the price of oil.

Finally, critics of inflation targeting *as a rule* might well ask what is gained by the loss of flexibility entailed by precommitting monetary policy in this way. The academic literature on rules argues that tying the hands of policymakers will reduce the inflation bias of discretionary policy and perhaps allow for less costly disinflations, as increased credibility leads inflation expectations to moderate more quickly. However, critics of inflation targeting could point out that, although inflation-targeting countries have generally achieved and maintained low rates of inflation, little evidence supports the view that these reduced rates of inflation have been obtained at a lower sacrifice of output and employment than disinflations pursued under alternative regimes (at least so far). Even the Deutsche Bundesbank and the Swiss National Bank, whose pursuit of low inflation over the last two decades has presumably given the maximum credibility, have been able to achieve inflation reductions only at high costs in lost output and employment (Debelle and Fischer, 1994; Posen, 1995). Nor is there evidence that the introduction of inflation targets materially affects private-sector expectations of inflation, as revealed either by surveys or by the level of long-term nominal interest rates. Inflation expectations have come down, in most cases, only as inflation-targeting central banks have demonstrated that they can deliver low inflation (Posen and Laubach, 1996).

These objections are certainly important, as far as they go. However, again, they derive much of their force from the assumption that inflation targeting is to be viewed as an ironclad rule. As we have said, we believe that interpreting inflation targeting as a type of monetary policy rule is a fundamental mischaracterization of this approach *as it is actually practiced by contemporary central banks*. First, at a technical level, inflation targeting does not qualify as a policy rule in that it does not provide simple and mechanical operational instructions to the central bank. Rather, the inflation targeting approach enjoins the central bank to use its structural and judgmental models of the economy, in conjunction with all relevant information, to determine the policy action most likely to achieve the inflation target, and then to take that action. Unlike simple policy rules, inflation targeting never requires that the central bank ignore information that bears on its achieving its objectives. Second, and more importantly, inflation targeting as it is actually practiced contains a considerable degree of what most economists would define as policy discretion. Within the general constraints imposed by their medium- to long-term inflation targets, central bankers have in practice left themselves considerable scope to respond to current unemployment conditions, exchange rates and other short-run developments.

The 1989 reform of the Reserve Bank of New Zealand, for example, is often held up as an example of the rule-making impulse. It is important to note that New Zealand is the most extreme of all the inflation-targeting countries in its use of formal institutional constraints on policy. Even so, the New Zealand law does provide the central bank some discretion and flexibility; for example, the target inflation series excludes movements in commodity prices; the target may be readjusted if necessary in the judgment of the bank in response to supply or terms-of-trade shocks; the inflation target is specified as a 3 percentage point range rather than as a single number; and there is an explicit escape clause that permits amending the target in the face of unexpected developments. In practice, inflation targeting in New Zealand has been implemented even more flexibly. Inflation was brought down to its current low level only gradually; and when inflation moved briefly above the target range in 1996, the Parliament did not seriously consider its option of replacing the governor of the central bank.

If inflation targeting is not a rule in the way this term is usually understood, then what is it, and what good is it? We believe that it is most fruitful to think of inflation targeting not as a rule, but as a framework for monetary policy within which "constrained discretion" can be exercised. This framework

READING 24 Inflation Targeting: A New Framework for Monetary Policy?

has the potential to serve two important functions: improving communication between policymakers and the public, and providing increased discipline and accountability for monetary policy.

In terms of communication, the announcement of inflation targets clarifies the central bank's intentions for the markets and for the general public, reducing uncertainty about the future course of inflation. (Of course, this assumes that the announcements are believable and believed; more on this later.) Arguably, many of the costs of inflation arise from its uncertainty or variability more than from its level. Uncertain inflation complicates long-term saving and investment decisions, exacerbates relative price volatility, and increases the riskiness of nominal financial and wage contracts. Uncertainty about central bank intentions may also induce volatility in financial markets—a common phenomenon in the United States, where stock market analysts parse every sentence uttered by the Fed chairman in search of hidden meanings. Inflation targets offer transparency of policy; they make explicit the central bank's policy intentions in a way that should improve private-sector planning, enhance the possibility of public debate about the direction of monetary policy, and increase central bank accountability. Transparency has been claimed as a positive feature of other policy strategies, such as money-growth targeting, but we doubt that concepts like the growth rates of particular money aggregates are nearly so understandable to the general public as is the predicted rate of change of consumer prices.

To see the practical advantage of policy transparency, consider the familiar scenario in which an upcoming election or a slow economic recovery induces the government to pressure the central bank to apply some short-run stimulus. In an inflation-targeting regime, the central bank would be able—indeed, would be required—to make explicit that the short-run benefits of this policy (faster real growth) may well be purchased at the price of medium- and long-term inflation. These projections could then be debated by politicians, press and public, but at least the issue of long-run inflation effects would be on the table, serving as an explicit counterweight to the short-run benefits of monetary expansion. Making the linkage of short-term policies and long-term consequences explicit would clarify for the public what monetary policy can and cannot do.

Aggregate supply shocks, such as oil price shocks, present a thornier policy problem. If a severe supply shock hits the economy, keeping medium-term inflation close to the long-run target could well be very costly in terms of lost output. However, in practice, a well-implemented inflation-targeting regime need not strongly constrain the ability of the monetary authorities to respond to a supply shock. Remember, the inflation target itself can be and typically is defined to exclude at least the first-round effects of some important supply shocks, such as changes in the prices of food and energy or in value-added taxes; the use of target ranges for inflation gives additional flexibility. Escape clauses, which permit the central bank to change its medium-term targets in response to major developments, are another possibility. We have seen, for example, that the Bundesbank's one-year inflation targets were often defined by its view of how much inflation was "unavoidable," rather than by its long-run objective of price stability. Thus, intermediate-run inflation targets can be used to define a transition path by which the temporary inflation induced by a supply shock is eliminated gradually over time. Relative to a purely discretionary approach, the inflation-targeting framework should give the central bank a better chance of convincing the public that the consequences of the supply shock are only a one-time rise in the price level, rather than a permanent increase in inflation. A relevant example occurred in Canada in 1991, shortly after their implementation of inflation targeting, when a sharp increase in indirect taxes caused a blip in the price level but had no apparent effect on the underlying inflation rate.

The idea that inflation targeting requires an accounting of the long-run implications of short-run "discretionary" actions is also central to the argument that inflation targeting helps to discipline monetary policy. In practice, exactly who needs disciplining may differ from country to country, depending on politics, institutional arrangements and personalities. In the macroeconomic literature on central bank credibility, it is the central bank that needs discipline, because it is assumed to desire an unemployment rate lower than the natural rate. This desire leads the monetary authority to try to "fool" the public with surprise inflation, inducing producers (who confuse nominal and real price increases) to increase output and employment above the natural rate. If the public has rational expectations, however, it will anticipate the central bank's actions, and producers will not be fooled, so that in equilibrium the economy will suffer higher-than-optimal inflation with no benefits in terms of lower unemployment.[9]

If a story along these lines describes the actual situation in a given economy, then an inflation-targeting framework will not *directly* prevent the counterproductive attempts of the central bank to engage in excessive short-run stimulus. In this respect, inflation targeting is inferior to an ironclad rule, if such could be implemented. However, in contrast to the purely discretionary situation with no explicit targets, under inflation targeting the central bank would be forced to calculate and to publicize the implications of its short-run actions for expected inflation in the long run (and again, these projections would be subject to scrutiny and debate). To the extent that the central bank governors dislike admitting publicly that they are off track with respect to their long-run inflation targets, the existence of this framework would provide an additional incentive for the central bank to limit its short-run opportunism.

Although the theoretical literature typically posits the central bank as the entity who chooses to inflate opportunistically, we suspect that in most cases the executive and legislative branches of the government have the greater incentive to engage in such behavior, often because of approaching elections. Central bankers, in contrast, tend to view themselves as defenders of the currency. This view may be the result of intentional appointments of "tough" central bankers (for reasons described by Rogoff, 1985), or it may just be that self-

READING 24 Inflation Targeting: A New Framework for Monetary Policy?

selection and socialization act to make central bankers relatively hawkish on inflation. But in either case, the existence of longer-term inflation targets can prove a useful device by which the central bank can protect itself politically from overexpansionist pressures. In particular, by making explicit the long-run, as well as the short-run, implications of overexpansionist policies, the central bank may be better able to get the support it needs to resist such policies. Our impression is that the Bank of England, for example, has on occasion used numerical inflation targets in precisely this way.

FURTHER ISSUES WITH INFLATION TARGETING

If viewed as a framework rather than as a rule, inflation targeting can confer some important advantages. It provides a nominal anchor for policy and the economy. By communicating the central bank's objectives and views, it increases the transparency of monetary policy. It has the potential to provide increased discipline and accountability for policymakers. Importantly, it may be able to achieve all this without entirely giving up the benefits of discretionary policies in the short run. These optimistic conclusions notwithstanding, important questions and controversies remain around inflation targeting, even when interpreted in the way that we prefer. Let us consider a few of these.

Which Inflation Measure? What Target Value?

A critical aspect of the design of an inflation-targeting regime is the definition of the price series to be used in the inflation target. The series needs to be considered accurate, timely and readily understood by the public, but may also need to allow for individual price shocks or one-time shifts that do not affect trend inflation, which is what monetary policy should influence. As Table 1 indicates, all inflation-targeting countries have chosen some variant of the consumer price index (CPI) as their target series. However, this choice is not typically the "headline" CPI figure, but an index that excludes some components or focuses on "core" inflation; clearly, it is incumbent on the central bank to explain its choice of index and to help the public understand its relation to the headline index.

In all inflation-targeting regimes, the inflation objective has been set at a low number, 4 percent or less. Is this the ideal range for the inflation target? Or would a somewhat higher range for inflation, which might involve lower initial output cost to attain, be acceptable?

Obtaining direct empirical confirmation of a link between inflation and economic performance is very difficult. Inflation is, after all, an endogenous variable; and so we rarely if ever see variation in inflation that is not associated with some third factor, such as supply shocks or political instability, which would plausibly affect other elements of economic performance as well.[10] As a result, economists' views on the subject have been based largely on prior arguments, intuition and indirect evidence. That conceded, it is nevertheless clear that the professional consensus, which at one time did not ascribe substantial costs to moderate inflation, has over the past few decades begun to take the costs of inflation more seriously. For example, Feldstein (1996) has emphasized the importance of inflation-induced inefficiencies, via the tax code, on capital formation. Fischer (1993) and others have provided some evidence that macroeconomic stability, including control of inflation, is an important precondition for economic growth. Shiller's (1996) opinion surveys of public attitudes about inflation, while confirming economists' suspicions that the public is confused about even the definition of inflation, also show that people believe inflation to be highly uneven in its distributional impacts and hence corrosive of the social compact. A strengthening preference for low inflation is quite visible in policy circles, perhaps most strikingly in the tough limits on inflation imposed by the Maastricht treaty on countries that want to join the European currency union.

Given the growing consensus that the long-term goal of monetary policy should be a low inflation rate, there remains the question of how low it should be. It seems clear that an inflation target of zero or near zero is not desirable, for several reasons. First, much recent research suggests that official CPI inflation rates tend to overstate the true rate of inflation, due to various problems such as substitution bias in the fixed-weight index and failure to account adequately for quality change. Studies for the United States have estimated this overstatement of inflation to be in the range of 0.5 to 2.0 percentage points per year.[11] Thus, as a practical matter, even if the central bank chooses to pursue a zero rate of true inflation, the target for the measured inflation rate should be greater than zero.

Putting aside measurement issues, there are other risks of setting the inflation target too low. In a much discussed recent article, Akerlof, Dickens and Perry (1996) point out that if nominal wages are rigid downward (a possibility that they argue is consistent with the evidence), then reductions in real wages can occur only through inflation in the general price level. Very low inflation therefore effectively reduces real-wage flexibility and hence may worsen the allocative efficiency of the labor market; indeed, the authors perform simulations suggesting that inflation rates near zero would permanently increase the natural rate of unemployment.[12] Another danger of setting the inflation target too low is that there is a greater chance that the economy will be tipped into deflation, with the true price level actually falling—as may have happened during the recent recession in Japan. As pointed out in the literature on financial crises, persistent deflation—particularly if unanticipated—can create serious problems for the financial system, interfering with its normal functioning and precipitating an economic contraction (Bernanke and James 1991; Mishkin, 1991).

These risks suggest that the inflation target, even when corrected for measurement error, should be set above zero, as has been the practice of all inflation-targeting countries to date. Indeed, a potentially important advantage of inflation targeting is that it provides not only a ceiling for the inflation rate, but also a floor. Inflation targeting thus acts to attenuate the effects of negative, as well as positive, shocks to aggregate demand. An interesting historical example is that of Sweden in the 1930s, which adopted a "norm of price stabilization" after leaving the gold standard in 1931. As a result, Sweden did not undergo the devastating deflation experienced by other countries during the Great Depression (Jonung, 1979).

Is Inflation Sufficiently Predictable and Controllable to be "Targeted"?

It has been noted by several authors that inflation is very difficult to predict accurately, particularly at both very short and very long horizons (Cecchetti, 1995). This lack of predictability poses two important problems for the inflation targeting strategy. The first is strictly operational: given the long lags between monetary policy actions and the inflation response, low predictability suggests that accurate targeting of inflation could be extremely difficult. The second issue has to do with the central bank's credibility: if inflation is largely unpredictable, and hence not finely controllable, then it will be difficult to judge whether the central bank has made its best effort to hit the inflation targets. For example, the central bank could always argue that wide misses were the result of bad luck, not bad faith; since central bank forecasts of inflation contain substantial judgmental components, such claims would be difficult to disprove. This possible escape hatch for the central bank weakens the argument that inflation targeting increases accountability of monetary policy and suggests that building up credibility for its inflation-targeting framework could be a long and arduous process.

While we agree that inflation targeting is less effective, the less predictable or controllable is the inflation rate, several observations should be made. First, statistical measures of predictability are themselves likely to be sensitive to the monetary policy regime in place. Inflation was no doubt difficult to predict during the 1970s, when monetary policymakers tried to deal with oil price shocks and other stagflationary pressures without a coherent, clearly articulated framework. In contrast, the stability of the inflation rate in the United States and other industrialized countries since the mid-1980s, a period during which the maintenance of low and steady inflation has received much greater weight in central bank decision making, suggests that inflation will be easier to predict in the future.

Second, the relative unpredictability of goal variables is not in itself an argument for the use of intermediate targets in the conduct of monetary policy. As Svensson (1997a) points out, from an optimal control perspective, the best possible intermediate target is the current forecast of the goal variable itself—in this context, inflation. Using an intermediate target such as money growth is acceptable in an optimal control framework only if the intermediate target contains all information relevant to forecasting the goal variable; in this extreme case, using the intermediate target is equivalent to targeting the forecast of the goal variable. However, if any variable other than the intermediate target contains marginal information about the future values of the goal variable, then targeting the inflation forecast strictly dominates using any single intermediate target. Thus, from a strictly operational point of view, while it is unfortunate if the goal variable is hard to predict or to control, no improvement is available by using an intermediate target.[13]

When the credibility of the central bank is at issue, the problem of whether to target inflation directly or to rely on an intermediate target becomes more complex. By Svensson's argument, use of the intermediate target must increase the variance of the goal variable, which is a cost of the intermediate targeting approach; the benefit, however, is that by hitting its announced target for the intermediate variable, the central bank can demonstrate the seriousness of its intentions to the public more quickly and reliably (Cukierman, 1995; Laubach, 1996). If credibility building is an important objective of the central bank, and if there exists an intermediate target variable—such as monetary aggregate—that is well controlled by the central bank, observed and understood by the public and the financial markets, and strongly and reliably related to the ultimate goal variable, then targeting the intermediate variable may be the preferred strategy. All of these are big "ifs," particularly the last one. However, this analysis may help to explain the continued use of money-growth targets by Germany and Switzerland, where financial institutions and hence velocity have evolved rather slowly, while countries such as the United Kingdom, with a history of unstable velocity, have opted for targeting inflation directly.

Is Inflation the Right Goal Variable for Monetary Policy?

The consensus that monetary policy is neutral in the long run restricts the set of feasible long-run goal variables for monetary policy, but inflation is not the only possibility. Notably, a number of economists have proposed that central banks should target the growth rate of nominal GDP rather than inflation (Taylor, 1985; Hall and Mankiw, 1994). Nominal GDP growth, which can be thought of as "velocity-corrected" money growth (that is, if velocity were constant, nominal GDP growth and money growth would be equal, by definition), has the advantage that it does put some weight on output as well as prices. Under a nominal GDP target, a decline in projected real output growth would automatically imply an increase in the central bank's inflation target, which would tend to be stabilizing.[14] Also, Cecchetti (1995) has presented simulations that suggest that policies directed to stabilizing nominal GDP growth may be more likely to produce good economic outcomes, given the difficulty of predicting and controlling inflation.

Nominal GDP targeting is a reasonable alternative to inflation targeting, and one that is generally consistent with the overall strategy for monetary policy discussed in this article. However, we have three reasons for mildly preferring inflation targets to nominal GDP targets. First, information on prices is more timely and frequently received than data on nominal GDP (and could be made even more so), a practical consideration that offsets some of the theoretical appeal of the nominal GDP target. Although collection of data on

READING 24 Inflation Targeting: A New Framework for Monetary Policy?

nominal GDP could also be improved, measurement of nominal GDP involves data on current quantities as well as current prices and thus is probably intrinsically more difficult to accomplish in a timely fashion. Second, given the various escape clauses and provisions for short-run flexibility built into the inflation-targeting approach, we doubt that there is much practical difference in the degree to which inflation targeting and nominal GDP targeting would allow accommodation of short-run stabilization objectives. Finally, and perhaps most important, it seems likely that the concept of inflation is better understood by the public than is the concept of nominal GDP, which could easily be confused with real GDP. If this is so, the objectives of communications and transparency would be better served by the use of an inflation target. As a matter of revealed preference, all central banks that have thus far adopted this general framework have chosen to target inflation rather than nominal GDP.

If It's Not Broke, Why Fix It?

Friedman and Kuttner (1996) decry the tendency of economists to want to impose restrictions and rules on central bank policymaking. They survey the problems with policy rules in the past, notably the failure of money-growth targeting to become a reliable policy framework in the United States, and they correctly point out that U.S. monetary policy has performed quite well in the recent past without the benefit of a formal rule or framework. Why, they ask, should we change something that is working well, especially given our inability to know what types of challenges will confront monetary policy in the future?

We would respond that a major reason for the success of the Volcker-Greenspan Fed is that it has employed a policymaking philosophy, or framework, which is de facto very similar to inflation targeting. In particular, the Fed has expressed a strong policy preference for low, steady inflation, and debates about short-run stabilization policies have prominently featured consideration of the long-term inflation implications of current Fed actions.

To take the next step and to formalize this framework would have several advantages. It would increase the transparency of the Fed's decision-making process, allowing more public debate and discussion of the Fed's strategy and tactics and, perhaps, reducing the financial and economic uncertainty associated with the Fed's current procedures. It would create an institutional commitment to the current approach that would be less dependent on a single individual's philosophy and might thus be expected to survive when, inevitably, new leadership takes over at the Fed. Finally, inflation targeting will be easiest to implement in a situation, like the current one, in which inflation is already low and the basic approach has been made familiar to the public and the markets. By adopting this approach now when it is relatively easy politically, we could ensure that the new procedures will be in place to provide guidance when the next difficult decisions about monetary policy have to be made.

CONCLUSION

It is too early to offer a final judgment on whether inflation targeting will prove to be a fad or a trend. However, our preliminary assessment is that this approach—when construed as a framework for making monetary policy, rather than as a rigid rule—has a number of advantages, including more transparent and coherent policymaking, increased accountability, and greater attention to long-run considerations in day-to-day policy debates and decisions.

ENDNOTES

1. Detailed analyses of experiences with inflation targeting can be found in Goodhart and Vinals (1994), Leiderman and Svensson (1995), Haldane (1995) and McCallum (1996), among others.
2. King (1996) adopts a similar view.
3. Technically, ensuring only that the inflation rate is stationary may leave a unit root in the price level, so that the forecast variance of the price level grows without bound. This problem is analogous to the issue of "base drift" in the literature on money-growth targeting.
4. However, Svensson (1996) gives examples in which price-level targeting actually reduces the volatility of output.
5. Svensson (1997b) relates inflation targeting to the contracting approach.
6. Another short-run objective that is almost always retained by inflation-targeting central banks is the maintenance of financial stability. For example, see Mishkin (forthcoming).
7. Users of the monetary conditions index would probably argue that treating the MCI simply as a forecasting variable is oversimple; they tend to view the MCI more specifically as a measure of how overall monetary conditions are affecting aggregate demand and thus as a potential guide to policy actions. See Freedman (1994) for further discussion.
8. Debelle and Fischer (1994) make the useful distinction between goal independence and instrument independence for the central bank. Goal independence implies the unilateral ability of the central bank to set its inflation targets and other goals, while instrument independence means that, although goals may be set by the government or by the government in consultation with the central bank, the central bank is solely responsible for choosing the instrument settings (for example, the level of short-term interest rates) necessary to achieve these goals. Instrument independence would seem to be the form of independence that maximizes central bank accountability and minimizes opportunistic political interference, while still leaving the ultimate goals of policy to be determined by democratic processes.
9. McCallum (1997) argues that the central bank can simply choose not to behave myopically, and the public's expectations will come to reflect this more farsighted behavior. He also points out, however, that to the extent time inconsistency is a problem, it will affect the government as well as the central bank; we agree, as we discuss below.
10. Studies that attempt to overcome these problems include Lebow, Roberts and Stockton (1992) and Barro (1995).
11. This bias was the subject of an official report to the Senate Finance Committee, the so-called Boskin report (Boskin et al., 1996). See also Moulton (1996) and Shapiro and Wilcox (1997).
12. The force of this argument should not be overstated. First, the inflation rates which Akerlof, Dickens and Perry (1996) argue would significantly affect the natural rate of unemployment are really quite low, for example, measured rates (as opposed to "true" rates) of inflation of 2 percent per annum or less. Second, their simulation studies do not take into account forces that may work in the opposite direction: for example, Groshen and Schweitzer (1996) point out that high and variable inflation rates may increase the "noise" in relative wages, reducing the efficiency of the process by which workers are allocated across industries and occupations; thus higher inflation can represent sand as well as grease in the wheels of the labor market.

READING 24 Inflation Targeting: A New Framework for Monetary Policy?

13. In characterizing the forecast of inflation as the intermediate target, Svensson (1997a) is careful to define "forecast" to mean the forecast derived internally by the central bank using its structural model of the economy. An intriguing alternative would be to try to "target" private-sector forecasts of inflation, that is, set short-run policy instruments so that private-sector forecasts of inflation equal the announced target. Unfortunately, as shown by Woodford (1994) and Bernanke and Woodford (1996), such a policy is usually not consistent with the existence of a unique rational expectations equilibrium. However, Bernanke and Woodford also show that, while targeting private-sector forecasts is not a good idea, private-sector forecasts can typically be combined with the central bank's own information to improve the efficiency of its operating procedure. Further, private-sector forecasts that the public observes to be close to the central bank's official targets may help to provide some validation of the bank's internal procedures for forecasting and controlling inflation.

14. Hall and Mankiw (1994) point out, however, that the equal weighting of real output growth and inflation implied by a nominal GDP targeting is not necessarily the optimal one; in general, the relative weight put on the two goal variables should reflect social preferences.

REFERENCES

Akerlof, George, William Dickens, and George Perry, "The Macroeconomics of Low Inflation," *Brookings Papers on Economic Activity*, 1996, 1, 1-59.

Barro, Robert, "Inflation and Economic Growth," *Bank of England Quarterly Bulletin*, May 1995, 35, 166-76.

Barro, Robert, and David Gordon, "Rules, Discretion, and Reputation in a Model of Monetary Policy," *Journal of Monetary Economics*, July 1983, 12, 101-21.

Bernanke, Ben, and Harold James, "The Gold Standard, Deflation, and Financial Crisis in the Great Depression: An International Comparison." In Hubbard, R.G., ed., *Financial Markets and Financial Crises*. Chicago: University of Chicago Press for NBER, 1991, pp. 33-36.

Bernanke, Ben, and Ilian Mihov, "What Does the Bundesbank Target?," *European Economic Review*, forthcoming 1997.

Bernanke, Ben, and Michael Woodford, "Inflation Forecasts and Monetary Policy," unpublished paper, Princeton University, September 1996.

Boskin, Michael J., Ellen R. Dulberger, Robert J. Gordon, Zvi Griliches, and Dale Jorgenson, "Toward a More Accurate Measure of the Cost of Living: The Final Report to the Senate Finance Committee from the Advisory Commission to Study the Consumer Price Index," December 4, 1996.

Calvo, Guillermo, "On the Time Consistency of Optimal Policy in a Monetary Economy," *Econometrica*, November 1978, 46, 1411-28.

Cecchetti, Stephen, "Inflation Indicators and Inflation Policy," *NBER Macroeconomics Annual*, 1995, 189-219.

Cukierman, Alex, "Towards a Systematic Comparison Between Inflation Targets and Money Targets." In Leiderman, L., and L. Svensson, eds., *Inflation Targets*. London: Centre for Economic Policy Research, 1995, pp. 192-209.

Debelle, Guy, and Stanley Fischer, "How Independent Should a Central Bank Be?" In Fuhrer, Jeffrey, ed., *Goals, Guidelines, and Constraints Facing Monetary Policymakers*. Boston: Federal Reserve Bank of Boston, 1994, pp. 195-221.

Deutsche Bundesbank, *The Monetary Policy of the Bundesbank*. Frankfurt am Main: Deutsche Bundesbank, 1995.

Feldstein, Martin, "The Costs and Benefits of Going from Low Inflation to Price Stability." NBER Working Paper No. 5469, February 1996.

Fischer, Stanley, "The Role of Macroeconomic Factors in Growth." NBER Working Paper No. 4565, December 1993.

Freedman, Charles, "The Use of Indicators and of the Monetary Conditions Index in Canada." In Balino, T., and C. Cottarelli, eds., *Frameworks for Monetary Stability: Policy Issues and Country Experiences*. Washington, D.C.: International Monetary Fund, 1994, pp. 458-76.

PART IV Central Banking and the Conduct of Monetary Policy

Friedman, Ben, and Kenneth Kuttner, "A Price Target for U.S. Monetary Policy? Lessons from the Experience with Money Growth Targets," *Brookings Papers on Economic Activity*, 1996, 1, 77-125.

Goodhart, Charles, and José Vinals, "Strategy and Tactics of Monetary Policy: Examples from Europe and the Antipodes." In Fuhrer, Jeffrey, ed., *Goals, Guidelines, and Constraints Facing Monetary Policymakers*. Boston: Federal Reserve Bank of Boston, 1994, pp. 139-87.

Groshen, Erica, and Mark Schweitzer, "The Effects of Inflation on Wage Adjustments in Firm-Level Data: Grease or Sand?" Staff Report No. 9, Federal Reserve Bank of New York, January 1996.

Haldane, Andrew G., ed., *Targeting Inflation*. London: Bank of England, 1995.

Hall, Robert, and N. Gregory Mankiw, "Nominal Income Targeting." In Mankiw, N.G., ed., *Monetary Policy*. Chicago: University of Chicago Press for NBER, 1994, pp. 71-94.

Howitt, Peter W., "Canada." In Fratianni, Michelle U., and Dominick Salvatore, eds., *Monetary Policy in Developed Economies, Handbook of Comparative Economic Policies*. Vol. 3, Westport: Greenwood Press, 1993, pp. 459-508.

Issing, Otmar, "Monetary Policy Strategies: Theoretical Basis, Empirical Findings, Practical Implementation." In Deutsche Bundesbank, ed., *Monetary Policy Strategies in Europe*. München: Verlag Franz Vahlen, 1996, pp. 197-202.

Jonung, Lars, "Knut Wicksell's Norm of Price Stabilisation and Swedish Monetary Policy in the 1930s," *Journal of Monetary Economics*, October 1979, 5, 459-96.

King, Mervyn, "Direct Inflation Targets." In Deutsche Bundesbank, ed., *Monetary Policy Strategies in Europe*. München: Verlag Franz Vahlen, 1996, pp. 45-75.

Kydland, Finn, and Edward Prescott, "Rules Rather than Discretion: The Inconsistency of Optimal Plans," *Journal of Political Economy*, June 1977, 88, 473-92.

Laubach, Thomas, "Signalling with Monetary and Inflation Targets," unpublished paper, Princeton University, August 1996.

Lebow, David, John Roberts, and David Stockton, "Economic Performance Under Price Stability." Working Paper No. 125, Division of Research and Statistics, Federal Reserve Board, 1992.

Leiderman, Leonardo, and Lars E. O. Svensson, eds., *Inflation Targets*. London: Centre for Economic Policy Research, 1995.

McCallum, Bennett, "Inflation Targeting in Canada, New Zealand, Sweden, the United Kingdom, and in General." NBER Working Paper No. 5579, May 1996.

McCallum, Bennett, "Crucial Issues Concerning Central Bank Independence." NBER Working Paper No. 5597; *Journal of Monetary Economics*, forthcoming 1997.

Mishkin, Frederic S., "Asymmetric Information and Financial Crises: A Historical Perspective." In Hubbard, R. Glenn, ed., *Financial Markets and Financial Crises*. Chicago: University of Chicago Press, 1991, pp. 69-108.

Mishkin, Frederic S., "What Monetary Policy Can and Cannot Do." In *Monetary Policy in Transition: Strategies, Instruments and Transmission Mechanisms*. Vienna: Oesterreichische Nationalbank, forthcoming.

Moulton, Brent, "Bias in the Consumer Price Index: What is the Evidence?," *Journal of Economic Perspectives*, Fall 1996, 10, 159-77.

Persson, Torsten, and Guido Tabellini, "Designing Institutions for Monetary Stability," *Carnegie-Rochester Conference Series on Public Policy*, 1993, 39, 53-84.

Posen, Adam, "Declarations are Not Enough: Financial Sector Sources of Central Bank Independence," *NBER Macroeconomics Annual*, 1995, 253-74.

Posen, Adam, and Thomas Laubach, "Some Comparative Evidence on the Effectiveness of Inflation Targets," unpublished paper, Federal Reserve Bank of New York, 1996.

Rogoff, Kenneth, "The Optimal Degree of Commitment to an Intermediate Monetary Target," *Quarterly Journal of Economics*, November 1985, 100, 1169-89.

Shapiro, Matthew, and David Wilcox, "Mismeasurement in the Consumer Price Index: An Evaluation," *NBER Macroeconomics Annual*, forthcoming, 1997.

READING 24 Inflation Targeting: A New Framework for Monetary Policy?

Shiller, Robert, "Why Do People Dislike Inflation?" Cowles Foundation Discussion Paper No. 1115, March 1996.

Svensson, Lars E.O., "Price Level Targeting vs. Inflation Targeting: A Free Lunch?" NBER Working Paper No. 5719, 1996.

Svensson, Lars E.O., "Inflation Forecast Targeting: Implementing and Monitoring Inflation Targets." NBER Working Paper No. 5797; *European Economic Review*, forthcoming 1997a.

Svensson, Lars E.O., "Optimal Inflation Targets, 'Conservative' Central Banks, and Linear Inflation Contracts." NBER Working Paper No. 5251; *American Economic Review*, forthcoming 1997b.

Taylor, John, "What Would Nominal GDP Targeting do to the Business Cycle?" In *Carnegie-Rochester Conference Series on Public Policy*. Vol. 22, Amsterdam: North-Holland, 1985, pp. 61-84.

von Hagen, Jurgen, "Inflation and Monetary Targeting in Germany." In Leiderman, L., and L. Svensson, eds., *Inflation Targets*. London: Centre for Economic Policy Research, 1995, pp. 107-21.

Walsh, Carl, "Optimal Contracts for Central Bankers," *American Economic Review*, March 1995, 85, 150-67.

Woodford, Michael, "Nonstandard Indicators for Monetary Policy: Can Their Usefulness be Judged from Forecasting Regressions?" In Mankiw, N.G., ed., *Monetary Policy*. Chicago: University of Chicago Press for NBER, 1994, pp. 95-116.

QUESTIONS

1. What is inflation targeting? Why have a number of countries adopted it as a framework for monetary policy? Does inflation targeting force policymakers to ignore other short-run stabilization goals? Explain.

2. How does the practice of inflation targeting in Germany and Switzerland differ from that in other countries?

3. According to Bernanke and Mishkin, why is a low inflation rate target preferable to both a zero inflation target and a nominal GDP target?

4. What problems for inflation targeting may arise from unpredictability and uncontrollability of the inflation rate?

5. Under what circumstances might the use of an intermediate target (such as the money supply) enhance policymakers' credibility more than targeting a goal variable (such as the inflation rate) would?

READING 25

A Predictable and Avoidable Mexican Meltdown

Joseph A. Whitt, Jr.

As 1993 drew to a close, Mexican prospects appeared good. The enactment of the North American Free Trade Agreement (NAFTA) culminated a series of reforms undertaken during the administration of President Carlos Salinas. To many observers, the only sign of trouble was Mexico's current account deficit, which ballooned from $6 billion in 1989 to more than $20 billion in 1992 and 1993.

Just a year later, in December 1994, the peso was devalued and a severe financial crisis ensued. Mexico's central bank blamed the crisis on a series of political shocks that occurred during 1994: the rebellion in Chiapas and the March 23 assassination of the ruling party's presidential candidate, Luis Donaldo Colosio (Salinas' expected successor).

Despite these tremors, Ernesto Zedillo (Colosio's replacement) was elected president in August. But by December 1, 1994—when Zedillo took office—the economic situation was precarious. Reserves were down to about $12.5 billion (from $25 billion at the end of 1993), and the government faced more than this amount in short-term liabilities. Foreigners were holding about $25 billion in government securities, 70 percent dollar-denominated. For the third consecutive year, the current account deficit was over $20 billion, and most forecasters did not expect much improvement in 1995. In addition, the exchange rate was close to the top of its target band against the dollar (see Chart 1).

STERILIZATION FUELED THE FIRE

The Mexican government and others insisted that the current account deficit was not a concern because it was caused by private capital inflows that were financing investment spending, not by fiscal deficits or excessive monetary expansion. In reality, a large portion of the capital inflows went into short-term financial investments, such as bank deposits and short-term government bonds (see Chart 2). Also, while the current and capital accounts moved together in the early 1990s, in 1994 capital inflows dropped dramatically as the current account deficit widened. As a fraction of gross domestic product (GDP), the current account deficit rose from 2.8 percent in 1989 to an average of more than 7 percent between 1992 and 1994.

READING 25 A Predictable and Avoidable Mexican Meltdown

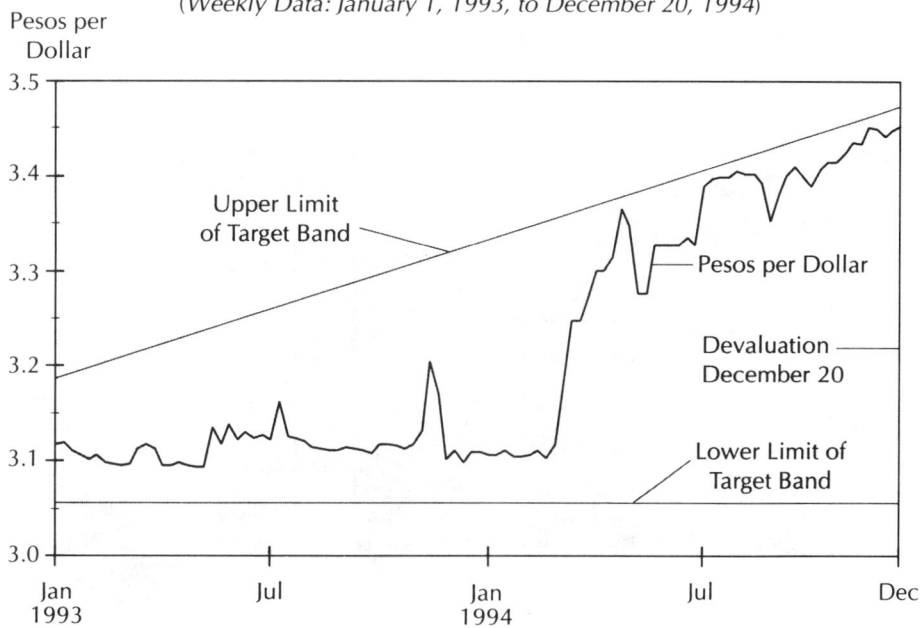

Chart 1
Mexican Peso Exchange Rate and Target Band Prior to Devaluation
(*Weekly Data: January 1, 1993, to December 20, 1994*)

Source: IMF, *International Financial Statistics*.

Even as the current account deficit widened, the growth of Mexican reserves (until early 1994) reinforced the government's false sense of security. Between 1990 and 1993, the central bank accumulated international reserves while reducing domestic credit. This policy, called "sterilizing" (matching central bank purchases of international reserves with sales of government bonds from its portfolio), prevents a rise in the monetary base and an expansion of the money supply. By the end of 1993 Mexico's international reserves totaled $25 billion, roughly four times their level at year-end 1989.

Mexico's central bank justified its sterilization on the basis that without it monetary expansion would have led to inflationary pressures. However, sterilization tends to keep domestic interest rates high, encouraging continued capital inflow. Moreover, in countries such as Mexico, where long-term bond markets are not well developed, sterilization through open-market operations can be done only with short-term instruments, thus biasing the capital inflows toward very short maturities. When Mexican reserves peaked in 1993, Mexico's ratio of highly liquid government and bank liabilities was at least four times the size of net

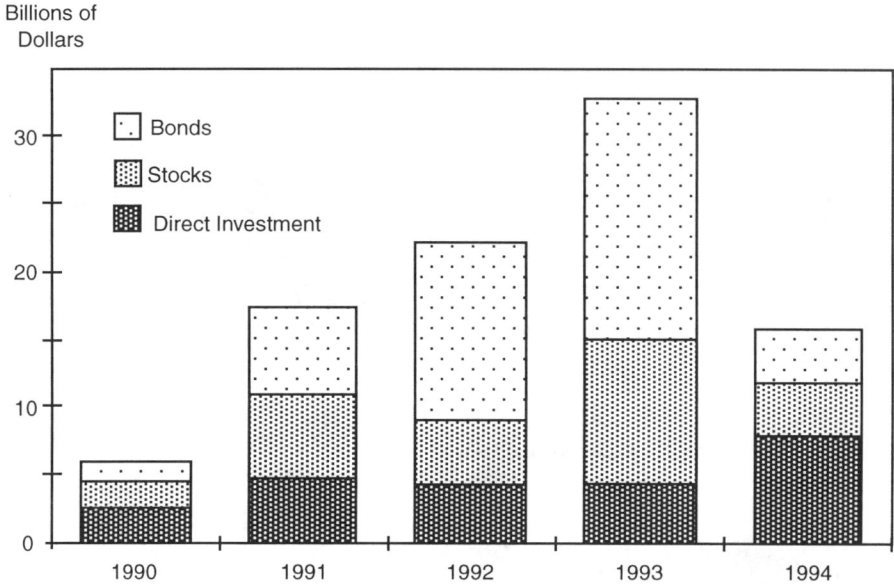

**Chart 2
Foreign Investment Flows to Mexico**

Source: Banco de Mexico.

international reserves, the highest ratio in Latin America.

A POLICY OF AVOIDANCE

In 1994 the U.S. Federal Reserve inadvertently added to Mexico's woes. Concerned that U.S. inflationary pressures were building, the Fed raised its federal funds rate target several times, reaching 5.5 percent by late November, a substantial increase from 1993's prevailing 3 percent. Other rates followed the funds rate.

Despite the economic and political shocks, Mexican policymakers continued massive sterilized intervention and avoided major changes in monetary or exchange-rate policy. The government also changed the composition of its debt, issuing large amounts of a short-term, dollar-denominated security called tesobonos. Over the next few months, the government converted a considerable portion of its debts into tesobonos. By November 1994, 70 percent of foreign holdings of Mexican government securities were in tesobonos.

By this time, with its dollar reserves dwindling, the government's policy options were limited: supporting the existing exchange rate by tightening monetary policy severely, floating the peso, or devaluation. On December 20 the government chose a 15 percent devaluation. In a best-case scenario, public confidence would have remained high enough to prevent a speculative attack on the new peg. However, the announcement of devaluation jolted public confidence, and diminished Mexican reserves added to the climate of vulnerability.

MUTED INITIAL MARKET REACTION TO DEVALUATION

Curiously, initial market reaction to the devaluation was generally positive. The government announced the devaluation before markets opened on December 20. The regular weekly auction of tesobonos occurred later that day and went quite well: average yield was 8.61 percent, only 38 basis points (bp) above the previous week's auction. The amount sold was $416 million, about the same as in the previous week.

The following day, the regular weekly auction of cetes was held. It too went reasonably well: average yield was 16.22 percent, up 142bp from the previous week. However, nervous investors shifted funds out of Mexico, resulting in a loss of $4.5 billion in reserves, the largest single-day decline of the year. On December 22, with reserves less than $6 billion, the government announced that it was abandoning the exchange rate target band and allowing the peso to float.

Market sentiment turned. At the next tesobono auction (December 27) the amount bid totaled only $28 million. The average yield was 10.23 percent, up about 1.5 percentage points from the previous week. The next cetes auction also went poorly: the amount bid fell well below the amount offered, as well as below the amount sold a week earlier, and the average yield soared to 31.41 percent, up 15 percentage points from the previous week. By the end of December the peso had depreciated to Ps5.3 per dollar, 35 percent below its value a month earlier.

As the Mexican government's access to credit dried up, market participants increasingly worried about the large quantity of tesobonos due to mature in 1995. Nearly $10 billion worth of tesobonos was slated to mature in the first quarter of 1995, and another $19 billion was due to mature before the end of the year.

The contrast between the severe market reaction to the move to a floating peso and the relatively mild response to the initial devaluation suggests that Mexico might have been better off increasing the target band's rate of crawl and making an earlier decision to devalue while reserves were still high enough to stave off at least a modest speculative attack on the peso.

In the weeks following the devaluation the U.S. and other governments made several efforts to help Mexico resolve the crisis. On January 2, 1995, an $18 billion line of credit was committed, half by the U.S. government and half by other governments and a few large private banks.

However, investors remained reluctant to roll over Mexican debt, primarily because the credit line was smaller than the amount of tesobonos maturing in the next few months. At the next two tesobono auctions, Mexico sold only small amounts (less than 20 percent of the amounts sold at the two auctions in December prior to the devaluation), even though it was offering higher and higher interest rates: the average yield at auction on January 10, 1995, was 19.63 percent.

On January 12 the Clinton administration proposed a larger assistance package, totaling $40 billion in loan guarantees. The proposal initially buoyed the financial markets, but it soon became clear that the U.S. Congress would be reluctant to approve it.

By January 31 the situation was desperate: Mexico needed quick cash to avoid default, but congressional approval of the $40 billion loan-guarantee package was nowhere in sight. At this point, the Clinton administration proposed a direct-loan package that included $20 billion from the United States and $18 billion from the International Monetary Fund (IMF), plus about $13 billion from the Bank for International Settlements (a quasi-governmental institution controlled by a consortium of central banks) and other commercial banks. In order to avoid a special congressional vote authorizing the assistance, the U.S. contribution was taken from the Exchange Stabilization Fund (ESF).

However, even following President Clinton's decision to tap the ESF, market participants remained extremely wary of Mexican debt. The tesobono auction on February 7 resulted in an average yield of 21 percent. The peso continued to weaken, bottoming out at Ps7.45 per dollar, until Mexico announced a stringent economic austerity package in early March.

LINGERING EFFECTS, BUT QUICKER RECOVERY

While Mexico's devaluation came as a surprise to many, there were signs that a crisis might be brewing. It seems likely that by early 1994 the peso was overvalued; the question was whether the overvaluation could be corrected without setting off a financial crisis that would set back Mexico's development for months, if not years. For months the government tried to avoid decisive action by maintaining the exchange rate peg while leaving other elements of policy largely unchanged. In the end the government opted for devaluation but was quickly forced to float the peso under panic conditions.

The ensuing crisis continues to affect the Mexican economy. Nevertheless, a relatively sound budget position, more effective economic policies, and the assistance arranged by the United States and the IMF should continue to enable Mexico to recover more quickly from this crisis than from the 1982 crash.

READING 25 A Predictable and Avoidable Mexican Meltdown

QUESTIONS

1. In early 1994 the Mexican peso stood at Ps3.1 per dollar. What evidence suggests that the peso was overvalued at this time?

2. What policy options were open to Mexican monetary authorities after the Fed began boosting U.S. short-term interest rates in 1994? Which option was chosen? How well did it work?

3. Why were Mexican authorities eventually forced to let the peso float? What repercussions flowed from this policy decision?

4. Illustrate the changes in the peso's value over the 1994-95 period using the exchange market diagram that Mishkin uses in Chapters 8 and 20.

READING 26

Mexico's Liquidity-Driven Financial Panic

Marco Espinosa and Steven Russell

Last year the Wall Street Journal posed the question, "How could so many smart people on Wall Street, in Mexico City, and in Washington have been so blind to so many warnings?" This query encapsulates the "conventional" wisdom regarding the late 1994 crisis, which is that it was the inevitable result of fundamental imbalances in the Mexican economy. However, certain evidence suggests a financial panic (reminiscent of 19th-century financial panics in the United States) explanation.

SHORT-TERM FINANCED GROWTH SET THE STAGE FOR FINANCIAL PANIC

In the late 1980s and early 1990s, Mexico pursued a development strategy of externally financed growth, capturing some $91 billion in net capital inflows between 1990-93. Between 1988 and 1992, this externally based financing strategy allowed the share of Mexican gross domestic product (GDP) devoted to domestic investment to rise from 20 percent to 23 percent, despite a fall in private savings from roughly 18 percent of GDP to below 9 percent.

However, much of this foreign capital inflow was short-term. For example, in 1993, the peak of the foreign-investment wave, only 32 percent of foreign funds went into the stock market, and only 13 percent took the form of direct foreign investment. Most of the rest went into short-term debt issued by Mexican commercial banks and the government. In 1993 Mexican borrowers made only 33 long-term bond issues (grossing $3.8 billion) on international markets. Only six of these involved private borrowers.

The financial panic explanation suggests that Mexico's exchange rate policies have been overemphasized and that a more important cause was the short-term nature of Mexican borrowers' liabilities. In particular, this alternative explanation does not necessarily imply that the Mexican peso was dramatically overvalued and does not interpret Mexico's large trade deficits as necessarily indicating that the country was borrowing or consuming at unsustainable rates.

Reprinted from Federal Reserve Bank of Atlanta *Economics Update*, 9, 3-4 (July-December 1996), 4-5.

READING 26 Mexico's Liquidity-Driven Financial Panic

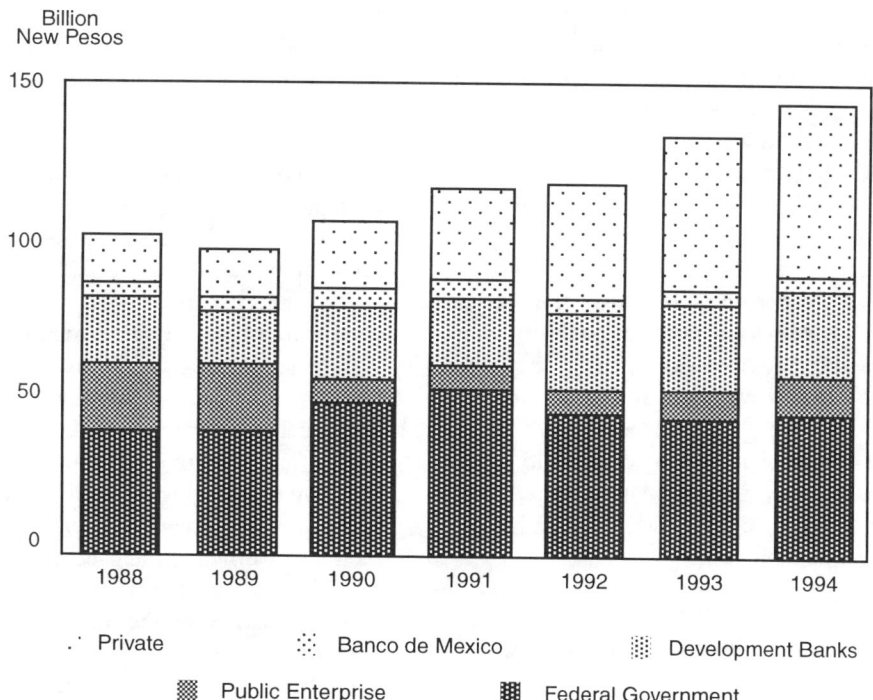

Mexico's Total External Debt, 1988–94
(With Components)

Source: Banco de Mexico.

IMPLICATIONS OF THE FINANCIAL PANIC EXPLANATION

According to the conventional view, the economic crisis occurred because the exchange rate pegging regime allowed the Mexican peso to become substantially overvalued. This overvaluation produced a situation in which Mexicans were consuming more than their incomes at international prices.

This overconsumption was financed by foreign borrowing and was reflected in Mexico's large trade deficit. The disequilibrium ended in December 1994 when the government was no longer able to defend its exchange rate peg because it had exhausted its foreign exchange reserves. Presumably, the Mexican government could prevent future problems of this sort by permanently abandoning its policy of exchange rate pegging and allowing the peso to continue to float. The exchange rate would then adjust to keep Mexico's domestic consumption in line with its domestic income.

But under the alternative financial panic explanation, the Mexican financial crisis was clearly an expectations-driven liquidity crisis. The immediate cause of the crisis was political turmoil that created concern among foreigners about the safety of their investments. As most of the deposits were short-term, millions of dollars were drawn off every day, producing a rapid deterioration in the government's reserve position and putting severe downward pressure on the dollar price of the peso. Ironically, in the weeks and months following the crisis it became clear that the various threats to Mexican political stability were considerably less serious than they had appeared in November and December of 1994. However, the vulnerability of the Mexican financial system to liquidity crises has been convincingly demonstrated, and foreign investors consequently remain hesitant to recommit their funds.

VULNERABLE PORTFOLIOS

Why did Mexican financial institutions allow themselves to acquire liability portfolios that made them so vulnerable to confidence shocks? An underlying reason is that the relatively low rate of domestic savings forced the Mexican financial system to look to foreign countries for funds to finance domestic investment. Moreover, both direct Mexican borrowers and the country's financial intermediaries were content to rely on short-term foreign credit.

Foreign short-term lenders had little reason to be concerned about long-term prospects, as it seemed certain that Mexican borrowers could continue to roll over their short-term debts using short-term funds provided by additional foreign lenders. As long as this was the case, the debts were perceived to have little default and the lenders were willing to purchase them at relatively low interest rates.

Long-term lenders, by contrast, would have recognized that the ability of borrowers to repay their loans was dependent on the long-term success of investment projects—a substantial risk—and would have demanded higher interest rates to compensate. The combination of higher interest rates and greater lender risk-consciousness would have forced Mexican firms to scale back investments, reducing both the firms' potential profits and the overall growth rate of the Mexican economy. Neither these firms nor the Mexican government was willing to accept such a slowdown in the pace of development.

Presumably, the desire to avoid these interest costs was the reason the Mexican government began pegging the exchange rate in the first place. Of course, the exchange rate pegging scheme introduced potential instabilities: any threat that the policy might have to be abandoned, whether real or imagined, could produce a self-perpetuating outflow of funds and a financial/economic disaster.

REMEDIES FOR MEXICO

What, if anything, could the Mexican government have done to avoid the problem of overreliance on short-term liabilities issued to foreign investors? What can it do to prevent similar crises in the future? One might argue that the problem will eventually solve itself as borrowers become more aware of the potential risks of heavy reliance on short-term credit. However, there are reasons to doubt that changes in private behavior stimulated by this crisis will be sufficient, in themselves, to prevent future crises.

One suggestion we offer is that the Mexican government impose reserve requirements on the short-term liabilities of banks and other financial intermediaries and also on any direct short-term liabilities of Mexican firms. The reserve assets would be medium-term bonds (bonds with terms of five to ten years) issued by the Mexican government.

The purpose of these graduated reserve requirements would be to discourage Mexican banks from issuing short-term liabilities, without forbidding them to do so. The lower reserve ratios on longer-term liabilities would give them a substantial interest-cost advantage relative to short-term liabilities—an advantage that would allow Mexican financial institutions to issue longer-term liabilities at rates that would increase their relative attractiveness to domestic and foreign investors. Allowing the peso to float might have made a financial crisis less likely. Therefore, Mexico should stick with its current flexible exchange rate regime—as it appears to have every intention of doing. However, exchange rate risk is certain to remain troubling to foreign investors and will provide a source of financial instability.

One approach to reducing the severity of the exchange rate risk problem would be for the Mexican government to encourage the country's banks and other borrowers to issue dollar-denominated debts. A second step might be to require that at least a minimum fraction of the foreign liabilities of Mexican financial intermediaries be dollar- or other-foreign-currency-denominated.

Clearly, one factor that contributed greatly to the financial crisis was Mexico's strategy of externally financed development. Unfortunately, it is unrealistic to expect Mexicans to increase their savings to the extent necessary to allow Mexico to resume its precrisis development path without relying on foreign funds. It is equally unlikely that the government will be willing to accept the much slower growth rate attainable through reliance on the current level of domestic savings.

Perhaps the most important step toward alleviating the credit squeeze would be continued progress toward deregulating the financial industry and exposing it to more vigorous domestic and foreign competition as well as drafting measures that help lengthen the country's borrowing term structure. Hopefully, deregulation would stimulate domestic investment enough to reduce the strong demand for foreign finance.

PART IV Central Banking and the Conduct of Monetary Policy

QUESTIONS

1. How does the "financial panic" explanation of Mexico's financial difficulties differ from the "overvalued peso" explanation?

2. Why did foreign lenders and Mexican borrowers prefer short-term over long-term lending?

3. What policies do Espinosa and Russell suggest to reduce Mecico's overreliance on short-term lending?

READING 27

The EMU: A Groundbreaking Monetary Experiment

Fiona Sigalla and David Gould

On January 1, 1999, the European Union (EU) is scheduled to introduce the euro, a first-of-its-kind currency designed to help blend 15 politically divergent countries into a unified economic area. The euro caps off the economic and monetary union (EMU), which requires that each country give up its national monetary policy and abide by the policies of a common central bank.

Never before have politically independent nations with histories of monetary independence and long-standing central banks given up that independence to form a common central bank and adopt a single currency. If successful, the EMU will be the biggest event in the world financial system since the Bretton Woods system of fixed exchange rates broke down in the early 1970s.

Many analysts remain skeptical about the EMU's potential for success. They believe the euro will be unpopular and the central bank will find it difficult to be tough on inflation without the benefit of a unified fiscal policy.

Although this historic union will not occur for nearly two years, preparations for the EMU are already greatly affecting the European economies. The outlook for the new currency's success and stability has also begun to impact financial markets.

ECONOMIC AND MONETARY UNION

The euro will essentially link the currencies of participating
countries with permanently fixed exchange rates. To increase the likelihood of the EMU's success, each country must meet strict monetary and fiscal criteria before joining. The economic strain on the EMU will be reduced if all the countries converge to roughly the same inflation and interest rates.[1] The countries also have to meet government debt and budget deficit criteria.[2] The hope is that if EMU countries have fairly healthy balance sheets, markets will not expect political pressure to force the central bank to print money to pay down a country's debt.

Of the 15 current members of the European Union, only those that meet the monetary and fiscal criteria will be eligible to join the EMU. The decision of which countries qualify, based on 1997 economic data, will take place in early 1998. Most

Reprinted from Federal Reserve Bank of Dallas *Southwest Economy*, Issue 3 (May/June 1997), 12-13.

likely, eight countries will be eligible to join in 1999: Germany, France, Belgium, Luxembourg, the Netherlands, Finland, Austria and Ireland. Italy, Greece and Portugal have begun EMU campaigns and may be able to join as well. Although the United Kingdom and Denmark will likely be eligible to join, it is not clear if those countries will participate in 1999.

THE EMU AND THE ECONOMY

The euro will effectively merge the Deutsche mark, the strongest European currency, with some weaker ones. For most countries, the newly formed European Central Bank will be much less likely to inflate because of political pressures than their current central banks. With a successful monetary union, these countries can achieve lower overall inflation and interest rates through a single coordinated policy. Already, the move to a single currency has motivated European countries to lower their inflation rates and get their fiscal policies in order.

If the move to a single currency is successful, it is expected to spur economic growth and stimulate export demand in Europe. The euro will make it cheaper and easier to transact business across Europe, reducing transactions costs and exchange rate risk. If the single currency generates more income and stability for Europe, it would also stimulate demand for U.S. goods.

On the downside, a lack of exchange rate flexibility and loss of national monetary policy may prolong regional economic downturns. A country cannot lower interest rates when it goes into a recession unless all the other countries agree that this is a good policy, perhaps prolonging a localized recession. For example, the fact that Texas could not lower interest rates when a collapse in oil prices sent its economy into recession in 1986 may have extended Texas' recession.

Several European countries have struggled with recessions during the push for a single currency, making convergence difficult. Their recessions have been blamed on the single-currency push because governments have been tightening fiscal policy and companies have cut costs in anticipation of a more competitive single market.

THE EURO AND U.S. FINANCIAL MARKETS

The euro could prove a strong alternative to the U.S. dollar. Financial markets will conduct transactions in euros, and central banks will want to hold some of their reserves in this currency. Both transactions will reduce the number of dollars held, but it is unclear by how much. How quickly the shift will occur is uncertain.

The EMU will create a broad bond market in which European governments and corporations will issue debt in euros. Roughly the size of the U.S. market, this will be the first alternative widely traded bond market available for issuers of debt. U.S. bond prices and interest rates will likely become more volatile as investors test the new market and then, perhaps, return to the U.S. market.

READING 27 The EMU: A Groundbreaking Monetary Experiment

If the euro takes off as a strong currency, it may affect the dollar's role as a reserve currency for the rest of the world. The European Union represents a big market. It is likely that the world will want to hold more euros and fewer dollars for international transactions. If fewer countries hold dollars, then it will be a loss for the U.S. Treasury because foreign holdings of U.S. dollars are interest-free loans to the United States from the rest of the world. But if the euro is unstable, then the dollar is likely to be seen as a safe haven and international holdings of dollars will grow.

As the birth of the EMU nears, uncertainty about its impact has already sent ripples through financial markets. In recent weeks, France, Germany and Italy have indicated that they may not meet some of the criteria for a single currency. Signs that the introduction of the euro may be delayed have pushed the dollar down against the mark. Many investors would prefer to hold dollars when the union occurs but are choosing to jump back into Deutsche marks on signs of a delay.

Still, the euro may go forward as planned because vagueness in the language of the Maastricht Treaty, which sets forth the parameters for the EMU, suggests that countries failing to meet the criteria can join if they show evidence of "sufficiently diminishing" debt and budget deficits. Essentially, if the EU believes it is advantageous to the EMU for a country to join, it will be allowed in.

The EMU's impact on the world's financial system could remain uncertain until it becomes clear to investors that the monetary union has either succeeded or failed.

ENDNOTES

1. To be eligible for convergence, the inflation rate cannot be more than 1.5 percentage points higher than the average of the three lowest-inflation countries, and long-term interest rates cannot be more than 2 percentage points higher than the average interest rate in the three lowest-inflation countries.
2. The fiscal criteria require government debt to be less than 60 percent of GDP and the budget deficit to be less than 3 percent of GDP.

PART IV Central Banking and the Conduct of Monetary Policy

QUESTIONS

1. What are the EMU and the euro?

2. What advantages and disadvantages for Europe are foreseen with the adoption of the EMU and the euro?

3. How might EMU and the euro affect the U.S. dollar and U.S. bond markets and interest rates? Why?

PART FIVE

MONETARY THEORY

Monetary theory considers the relationship between money supply and interest rates, which the Fed can influence with its monetary policy, and aggregate output, employment, the price level and the inflation rate. The readings for Part Five discuss some of the central topics and controversies of monetary theory: the relationship between inflation and unemployment; the transmission mechanisms of monetary policy; monetary policy's short-run and long-run effects; the causes of inflation; efficient markets; and the activist/nonactivist policy debate.

Reading 28, **"Nobel Views on Inflation and Unemployment"** by Carl E. Walsh, examines the Nobel Lectures of Milton Friedman and Robert Lucas to reveal how economists' thinking about the short-run and long-run relationships between inflation and unemployment has changed over recent decades. Walsh also addresses the roles that both theoretical advances and empirical evidence have played in promoting greater understanding of the relation between money and output. Instructors should find this reading to be a useful summary of these topics to accompany discussion of monetary policy in Chapters 23, 24, 26 and 28.

Owen F. Humpage, in Reading 29, **"Monetary Policy and Real Economic Growth,"** discusses various monetary policy transmission mechanisms and money's short-run relationship with output and long-run relationship with inflation. He emphasizes that money supply growth is not one of the key determinants of long-run economic growth. This reading can be used with Chapter 24's discussion of the Phillips Curve and Chapter 26's treatment of monetary policy and inflation.

"What Causes Inflation?" by Laurence Ball, Reading 30, also supplements Chapter 26's discussion of inflation. Ball summarizes modern inflation theory: long-run inflation trends are determined by the extent to which the rate of money supply growth exceeds the growth rate of output, and short-run fluctuations in the inflation rate are influenced by demand and supply shocks. He mentions the roles of price inertia, budget deficits, inflationary expectations, and accommodating monetary policy in the inflation process and explains why price increases for specific items do not *cause* inflation.

In Reading 31, **"Stock Market Fundamentals,"** Joseph G. Haubrich explains that share prices are determined by the present value of future dividend streams and fluctuate when expectations about dividends change or the rate of return investors require changes. He uses this model to assess whether stocks are presently overvalued. This reading augments Chapter 27's discussion of efficient markets.

Reading 32 is **"Activist Monetary Policy for Good or Evil? The New Keynesians vs. the New Classicals"** by Tom Stark and Herb Taylor. This reading delineates the essential elements of these two schools and explains why their positions on activist policy differ. It ties in with Chapter 28's discussion of New Classical and nonclassical rational expectations models. Alternatively, instructors may wish to use this reading when they cover the activist/nonactivist policy debate in Chapter 26.

READING 28

Nobel Views on Inflation and Unemployment

Carl E. Walsh

Is current monetary policy consistent with maintaining a low rate of inflation? Would the establishment of price stability as the Fed's sole objective hinder long-run growth prospects for the U.S. economy? The answers to these questions are critical for the design and implementation of monetary policy, and one means of assessing the progress economists have made in recent years in addressing them is to examine the views of two Nobel laureates in economics; the Nobel Lectures of Milton Friedman (1977) and Robert Lucas (1996), separated by almost 20 years, provide benchmarks for reviewing developments in the way economists think about inflation and unemployment.

Friedman and Lucas are two of the giants of monetary economics. Friedman, the winner of the Nobel Prize in Economics in 1976, is most widely known for his emphasis on the role of monetary policy as a force in shaping the course of inflation and business cycles; outside the field of economics, he also is known for his advocacy of free markets. Lucas, who will be honored at the American Economic Association's annual meetings in January, was probably unfamiliar to most non-economists when he was awarded the Nobel Prize in 1995. Like Friedman, he too has made fundamental contributions to the study of money, inflation, and business cycles.

INFLATION AND UNEMPLOYMENT IN THE SHORT RUN

When Friedman gave his lecture in 1976, the long-run relationship between inflation and unemployment was still under debate. During the 1960s, most economists believed that a lower average unemployment rate could be sustained if one were just willing to accept a permanently higher (but stable) rate of inflation. Friedman used his Nobel lecture to make two arguments about this inflation-unemployment tradeoff. First, he reviewed the reasons the short-run tradeoff would dissolve in the long run. Expanding nominal demand to lower unemployment would lead to increases in money wages as firms attempt to attract additional workers. Firms would be willing to pay higher money wages if they expected

---

Reprinted from Federal Reserve Bank of San Francisco *Economic Letter*, No. 97-01, January 10, 1997. The opinions expressed in this article do not necessarily reflect the views of the management of the Federal Reserve Bank of San Francisco, or of the Board of Governors of the Federal Reserve System.

prices for output to be higher in the future due to the expansion. Friedman assumed, however, that workers would initially perceive the rise in money wages to be a rise in real wages. They would do so because their "perception of prices in general" adjusts slowly, so nominal wages would be perceived to be rising faster than prices. In response, the supply of labor would increase, and employment and output would expand. Eventually, workers would recognize that the general level of prices had risen and that their real wages had not actually increased, leading to adjustments that would return the economy to its natural rate of unemployment.

Friedman's second argument was that the Phillips Curve slope might actually be positive—higher inflation would be associated with higher average unemployment. In the 1970s, many economies were experiencing rising inflation and unemployment simultaneously. Friedman attempted to provide a tentative hypothesis for this phenomenon. In his view, higher inflation tends to be associated with more inflation volatility and greater inflation uncertainty. This uncertainty reduces economic efficiency as contracting arrangements must adjust, imperfections in indexation systems become more prominent, and price movements provide confused signals about the types of relative price changes that indicate the need for resources to shift.

The positive correlation between inflation and unemployment that Friedman noted was subsequently replaced by a negative correlation as the early 1980s saw disinflations accompanied by recessions. Today, most economists would view inflation and unemployment movements as reflecting both aggregate supply and aggregate demand disturbances as well as the dynamic adjustments the economy follows in response to these disturbances. When demand disturbances dominate, inflation and unemployment will tend to be negatively correlated initially as, for example, an expansion lowers unemployment and raises inflation. As the economy adjusts, prices continue to increase as unemployment begins to rise again and return to its natural rate. When supply disturbances dominate (as in the 1970s), inflation and unemployment will tend to move initially in the same direction.

Almost all economists have followed Friedman in accepting that there is no long-run tradeoff that would allow permanently lower unemployment to be traded for higher inflation. And a part of the reason for this acceptance is due to the contributions of Lucas.

DOES MONETARY POLICY PREDICTABLY AFFECT UNEMPLOYMENT?

In his Nobel lecture, Lucas notes that while clear evidence exists that average inflation rates and average money growth rates are tightly linked: "The observation that money changes induce output changes in the same direction receives confirmation in some data sets but is hard to see in others. Large-scale reductions in money growth can be associated with large-scale depressions or, if carried out in the form of a credible reform, with no depression at all" (p. 668). Lucas draws this conclusion largely from work on episodes of hyperinflations (Sargent 1986) in which major institutional reforms have been associated with large changes in inflation; when major reforms are not involved, the evidence shows a more consistent effect of monetary policy expansions and contractions on real activity.

While Friedman also stressed that the real effects of changes in monetary policy would depend on whether they were anticipated or not, Lucas demonstrated the striking implications of assuming that individuals form their expectations rationally. Lucas abandoned Friedman's notion of a gradual adjustment of expectations based on past developments and instead stressed the forward-looking nature of expectations. Expectations of future monetary easing or tightening will affect the economy now. And this means that the real effects of, say, an increase in money growth could, in principle, be expansionary or contractionary, depending on the public's expectations.

One consequence of this insight has been a new recognition of the importance of credibility in policy; that is, a credible policy—one that is explicit and for which the central bank is held responsible—can influence the way people form their expectations. Thus, the effects of policy actions by a bank with credibility may be quite different from those of a central bank that lacks credibility. Even though the empirical evidence for credibility effects is weak, the emphasis on credibility has been one factor motivating central banks to design policy frameworks that embody credible commitments to low inflation.

Some economists have begun to question the natural rate result that Lucas's work helped to promote. Akerlof, Dickins, and Perry (1996), for example, argue that even credible low-inflation policies are likely to carry a cost in terms of permanently higher unemployment and that a stable Phillips Curve tradeoff exists at low rates of inflation. They argue that employee resistance to money wage cuts will limit the ability of real wages to adjust when the price level is stable. But the contributions of Friedman and Lucas have clearly shifted the debate since the early 1970s. Now it is proponents of a tradeoff who represent the minority view.

THEORY, EVIDENCE, AND POLICY

Both Friedman and Lucas motivated their discussions of the relationship between monetary policy and unemployment by presenting empirical evidence. This similarity reveals an important characteristic of macroeconomics—theory is tightly linked with empirical evidence. Yet, while sharing a common approach, the two Nobel laureates stress different aspects of the connection between theory, evidence, and policy.

For example, Friedman and Lucas differ in their views on what is responsible for advances in our understanding of money and output. Friedman stresses the role of empirical evidence. He argues that the growing evidence that the 1960s vintage Phillips Curve was unstable was instrumental in forcing the profession to adjust its thinking. As Friedman puts it, "the drastic change that has occurred in accepted professional views was produced primarily by the scientific response to experience that contradicted a tentatively accepted hypothesis—precisely the classical process for the revision of a scientific hypothesis" (p. 453).

In contrast, Lucas stresses the role played by mathematical tools in leading to advances in economics. As he notes, the effects of money on the economy involve the *dynamic* response of economic agents to changes in prices, interest rates, and income. Much of modern macroeconomics consists of working out the implications of these dynamic responses, and the development of theoretical models of these responses would be futile "without any of the equipment of modern mathematical economics" (p. 669). Economists needed the appropriate formal tools before progress could be made in understanding the dynamic nature of the individual decisions that affect the economy's behavior over time.

Lucas also emphasizes the role of theory in influencing practical macroeconomics: "All one can be sure of is that progress will result from the continued effort to formulate explicit theories that fit the facts, and the best and most practical macroeconomics will make use of developments in basic economic theory" (p. 680). In contrast, Friedman's stress is on the role of evidence in the battle among competing theories: "... brute experience proved far more potent than the strongest of political or ideological preferences" (p. 470).

The insights of Friedman and Lucas continue to guide developments in macroeconomics. Their work on the links between inflation and unemployment has influenced the course of economic theory and the most practical of policy discussions. For example, Lucas's development of a theory of expectations served to emphasize the role of credibility in the conduct of policy, an emphasis that continues to have a major impact on discussions dealing with proposals for inflation targeting and for legislative mandates to require central banks to treat price stability as their sole objective.

THE FUTURE

Both Friedman and Lucas speculated on promising areas for research. Friedman emphasized the need to incorporate more explicit models of political behavior in order to understand the determinants of policy. This was quite natural; once economists gained a clear understanding of the effects of monetary policy on the economy, understanding why nations had undergone differing inflation experiences became an issue of understanding how different political structures had generated differing policy outcomes.

Friedman was amazingly prescient; the very article following his Nobel Lecture in the *Journal of Political Economy* was a paper by Kydland and Prescott (1977) that lay the groundwork for the huge literature on time inconsistency of discretionary policy. By providing a framework for analyzing the way in which the economic structure can interact with the incentives faced by policymakers, Kydland and Prescott provided the foundations of a political theory of inflation consistent with the natural rate models of Friedman and Lucas and set the language of debate for most current discussions of central banking reform.

Lucas noted that the specific models developed during the first generation of the rational expectations revolution have not proven successful as theories of the business cycle and that more work incorporating monetary phenomena into general equilibrium real business cycle models was likely to occupy the research agendas of monetary economists in the near future. However, he also expressed the view that speculating on future directions was difficult: "... who can say how the macroeconomic theory of the future will develop, any more than anyone in 1960 could have foreseen the developments I have described in this lecture?" (p. 680).

REFERENCES

Akerlof, George, William Dickens, and George Perry. 1996. "The Macroeconomics of Low Inflation." *Brookings Papers on Economic Activity* 1, pp. 1-59.

Friedman, Milton, 1977. "Nobel Lecture: Inflation and Unemployment." *Journal of Political Economy* 85, pp. 451-472.

Kydland, F.E., and E.C. Prescott. 1977. "Rules Rather than Discretion: The Time Inconsistency of Optimal Plans." *Journal of Political Economy* 85, pp. 473-491.

Lucas, Robert E., Jr. 1996. "Nobel Lecture: Monetary Neutrality." *Journal of Political Economy* 104, pp. 661-682.

Sargent, Thomas J. 1986. "The Ends of Four Big Inflations." In his *Rational Expectations and Inflation*, New York: Harper and Row.

QUESTIONS

1. In Friedman's view, why is there a short-run inflation-unemployment tradeoff but not a long-run tradeoff?

2. How did Lucas's work modify economists' views of the short-run inflation-unemployment tradeoff?

3. What factors do Friedman and Lucas cite as responsible for advances in economists' understanding of the relationship between money and output?

READING 29

Monetary Policy and Real Economic Growth

Owen F. Humpage

The media frequently take central banks to task for failing to encourage real economic growth. Usually, such criticisms center on the business cycle, with analysts calling for monetary ease when growth falls below its recent trend and, somewhat ironically, chiding policymakers for responding too quickly when growth rises above trend.

Recently, with long-term U.S. economic growth apparently slowing, the focus of these criticisms has shifted somewhat. News reports are now increasingly asking whether an easier monetary policy stance might not boost investment and the nation's economic potential.

Most economists will concede that monetary policy can affect real economic growth, at least in the short term, but caution that it may do so only when the public fails to anticipate the policy change and then misinterprets the accompanying price adjustments. Frequent attempts to exploit such connections will eventually be noticed. Then, an expansionary monetary policy could actually backfire.

This *Economic Commentary* traces the connections between policy changes, shifts in aggregate spending, and adjustments to production. In response to those who advocate monetary ease as a stimulant for growth and employment, I emphasize the precarious nature of the assumptions about price expectations that typically underlie their beliefs.

MONETARY POLICY TRANSMISSION

According to the standard view, monetary policy affects total spending primarily by altering interest rates.[1] The Federal Reserve System's main instrument for conducting monetary policy is the purchase and sale of government bonds in the secondary market (open-market operations).[2] When the Fed buys government bonds, it pays for them by crediting the reserve accounts of the appropriate commercial banks. These banks then have additional (excess) reserves, which they will lend or invest in other securities. To expand their lending (and through the act of purchasing other securities), commercial banks reduce interest rates. This in turn encourages an expansion of such interest-sensitive spending as business fixed investment and residential construction, according to the conventional view.

Reprinted from Federal Reserve Bank of Cleveland *Economic Commentary*, December 1996.

READING 29 Monetary Policy and Real Economic Growth

Under our present system of floating exchange rates, an exchange-rate change can augment the traditional interest-rate channel of monetary policy. As U.S. interest rates fall, international investors may shift their portfolios from dollar-denominated assets to foreign-currency-denominated assets, which now have higher yields. As they do, dollar exchange rates will fall, making U.S. exports more attractive than foreign goods and services. World demand will shift toward the U.S. market.

Many economists believe that connections between aggregate spending and monetary policy are substantially broader and more complicated than those described by the conventional interest-rate view, even as modified with an exchange-rate effect. Following an expansionary open-market operation, for example, individuals may find themselves with too much liquidity and may attempt to acquire additional assets, both financial (stocks and bonds) and real (houses and durable goods). This reshuffling of portfolios can also raise stock prices. A rise in the market value of firms (as reflected in equity prices) relative to the replacement costs of capital offers businesses another incentive to undertake new investments. In addition, the higher stock prices also increase household financial wealth, which could further stimulate consumption spending. Likewise, if land and housing prices rise, household wealth and consumption may get an additional boost.

An expansionary open-market operation may have an independent effect on financial institutions' willingness to make loans, quite apart from their gain of additional excess reserves. By raising equity prices and lowering interest rates, a policy change can increase the net worth and cash flow of businesses and households. As net worth and cash flow improve, these borrowers become better credit risks, so banks are more likely to lend to them. Investment (business and residential) and durable-goods spending will rise.

THE SHORT RUN: SPENDING TO PRODUCTION

That monetary policy can affect the overall level of spending through these myriad connections does not necessarily imply that it can increase real output and employment. A shift in spending may simply lead to higher prices rather than to additional output. The upshot depends on whether individuals correctly anticipate the monetary change and the resulting price pressures.

Most economists believe that a nation's long-term economic growth depends on its ability to accumulate capital, the expansion of its workforce, and improvements in its productivity. They also contend that ultimately, money determines only the price level. Nevertheless, the majority of economists concede a short-term connection between money and output. Indeed, in most of the largest industrialized countries, faster money growth seems to precede faster economic growth by one year (see table 1).

The causal connection, however, requires that information about policy-induced price changes be imperfect. This may happen if some sectors of the economy have embedded

PART V Monetary Theory

TABLE 1: SHORT-RUN GROWTH OF MONEY AND OUTPUT
(Correlation, year-over-year percent change)

	M2 lagged one year	M2 lagged two years
France	0.17	0.06
Germany	0.74[a]	−0.13
Japan	0.72[a]	0.51[a]
United Kingdom	0.18	−0.19
United States	0.35[a]	0.16
Canada	−0.17	−0.11
Italy	0.62[a]	0.42[a]

a. Indicates that the correlation coefficient is more than two standard deviations away from zero. For the United States, the correlation coefficient falls within the two-standard-deviation band by 0.004. *Source:* International Monetary Fund, *International Financial Statistics*.

outdated price expectations in contracts that cannot be broken, if certain segments of the economy have better access to current price information than others, or if people generally have complete knowledge about the wages they earn and the prices they charge, but not about other prices. When this information is neither perfect nor equally shared, a monetary expansion will initially create profit opportunities (or the perception of such) for some individuals, inducing them to work more and to expand production.

Essentially, two versions of this story exist.[3] The first interpretation, which relies on contracts and assumes that prices and wages are set in noncompetitive markets, seems to be a plausible description of the behavior of big labor unions and large producers.[4] According to this model, workers set a wage rate based on the inflation rate they expect over the duration of the contract. If the actual rate of inflation turns out to be higher, the cost of labor falls relative to the prices received for their output. This increased profitability causes firms to lengthen work hours, hire more crews, and expand production. Only when workers renegotiate their contracts will wages rise as high as goods prices and dissipate profit opportunities. In this scenario, when monetary policy expands, firms benefit temporarily relative to workers.

Similarly, faced with an increase in demand, firms with noncompetitive market power may delay raising their prices simply because small, frequent price changes are costly to institute. They may instead accommodate an increase in aggregate spending through additional short-run production, even though their profits, which exceed competitive levels to begin with, may suffer. Such firms will eventually adjust their prices when they can do so advantageously. In this scenario, output expands temporarily at the expense of profits.

Another explanation relies on asymmetric information about price changes and applies to more competitive labor and goods markets. As applied to labor, this explanation assumes that workers have less reliable information about prices than producers do. Firms initially perceive price increases and raise wages, but by less than the increase in prices. Workers, uncertain about the overall rise in prices and believing that their wages have outpaced prices, agree to work longer hours. Employment and output expand, but only until workers learn that prices in general have actually risen by more than their wages; then labor supply declines.

To apply the same argument more generally, assume that all individuals have good information about the prices of things in which they specialize (that is, their wages and the goods they produce), but that they have rather imprecise information about other goods and services. Therefore, they quickly perceive a change in their special prices, and believe that it represents a relative gain to them. They produce more until they discover their mistake.

THE LONG RUN: SPENDING TO INFLATION

In economics, the long run is not a specific period of time, but an interval over which all economic adjustments are feasible. In our case, it implies a period in which all individuals have complete access to information and can adjust contracts for changes in their expectations. This may be many years. Nevertheless, in the long run, after expectations adjust, an increase in the money supply will raise neither output nor employment. Across the sample of 45 countries portrayed in figure 1, faster rates of money growth are not correlated with higher rates of long-term real economic growth.[5]

In the long run, a monetary-policy-induced increase in aggregate demand seems only to raise prices. Figure 2 illustrates a tight, proportional relationship between money growth and inflation across these same 45 nations.

If anything, attempting to promote economic prosperity through expansionary monetary policies could have a detrimental effect on long-term economic growth. Money contributes to economic efficiency by reducing the transaction costs associated with economic exchange. In so doing, money plays its familiar textbook roles as a medium of exchange, a unit of account, and a temporary store of value.

The ability of money to reduce transaction costs ultimately depends on its general acceptance. If people question the stability of a monetary asset's purchasing power, they will reduce their holdings of it, look for substitute monetary assets, and devise alternative, less efficient, methods of exchange. When the efficiency of money is compromised, transaction costs rise. Moreover, as inflation accelerates, households and businesses will spend more time, energy, and resources protecting their financial wealth from inflation. Fewer resources will go into capital accumulation or productivity-enhancing

PART V Monetary Theory

FIGURE 1 MONEY AND REAL OUTPUT GROWTH[a]

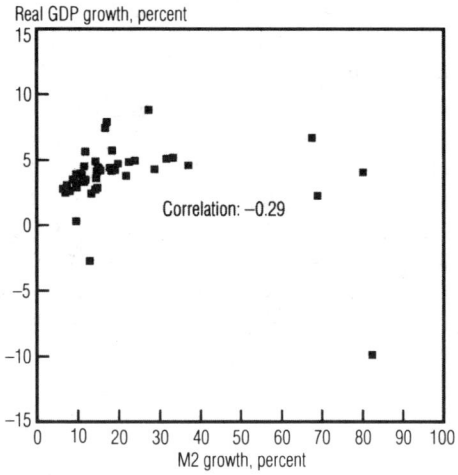

FIGURE 2 MONEY GROWTH AND INFLATION[a]

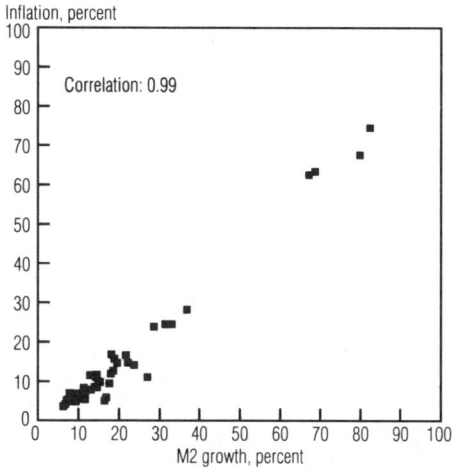

FIGURE 3 INFLATION AND REAL OUTPUT GROWTH[a]

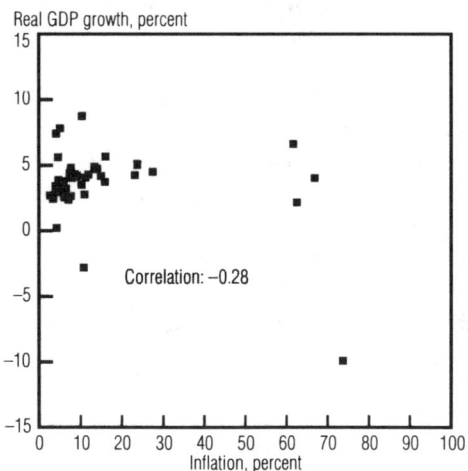

a. Average annual percent change.
SOURCE: International Monetary Fund, *International Financial Statistics.*

innovations. To the extent that the government bases taxes on nominal values, inflation levies an unlegislated tax, further crimping the resources available for private investment.

How extensive these costs are for society is not clear. Although the correlation between inflation and real output growth in figure 3 is negative, as the discussion above predicts, it is not significantly different from zero. Other studies have found that a 10-percentage-point increase in the long-run average inflation rate is associated with declines of 0.2 to 0.7 percentage point in long-term economic growth. While seemingly small, the implied output loss cumulates through the years.[6]

CONCLUSION

The short-term connection between monetary expansions and real economic growth capitalizes on imperfections in the public's information about prices. People respond inefficiently in the sense that under perfect information, they would not have altered their behavior. At best, one party gains at another's expense.

A central bank may periodically exploit this connection, but frequent attempts—as some seem to advocate—may ultimately distort the allocation of resources from productive uses to protective enterprises. Countries with high inflation rates tend to have larger financial sectors relative to GDP, not faster rates of economic growth.[7] In the long run, money growth seems to translate only into proportionally higher inflation; it does not foster real economic growth or employment. Ultimately, a central bank can best contribute to a nation's economic health by eliminating the price uncertainties associated with inflation.

ENDNOTES

1. See Frederic S. Mishkin, "Symposium on the Monetary Transmission Mechanism," *Journal of Economic Perspectives*, vol. 9, no. 4 (Fall 1995), pp. 3–10. See also the associated articles printed in this volume.
2. The Federal Reserve can also conduct monetary policy by changing either its discount rate (the rate at which it makes temporary loans to financial institutions) or its reserve requirements.
3. This exposition generally follows N. Gregory Mankiw, *Macroeconomics*, New York: Worth Publishers, 1992. His work contains references to many original contributions in this area.
4. These models assume that wages or prices exceed their competitive market level. This results in an excess supply of workers at current wage levels in the labor-market model and a cushion of profits in the goods-market model.
5. Detailed cross-country evidence on the relationships between money, prices, and output is found in George T. McCandless, Jr. and Warren E. Weber, "Some Monetary Facts," Federal Reserve Bank of Minneapolis, *Quarterly Review*, vol. 19, no. 3 (Summer 1995), pp. 2–11.
6. See V.V. Chari, Larry E. Jones, and Rodolfo E. Manuelli, "The Growth Effects of Monetary Policy," Federal Reserve Bank of Minneapolis, *Quarterly Review*, vol. 19, no. 4 (Fall 1995), pp. 18–32.
7. Moreover, the effect of inflation on the size of the financial sector is bigger in high-income countries. See William B. English, "Inflation and Financial Sector Size," Board of Governors of the Federal Reserve System, Finance and Economics Discussion Series No. 96-19, April 1996.

PART V Monetary Theory

QUESTIONS

1. Identify and explain the individual monetary policy transmission mechanisms discussed in the reading.

2. What are the key determinants of an economy's long-run growth? Why isn't money supply growth one of them?

3. "The short-run positive relationship between money supply and output growth is the result of imperfect information." Is this statement true, false, or uncertain? Explain.

4. How can an expansionary monetary policy harm an economy's prospects for long-run growth?

READING 30

What Causes Inflation?

Laurence Ball

Inflation is universally unpopular; everyone from ordinary consumers to top government officials bemoans the perpetual process of rising prices. Frequently, discussions of inflation have an air of resignation. Inflation is like bad weather: we can complain about it, but it seems to be a fact of life. For most people, the causes of inflation are murky. Popular writers lay the blame on a variety of scapegoats: governments that spend too much money, the OPEC cartel, skyrocketing costs of medical care. What causes inflation, and is there any way to eliminate it?

Economists have both good news and bad news about inflation. The good news is that we know a lot about its causes and how it could be ended. The bad news—and the reason that inflation has not been ended—is that doing so could be costly. This article describes what economists understand about inflation and what issues remain mysterious. There is a clear consensus about the long-run causes of inflation—the determinants of average inflation over a decade or more. The short-run behavior of inflation—the ups and downs from year to year—is only partly understood.

INFLATION IN THE LONG RUN

The year-to-year movements in inflation that make newspaper headlines are small compared with the differences in inflation across different eras or different countries. In the United States, inflation as measured by the gross-national-product deflator averaged 7.4 percent per year from 1970 through 1979, but only 2.4 percent from 1950 through 1959.[1] From 1930 through 1939, inflation averaged -1.7 percent per year—the price level was lower at the end of the decade than at the beginning. And these differences across periods in the United States, while substantial, are dwarfed by differences across countries. From the 1950s to the mid-1980s, inflation averaged 4.2 percent per year in the United States, only 2.7 percent in Switzerland, but 8.0 percent in Italy, 21.2 percent in Israel, and 54.4 percent in Argentina (see Ball, Mankiw, and Romer, 1988).[2] What causes these differences in inflation over long periods?

The Culprit: Too Rapid Money Growth. While economists disagree about many issues, there is near unanimity about this one: continuing inflation occurs when the

Reprinted from Federal Reserve Bank of Philadelphia *Business Review*, March/April 1993, 3-12.

rate of growth of the money supply consistently exceeds the growth rate of output. In the long run, as Milton Friedman puts it, "inflation is always and everywhere a monetary phenomenon." When the money supply grows much more quickly than output of goods and services, inflation is high; when it grows only slightly faster than output, inflation is low; and when it consistently decreases relative to output there is deflation: the price level falls. (The most recent example of deflation in the United States is the early 1930s).

Why does too rapid growth in the money supply cause inflation? To see the answer, consider how the economy responds when the money supply rises. According to mainstream economics, firms do not immediately adjust their prices in response to an increase in the money supply. Because prices do not respond immediately, there is an increase in the real money supply—the money supply relative to the price level. The increase in the real supply of money pushes down the price of money—that is, the interest rate. Over time, lower interest rates stimulate borrowing and spending by firms and consumers, and the economy expands. The story ends when firms react to the booming economy and their strained capacity by raising prices. Prices rise until they match the increase in the money supply, pushing the real money supply back to its original level and choking off the boom. That is, the long-run effect of a 10 percent increase in the money supply relative to output is a 10 percent increase in the price level and no change in the ratio of money to prices. It follows that if the money supply increases 10 percent faster than output every year, prices must eventually rise 10 percent per year. The gap between the average rate of money growth and the average growth rate of output determines average inflation.[3]

In principal, differences in inflation across countries or time periods could be explained by differences in either money growth or output growth, since the gap between the two determines inflation. In practice, however, the most important factor is money growth, which varies widely, with levels near zero in some countries and over 100 percent per year in others. Variation in output growth is smaller and thus is a secondary factor in explaining differences in the gap between money growth and output growth. As a first approximation, then, differences in inflation across time periods or countries can be explained by differences in money growth.

To provide evidence for this point, Figure 1 plots average inflation and money growth in the United States for various decades. Figure 2 presents average inflation and money growth from 1986-89 for a number of countries.[4] In Figure 1, the decades with the highest inflation, such as the 1910s and the 1970s, are those with the highest money growth. Similarly, Figure 2 shows a close relationship between inflation and money growth across countries. Countries such as Switzerland and France produce low inflation through low money growth; countries such as Turkey and Mexico produce high inflation through high money growth. Along with the theoretical arguments discussed above, this evidence has convinced economists that trend or average inflation is determined by money growth.

Why Is Money Growth Excessive? The question of what causes inflation has, at one

READING 30 What Causes Inflation?

FIGURE 1
Money Growth and Inflation (U.S.)
(1870 - 1980)

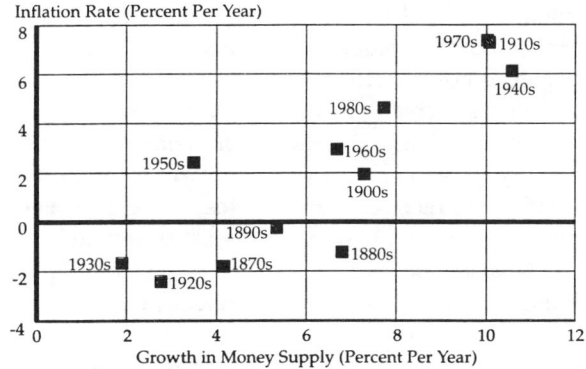

Recreated from: Milton Friedman and Anna J. Schwartz, *Monetary Trends in the United States and the United Kingdom*. Chicago: University of Chicago Press, 1982, with permission.

FIGURE 2
Money Growth and Inflation Across Countries
(1986 - 1989)

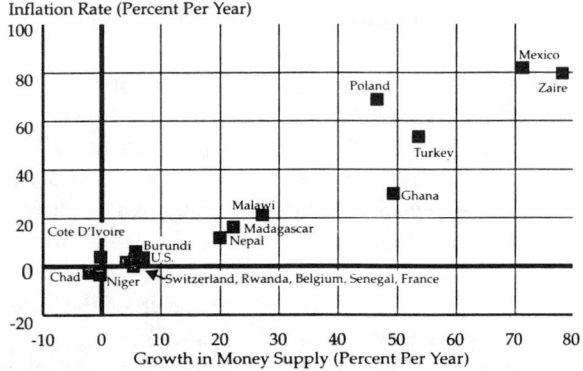

Recreated from: Andrew B. Abel and Ben S. Bernanke, *Macroeconomics*. Reading, MA: Addison-Wesley, 1992, p. 141, with permission.

PART V Monetary Theory

level, an easy answer: money growth. This answer, however, raises another, deeper question: why do policymakers allow the money supply to grow quickly? The Federal Reserve and corresponding monetary authorities in other countries possess effective techniques for controlling the average growth rate of the money supply.[5] Policymakers could slow average money growth enough to keep the average inflation rate at zero (although shocks to the economy would cause temporary movements above and below zero). Since both the public and the Federal Reserve dislike inflation, why isn't it eliminated?

The answer to this question is different in different types of economies. In some countries, the answer is simple: the government prints money at a rapid rate to finance budget deficits. This explains most episodes of very high inflation—the annual inflation of several hundred percent or more that has affected South American countries and Israel within the past decade. These countries have had high levels of government spending and have been unable politically to match this spending with tax revenues; thus they have financed their spending by creating new money. Predictably, rapid money creation has produced high inflation. Inflation has been brought under control only when the underlying budget deficit was reduced. (In Israel, for example, such a stabilization occurred in 1985.)

Budget deficits are not, however, the basic source of inflation in the United States or in most European economies. The U.S. government has, of course, run large deficits over the past decade. But these deficits have been financed primarily by borrowing, not by printing money. That is, the government covers its deficit mostly by issuing bonds. The Federal Reserve contributes to government revenue by creating new money, but this "seignorage" is small: less than 1 percent of total revenue. In countries like the United States, policymakers would gladly eliminate inflation through lower money growth if the only cost were a small revenue loss. The deterrent to lowering inflation must arise from a different source.

The reason U.S. policymakers are reluctant to push inflation to zero is that doing so is likely to cause a recession, or at least slower economic growth. This fear is supported by both macroeconomic theory and historical experience. Slower money growth reduces inflation in the long run, but there is a lag, as discussed earlier. When money growth falls, firms initially continue to raise prices at the rate to which they are accustomed. With money growing more slowly than prices, the real money supply falls, causing a recession. Only the experience of the recession causes inflation to fall.

This theoretical story fits much of the U.S. experience. One cause of the recession that began in 1990 was, arguably, the Fed's efforts to reduce inflation in the late 1980s. More clearly, disinflation was a major cause of the recession of 1981-82—the worst recession since the 1930s. Paul Volcker, the chairman of the Federal Reserve from 1979 to 1986, moved decisively to eliminate the double-digit inflation of the late 1970s. He succeeded, but at a price: inflation fell from 10.1 percent in 1980 to 4.0 percent in 1983, but unemployment rose from 5.8 percent in

1979 to 9.5 percent in both 1982 and 1983. Research by economic historians has shown that this experience is part of a regular pattern: when the Fed slows money growth substantially to reduce inflation, a recession occurs almost invariably.[6]

While some policymakers are willing to pay this price to reduce inflation, others are not. And the Fed's eagerness to fight inflation appears to depend on the severity of the inflation problem. Volcker was sufficiently concerned about double-digit inflation to implement the monetary tightening needed to reduce inflation. But inflation of around four percent, the level through much of the 1980s, did not create enough distress to prompt a further tightening. Thus inflation continued. (For more on this subject, the reader is referred to "What Are the Costs of Disinflation?" by Dean Croushore, in the May/June 1992 issue of the Federal Reserve Bank of Philadelphia *Business Review*.)

SHORT-RUN FLUCTUATIONS IN INFLATION

Although money growth determines average inflation in the long run, the short-run behavior of inflation is more complicated. Inflation fluctuates around its long-term trend from year to year; for example, annual inflation rates in the second half of the 1980s varied around their average of 3.6 percent, with annual rates from 1985 to 1989 of 3.6, 2.5, 3.3, 4.3, and 4.2 percent. Short-term fluctuations in inflation were larger in the 1970s: the annual rates from 1970 to 1974 were 4.7, 5.6, 5.0, 7.6, and 9.6 percent. One source of these inflation movements is temporary fluctuations in the growth of the money supply. In contrast to the long run, however, too rapid money growth is not the only, or even the primary, determination of inflation. Figure 3 plots inflation against money growth for each year during the 1970s and 1980s. Clearly, annual inflation can differ considerably from money growth. What causes this short-run divergence?

Demand Shocks. One source of short-run changes in inflation is shifts in aggregate demand—in desired spending by government, businesses, and consumers. Suppose that the government spends more to finance a war or businesses become more confident about the future and invest in factories and machines. As the demand for military hardware or for factories rises, the economy expands: firms increase production and hire more workers, cutting unemployment. But again, high output and low unemployment eventually spur faster increases in wages and prices: inflation rises. Similarly, a fall in aggregate demand causes a recession, leading firms to raise prices more slowly. The economy's short-run movements between booms and recessions produce fluctuations in inflation as well.

A good example of inflation arising from a shift in aggregate demand—a shift that was not initiated by monetary policy—is the increase in inflation in the late 1960s. Annual inflation varied from 0.8 percent to 2.3 percent over the period of 1960-64, but rose to 5.3 percent in 1969. The consensus explanation for this experience is increased government spending. As the Vietnam War escalated, the Johnson administration raised

PART V   Monetary Theory

FIGURE 3
Money Growth and Inflation During the 1970s (U.S.)

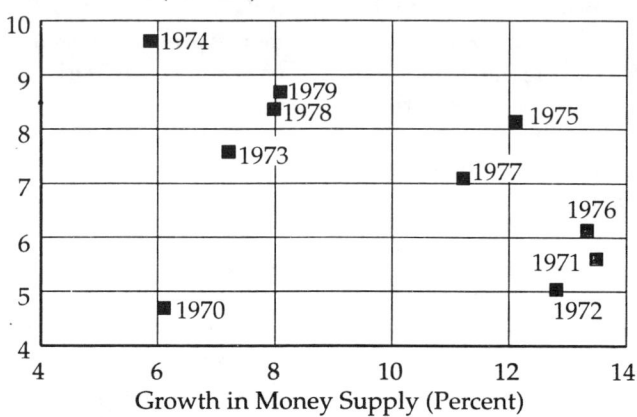

Money Growth and Inflation During the 1980s (U.S.)

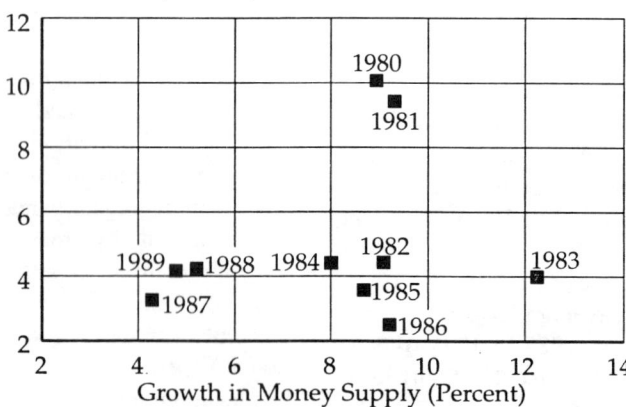

military spending while also continuing the social programs of the "Great Society." As a result, the federal budget deficit grew from $1.4 billion in fiscal year 1965 to $25.2 billion in 1968, and the economy overheated: unemployment fell, but inflation rose.

Price Shocks. Until the 1970s, most economists believed that shifts in aggregate demand were the dominant source of short-run movements in inflation. This view had to be modified, however, after the experience of the 1970s, when price shocks—a.k.a. "supply shocks"—caused large increases in inflation. These shocks were sharp increases in the prices of particular goods, namely food and energy products, arising ultimately from poor weather and the emergence of the OPEC cartel. These shocks created "stagflation": inflation rose while unemployment rose and real output fell (in contrast to the experience of demand shocks, which push inflation and unemployment in opposite directions). From 1972 to 1974, annual inflation rose from 5.0 percent to 9.6 percent as a result of a rise in food prices and the first OPEC price increase. OPECII raised inflation from 7.1 percent in 1977 to 10.1 percent in 1980. These increases dwarfed the fluctuations in inflation arising from the demand shocks of the previous 20 years. More recently, the spike in oil prices during the gulf crisis raised inflation in the second half of 1990.

Why do rises in food and energy prices create inflation? The reader will be forgiven for thinking that the answer is obvious: food and energy are a significant fraction of the economy, and rises in prices are the *definition* of inflation. Economists, however, believe that the issue is not so simple because of the distinction between the overall price level and *relative* prices.

In classical economic theory, the price level is determined by the money supply, as described above. Changes in supply and demand for various products arising from weather conditions, cartel decisions, and so on affect not the price level but relative prices: OPEC makes oil more expensive *relative* to other goods. Theoretically, this is accomplished partly by an increase in the absolute price of oil and partly by *decreases* in all other prices. With these price adjustments, oil can become relatively more expensive while the price level remains unchanged at the equilibrium level determined by the money supply. In practice, this is not what happens: OPEC in fact raised the average price level. But it is not obvious why this is so.[7]

This issue is the subject of recent research by me and Gregory Mankiw of Harvard University (Ball and Mankiw, 1992). Our explanation for the inflationary effects of price shocks rests on two ideas. First, there is some inertia in prices. Firms do not instantly adjust prices to every change in circumstances; instead, they adjust only if their desired price change is large enough to justify the costs of adjustment. For example, a mail-order company will print a new catalog to announce a 50 percent sale, but it is not worth the effort to announce a one-cent price change arising from a tiny change in costs; instead, the firm will simply keep its prices fixed. This behavior implies that large shocks have disproportionately large effects on prices: firms adjust to them quickly, while they make smaller adjustments more slowly.

PART V   Monetary Theory

The second key idea is that "price shocks" are episodes in which certain relative prices rise or fall by unusually large amounts. In the OPEC episodes, for example, some relative prices—those for oil-related products—rose 50 percent or more in response to the trebling of oil prices. By definition, other relative prices went down to balance these increases: if some prices are relatively higher, others must be relatively lower. It was not the case, however, that equilibrium prices of some nonoil products needed to fall by more than 50 percent. Instead, the relative price decreases were spread over all nonoil goods: a fraction of relative prices rose a large amount, balanced by smaller relative decreases in the majority of prices.

Combining this idea with the previous one—that large shocks have disproportionate effects—explains why OPEC was inflationary. The large relative shocks to oil-related prices triggered quick upward adjustments. For example, given the large increase in oil prices, gas stations would have suffered huge losses had they not quickly raised prices at the pump. In contrast, while prices of many other goods came under downward pressure, the required price decreases were small and hence occurred more slowly.

When consumers spend more money on oil, they had less available for toothbrushes, soft drinks, and all other nonoil goods, creating an incentive for the sellers of these products to reduce prices. But the desired decreases were only a few percentage points because OPEC did not cut heavily into toothbrush or soft drink demand. Thus firms were slow to adjust prices downward. In the short run, oil-related prices rose, and the offsetting decreases did not fully occur. Thus prices rose on average: there was inflation.

This theoretical story explains a large number of rises and falls in inflation in the United States. The oil and food price episodes in the 1970s are examples. Another example is the large *decrease* in oil prices in 1985-86. Our theory predicts that inflation should fall in this episode because the decreases in oil prices occur more quickly than the smaller increases in other prices. And, indeed, inflation fell from 4.4 percent in 1984 to 2.5 percent in 1986.

Our theory also explains episodes before the famous supply shocks of the 1970s. For example, inflation rose above 10 percent in 1951, largely due to a demand shock: the Korean War. Inflation then plummeted to near zero in 1952, and the cause appears to be a price shock. Specifically, the prices of meat, rubber, vegetable oil, and several other products fell steeply. More generally, my research with Mankiw suggests that a combination of demand and price shocks explains most of the year-to-year fluctuations in U.S. inflation since 1950.

Although some relative price increases are inflationary according to our theory, others are not. One example is the steady increase in the cost of medical care. These price increases probably have little to do with inflation, despite frequent claims to the contrary in popular discussions. A relative price increase affects inflation only if there is an unusually large shock during a particular year, so that the upward price adjustment occurs more quickly than the offsetting downward adjustments. Medical costs have risen faster than the overall price level for several decades, but the rise has been steady; there are no cases of 50 percent or 100 percent increases within a year, as in the case of oil. This smooth adjustment of relative prices could occur without inflation. If the Federal Reserve pursued noninflationary monetary policy, the average price level would remain steady, with rises in the price of medical care offset by price decreases in other industries.

FROM THE SHORT RUN TO THE LONG RUN

According to the analysis so far, the average rate of inflation over a long period is determined by the amount that average growth of the money supply exceeds average output growth. Inflation fluctuates around its trend from year to year in response to various demand and price shocks. We have seen that these ideas explain much of the U.S. inflation experience, but they do not capture one aspect: the link between the short run and the long run.

Suppose that inflation is proceeding at the level determined by trend money and output growth and that oil prices rise sharply. The theories reviewed so far suggest that this price shock should raise inflation in the short run but that inflation should then return to its long-run trend if trend money growth is unchanged. In fact, shifts in inflation arising from demand or price shocks appear quite persistent. When government spending raised inflation in the late 1960s, and when OPEC raised inflation in the 1970s, there was little sign that inflation would naturally return to its previous level. Instead, inflation continued until the Federal Reserve became sufficiently concerned to tighten policy, producing a recession. (Such policy tightenings occurred in 1970 in response to the high inflation of the late 1960s and in 1974 and 1978-79 after the OPEC shocks. See Romer and Romer, 1989.) Absent a policy tightening and recession, inflation arising from price or demand shocks seems to continue indefinitely: short-run shifts in inflation have long-run effects on trend inflation. How can this evidence by squared with our earlier theories?

Recall the crucial fact that trend inflation is ultimately caused by faster growth in the money supply than in output. Logically, if shocks such as OPEC shift trend inflation, they must induce the Federal Reserve to raise trend money growth (until the point when policymakers decide that inflation is too high and accept the cost of disinflation). Why does a short-run spurt in inflation lead the Fed to raise the average level of money growth?

The usual answer to this question focuses on the behavior of inflationary expectations. In past experience, individuals have seen that increases or decreases in inflation usually persist for a substantial period. Thus, when they see a new rise in inflation (because of an OPEC shock, for example), they expect inflation to stay high. Crucially, this expectation is self-fulfilling: the expectation that inflation will stay high causes it to stay high. The reason expectations affect actual inflation is that they affect decisions about wage- and price-setting. If everyone expects a 10 percent rate of inflation to continue, workers will demand 10 percent wage increases to keep up. Firms will raise prices 10 percent to match the higher wages they pay and also the 10 percent increases they expect from their competitors. Thus inflation will continue at 10 percent, fulfilling expectations.

The Federal Reserve is not helpless in the face of this self-fulfilling inflationary spiral. The spiral can continue only as long as it is "accommodated" by the Fed—as long as the Fed raises money growth as much as inflation has risen. However, a price shock such as that caused by OPEC is not only inflationary for the U.S., it also is contractionary. Because the higher price of imported oil leaves Americans with less of their incomes to spend on domestic goods and services, it causes output and employment to fall, at least temporarily. The Federal Reserve could bring inflation back down by slowing money growth. The result will be to reduce output further, causing a recession that eventually forces inflation down. Over substantial periods, however, such as the 1970s, the Fed has been unwilling to impose this cost on the economy. Thus, once a shock such as OPEC raises inflation, it can stay high for a long period before a Paul Volcker takes charge and disinflates. The price shock creates a vicious circle in which persistence in inflation creates the expectation of persistence, which in turn creates persistence.

While this story is widely accepted, it is not airtight. At an empirical level, it appears true that changes in inflation are expected to persist. Surveys of the expectations of forecasters and of ordinary citizens show that a rise in current inflation leads to higher forecasts of future inflation. At a deeper level, however, it is not clear *why* expectations behave that way. Since the expectation of persistence is self-fulfilling, it proves itself correct. But there are other expectations that would also be self-fulfilling. Suppose that a price shock raised inflation in one year, but everyone expected that inflation would return to its original level in the next year. With the expectation of moderate inflation, workers would moderate their wage demands, and firms would moderate their price increases. Thus the expectation of low inflation would also prove itself correct. Since expectations of either persistent or nonpersistent inflation are self-fulfilling, it appears that either expectation would be rational. The U.S. economy has settled into a situation in which people expect inflation to persist, perhaps only because it has in the past.

CONCLUSIONS

The behavior of inflation is one of the better-understood areas of macroeconomics. There is a wide consensus about the long-run determinants of inflation and, arguably, a consensus about much of its short-run behavior. The average inflation rate over long periods is determined by the extent to which the average rate of money growth (which, in the United States, is chosen by the Federal Reserve) exceeds the average growth rate of real output. Short-run inflation fluctuates around its long-run average because of demand shocks, such as large increases in government spending, and supply shocks, such as sharp rises in the prices of food and energy.

Some countries have persistently high inflation because they continuously create new money to finance large, ongoing budget deficits. Such countries are unable to reduce money growth enough to halt inflation because their governments have been unable to eliminate budget deficits and because they do not have effective alternatives for financing those deficits. In the United States, however, the government budget deficit is financed almost entirely with Treasury debt, not money creation. The United States had low average inflation in the 1980s because money growth, on average, only slightly exceeded output growth.

Finally, the distinction between short-run and long-run determinants of inflation is blurred by the fact that short-run changes often influence the long-run trend. When a demand or price shock raises short-run inflation in the United States, expectations of future inflation rise. Historically, the Fed often accommodated these expectations by allowing money growth to rise, so expectations were fulfilled. Not allowing money growth to rise would have slowed output growth and perhaps caused a recession.

These conclusions—a summary of the thinking of mainstream economists—partly fit ideas that are popular among journalists and the public and partly contradict such ideas. It is common, for example, to blame inflation on excessive deficit spending by the government. This view is on target for the case of Argentina, but not for the United States. Little of the U.S. deficit is financed by printing money. Thus it was possible for U.S. inflation to fall between the 1970s and the 1980s even though the U.S. budget deficit rose substantially. On the other hand, the view that government spending fuels U.S. inflation has a grain of truth. There are periods, notably the Vietnam era, when too much spending overheats the economy, producing inflation that persists as long as monetary policy is accommodative.

Perhaps the most common scapegoats for inflation are the particular prices that the public observes to rise most rapidly. In some eras, these are oil or food prices; a current favorite is medical care. When journalists and citizens blame individual prices for inflation, they confuse average and relative prices. Particular prices could rise just as much in relative terms even if the overall price level were constant. Again, however, there is a grain of truth in conventional thinking. Particularly sharp increases in prices, such as OPEC shocks, are inflationary.

ENDNOTES

1. Unless otherwise noted, all inflation figures refer to the percentage change in the GNP deflator. This variable is a broad index of the level of all prices in the economy. The more famous Consumer Price Index covers only prices paid by consumers, not those paid by governments or businesses.
2. Citations to all papers mentioned in the text are included in the "References" section at the end of this article.

PART V Monetary Theory

3. To be complete, inflation depends on the growth rate of the "velocity" of money—the frequency with which money is turned over—as well as on the gap between the average growth rates of money and output. For the United States, the average growth rate of velocity (for the M2 measure of money) has been zero over the past 40 years. In practice, then, money growth of 2 or 3 percent per year is consistent with stable prices. This rate of money growth matches the natural growth of output and spending.
4. The data for Figures 1 and 2 are taken from Friedman and Schwartz (1982) and Abel and Bernanke (1992), respectively.
5. Specifically, the Fed manipulates the supply of money through "open market operations"—purchases and sales of government bonds. Buying bonds with money adds to the economy's money stock, and selling bonds drains money out of the economy.
6. Romer and Romer (1989) identify six episodes since World War II in which the Fed sharply tightened policy to reduce inflation. In each case, a recession occurred within two or three years.
7. Writing in 1975, Milton Friedman puts the point this way: "It is essential to distinguish changes in *relative* prices from changes in *absolute* prices. The special conditions that drove up the prices of oil and food required purchasers to spend more on them, leaving them less to spend on other items. Did that not force other prices to go down or to rise less rapidly than otherwise? Why should the *average* level of prices be affected significantly by changes in the price of some things relative to others?"

REFERENCES

Abel, Andrew, and Ben Bernanke. *Macroeconomics*. Addison-Wesley, 1992.

Ball, Laurence, and N. Gregory Mankiw. "Relative-Price Changes as Aggregate Supply Shocks," mimeo, Princeton University (April, 1992).

Ball, Laurence, N. Gregory Mankiw, and David Romer. "The New Keynesian Economics and the Output-Inflation Trade-off," *Brookings Papers on Economic Activity* (1988:1).

Croushore, Dean. "What Are the Costs of Disinflation?" Federal Reserve Bank of Philadelphia *Business Review* (May/June, 1992).

Friedman, Milton. "Perspectives on Inflation," *Newsweek* (June 24, 1975).

Friedman, Milton, and Anna J. Schwartz. *Monetary Trends in the United States and the United Kingdom*. University of Chicago Press, 1982.

Romer, Christina, and David Romer. "Does Monetary Policy Matter? A New Test in the Spirit of Friedman and Schwartz," *NBER Macroeconomics Annual*, 1989.

READING 30 What Causes Inflation?

QUESTIONS

1. Why does excessive monetary growth cause inflation? What evidence does Ball present to support this argument?

2. Do increases in the prices of particular goods or services necessarily cause inflation? Under what circumstances may they be the cause of inflation?

3. What causes short-run fluctuations of inflation rates around the long-run trend?

4. Suppose the inflation rate increases above its long-run trend. Is the inflation rate likely to persist at this higher level or return to its long-run trend? Why?

READING 31

Stock Market Fundamentals

Joseph G. Haubrich

The Great Bull Market of 1996–97 has caught the attention of stock market professionals and individual investors alike. Because the stock market serves as an economic indicator and a possible source of economic disturbances, its recent movements have captured the interest of policymakers as well.

Most of this concern has centered around whether current stock prices are justified by economic "fundamentals," or whether they indicate a speculative "bubble."[1] Investors worry that such a bubble may burst, leaving their recent gains a mirage. Policymakers worry about how stock market wealth impacts consumer spending, whether a bull market is driven by fears of inflation, and how they should respond if the recent correction becomes a full-fledged bear market.

This *Economic Commentary* looks at the major factors behind stock price fundamentals and examines how well those factors explain—or fail to explain—market fluctuations.[2] As in many prognoses, there are reasons for both optimism and pessimism. Keep in mind, however, that while economic analysis may offer insights into the stock market, it by no means guarantees profits.

A SHIFT IN PERSPECTIVE

Before their recent losses, stock prices had been surging, with market averages soaring to new heights (sometimes on a daily basis). These gains can be exaggerated, however, if one ignores the previously high level of the market. If the Dow Jones industrial average moves up 1,000 points to a level of 2,000, investors double their money. A move from 5,000 to 6,000 means a return of 20 percent, and a similar jump to 7,000 translates into a 17 percent gain. Figure 1 exploits this insight by plotting the Standard & Poor's (S&P) 500 index on a proportional (logarithmic) scale, where straight lines indicate constant percentage growth rates. To provide the same return, prices must rise more when they are high than when they are low. From this perspective, the market's recent increases look more typical.

MARKET FUNDAMENTALS

Why are people willing to buy a share of stock? The fundamental approach argues that investors value the dividends the stock will

Reprinted from Federal Reserve Bank of Cleveland *Economic Commentary*, January 15, 1997.

READING 31 Stock Market Fundamentals

FIGURE 1 S&P 500 PRICE PER SHARE

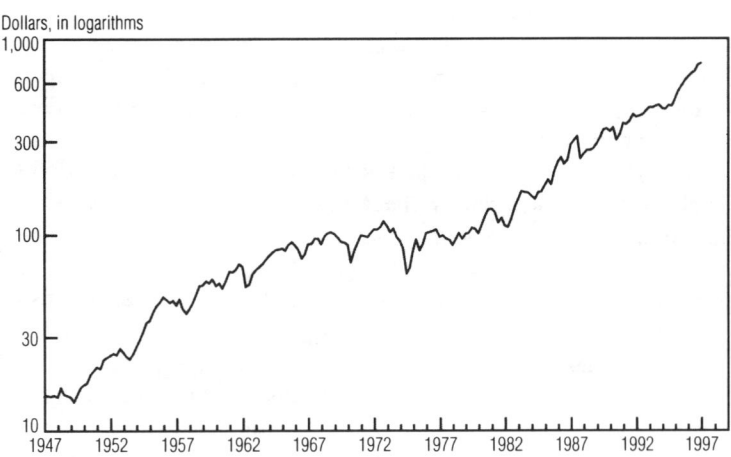

SOURCE: Standard & Poor's Corporation.

pay.[3] (More generally, they value the income from the stock, which might also come from buy-backs or, in closely held firms, from cushy jobs given to shareholders.) The value of this dividend stream should be the value of the stock.

The value of the dividend stream has two components. The first is the dividend stream itself, which, given the uncertainty of its future, entails an educated guess about what the firm will pay at some later date. It is by nature a forward-looking, expected-value calculation that buyers must make. Will your favorite biotechnology company find the cure for the common cold? Is that gold stock in your portfolio running low on ore? Will the software firm you own get its new operating system out on time? The answers to these questions matter for the dividend stream, and thus for stock prices. More general macroeconomic factors, such as inflation, unemployment, or productivity, impact many firms and hence affect the market as a whole. For example, a general inflation would also boost dividends (in dollar, although perhaps not real, terms) and lead to an adjustment in stock prices.

Buying a stock is riskier, however, than putting your money in the bank. This means that investors will demand a higher average return on stocks to compensate for the greater uncertainty and chance of loss. People assign a lower value to a stock that is expected to pay $1 per year than to a bank account that pays $1 a year, because the stock dividend is uncertain. One way to express this is to say that the interest rate used to discount the dividend stream is higher.[4] This interest rate is the second component affecting the value of the dividend stream.

PART V Monetary Theory

The fundamental price of a stock may thus fluctuate for two reasons. Expectations about dividends may change, or the required rate of return may change. That is, future cash flows may vary, or the way investors value those flows may vary. It's common knowledge that slow dividend growth may depress a stock's price, but it is also true that uncertainty about those dividends or an increase in bond and bank rates can have the same effect.

Combining both of these factors allows us to calculate a "warranted" stock price, or one justified by market fundamentals. Such a calculation must be treated as a rough estimate because it purports to measure something unobservable: people's expectations. Seemingly small changes in the method could yield substantially different results. Still, the effort is instructive. By using a five-year average of dividend growth, we can obtain an estimate of expected dividend growth (under the potentially dangerous assumption that the future will be similar to the past). By using Moody's composite return on long-term bonds plus a risk premium of 2.5 percent, we can generate an estimate of the return investors demand on stocks.[5]

Putting these two estimates together allows us to compare actual with warranted stock prices based on the estimated fundamentals. Figure 2 shows the pessimist's side of the story: Stocks look overvalued because dividend growth has been too slow to justify the recent surge in prices. This relationship is not perfect, of course, but the current gap seems particularly large. Recent dividend growth of less than 4 percent is far below the 8 percent posted in the early 1990s, let alone the 11 or even 12 percent growth of earlier years.

Optimists take a somewhat different view. Dividends do not appear out of thin air. Rather, they are one destination for a firm's earnings. This makes earnings growth more fundamental than dividend growth, and earnings growth has been explosive in recent years (see figure 3). The optimist maintains that increased earnings will eventually result in larger dividends, justifying today's high stock prices. The price-to-earnings (P/E) ratio, at a relatively high 19, seemingly contradicts this point, but it ignores the important distinction between the level and the growth rate of earnings. It's not the height but the speed of a rocket that keeps it moving forward. The optimist focuses on earnings growth. If growth remains strong, the P/E ratio may likewise stay at a consistently high level, since investors expect earnings to continue rising.

The argument between optimists and pessimists also involves another statistic, the payout ratio, which tracks the fraction of earnings paid out as dividends. Historically, it averages around 50 percent, but the current figure is closer to 35 percent. Pessimists think that recent earnings growth is unsustainable and that firms, knowing this, have kept dividends stable. And shouldn't firms have the best forecast of their own earnings? The payout ratio will return to its long-run level when earnings fall. Optimists believe that firms have merely delayed dividend increases, and that the low payout ratio leaves a lot of room for dividend growth, even if earnings slow.

FIGURE 2 S&P 500 STOCK PRICES: WARRANTED VS. ACTUAL

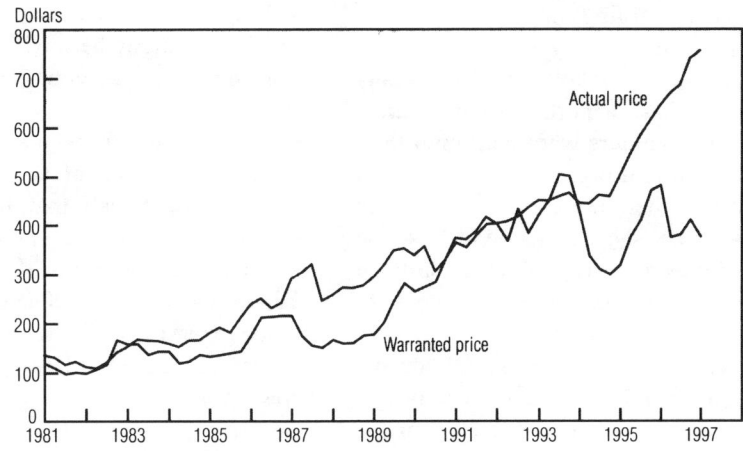

SOURCES: Standard & Poor's Corporation; and author's calculations.

FIGURE 3 S&P 500 EARNINGS PER SHARE

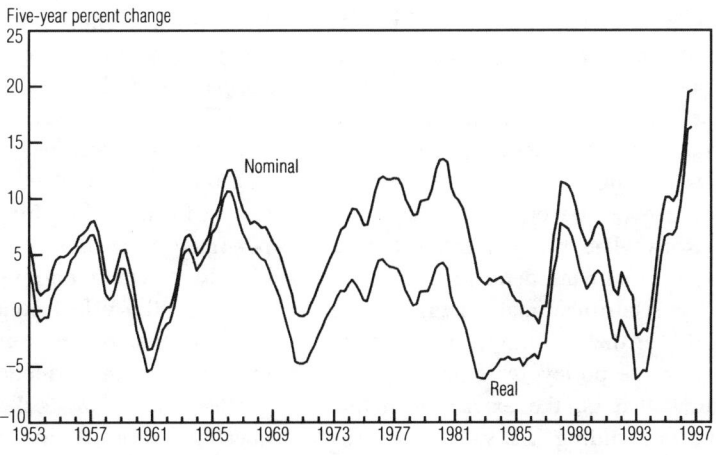

SOURCE: Standard & Poor's Corporation.

Optimists have one more reason to prefer the message from earnings: stock repurchases. Dividends are not the only way to get cash into the hands of shareholders. A company may also repurchase a portion of its shares. Even those stockholders who hang onto their shares benefit from a higher stock price, and perhaps from higher future dividends. Stock repurchases do not show up as dividends, and thus low dividends may reflect a shift to repurchases rather than a low payout to shareholders.

As noted above, however, dividends, earnings, and repurchases represent only half the fundamental story. The risk factor, or the higher expected return that people demand on stocks, also changes over time. If that number falls, it pushes stock prices higher.

A generation ago, most people attributed shifts in stock market fundamentals to dividends or earnings, but one of the clearest messages coming out of the academic finance literature over the past 15 years is the importance of time-varying expected returns.[6] That is, more variation in fundamentals, and hence in stock prices, results from variation in the risk factor and the expected return than was previously thought.

The return expected on stocks may vary for two reasons. The riskless interest rate, measured by insured bank deposits or default-free Treasury securities, may change along with the health of the economy, productivity, or Federal Reserve policy. Alternatively, the risk premium—that is, the extra return that people get for holding risky stocks—may change. A lower risk premium reflects either a less risky market or investors who are more willing to bear such risk, much as a boom in skydiving might be attributed to either safer parachutes or a younger, more daredevil population.

From the pessimist's viewpoint, the evidence for both of these possibilities is at best mixed. Recall that figure 2 includes a changing interest rate in the calculation of the warranted price, yet still reveals a large gap between warranted and actual stock prices. By some measures, such as yearly standard deviation, market volatility has been relatively low over the past five years, but it has also been rising since 1994.

The optimists do have some evidence on their side. An excellent predictor of future stock market returns is the dividend-to-price (D/P) ratio. For returns based on holding a stock for five years, the D/P ratio accounts for more than 40 percent of the variation.[7] This figure is now at a post–World War II low, which strongly suggests that investors are accepting a smaller return on stocks than in the past, for whatever reason.[8]

This phenomenon has consequences that both optimists and pessimists can appreciate. The optimist sees the low expected return as a justification for high stock prices; the pessimist sees the low expected return as exactly that and nothing more. But there is also a subtler effect concerning the influence of dividends. A lower expected return means that changes in dividend growth will have a greater impact on stock prices. It thus makes questions about dividends and earnings more important than before.

CONCLUSION

Asset pricing is not an exact science. The market has crushed the bones of many a surefire scheme under the iron heel of its random walk. This is not to deny that there are many good investment opportunities available, but only to emphasize that pitfalls exist as well. A better appreciation of the forces driving market fundamentals may give investors (and policymakers) the sagacity to find one and avoid the other.

ENDNOTES

1. This *Economic Commentary* went to press on May 8, 1997.
2. Nothing in this article should be construed as investment advice, either on behalf of particular stocks or in regard to overall investment strategies.
3. The classic discussion of this issue can be found in John Burr Williams (first published in 1938), "Evaluation by the Rule of Present Worth," in James Lorie and Richard Brealey, eds., *Modern Developments in Investment Management: A Book of Readings*, 2d ed., Hinsdale, Ill.: Dryden Press, 1978, pp. 471-91. (If the equations are not to your taste, memorize the poem.) A particularly clear and comprehensive modern treatment is presented in John Y. Campbell, Andrew W. Lo, and A. Craig MacKinlay, *The Econometrics of Financial Markets*, Princeton, N.J.: Princeton University Press, 1997, pp. 253-89.
4. For a helpful discussion of this point, see Timothy Cogley, "Why Do Stock Prices Sometimes Fall in Response to Good Economic News?" Federal Reserve Bank of San Francisco, *Economic Letter* No. 96-36, December 13, 1996.
5. The 2.5 percent equity premium represents a rough guess that is in line with historical measures and that also provides a sensible warranted-price series. For a more sophisticated approach, see R. Glen Donaldson and Mark Kamstra, "A New Dividend Forecasting Procedure that Rejects Bubbles in Asset Prices: The Case of the 1929 Stock Crash," *Review of Financial Studies*, vol. 9, no. 2 (Summer 1996), pp. 333-83.
6. See, for example, Robert F. Whitelaw, "Time Variations and Covariations in the Expectation and Volatility of Stock Market Returns," *Journal of Finance*, vol. 49, no. 2 (June 1994), p. 515.
7. See John Y. Campbell, Andrew W. Lo, and A. Craig MacKinlay, *The Econometrics of Financial Markets* (footnote 3), section 7.2.
8. For more evidence supporting this point, see Olivier J. Blanchard, "Movements in the Equity Premium," *Brookings Papers on Economic Activity*, vol. 2 (1993), pp. 75-118.

PART V   Monetary Theory

> **QUESTIONS**
>
> 1. What determines the price investors are willing to pay for a particular share of stock?
>
> 2. What does Haubrich mean by a stock's "warranted price" and how does he estimate it?
>
> 3. Are stocks overvalued? Present both the optimists' and the pessimists' perspectives on this question.
>
> 4. What factors determine the return investors expect on stocks? How will an increase in this expected return affect the impact that changes in earnings and dividends will have on a stock's price?

READING 32

Activist Monetary Policy for Good or Evil? The New Keynesians vs. the New Classicals

Tom Stark and Herb Taylor

Economic analysts and policy practitioners argue endlessly about how long it takes for monetary policy actions to affect output or employment, how long the effects will last, or how large they will be. But underneath it all, the truth is that economists cannot agree on how monetary policy affects the real economy in the first place. Theoreticians are offering two different explanations, each with its own implications for the way monetary policy ought to be conducted.

Perhaps the most popular explanation for money's impact was first proposed about 15 years ago by a group of economists now known as the New Classicals. These economists see episodes of money affecting economic activity as temporary aberrations that occur only when monetary policy actions happen to catch the public by surprise. Because they see these episodes as harmful, the New Classical economists think that central banks should avoid such surprises. They think that a central bank should just announce a simple money growth plan and stick to it. Such a policy, they say, would minimize economic disruptions and make inflation predictable.

In the last few years a group of economists labeled the New Keynesians has begun mounting a challenge to the New Classical view. The New Keynesians claim that under the right circumstances even widely publicized monetary policy actions can have a sustained impact on output and employment. And they claim that this impact can be used to help counteract what they see as the ecomomy's tendencies toward excessive volatility and unemployment. So the New Keynesians think that a good central bank conducts an activist monetary policy—it actively manages the supply of money and credit to keep the economy close to full employment.

Which side is right? Is an activist monetary policy good or evil? Neither side has all the answers, but both command serious attention in a very important policy debate.

THE NEW CLASSICALS' CASE AGAINST ACTIVIST POLICY

Like the great Classical economists of the last century, the New Classicals see the

Reprinted from Federal Reserve Bank of Philadelphia *Business Review*, March/April 1991, 17-25.

PART V Monetary Theory

market system naturally bringing the economy to its peak level of efficiency. They see markets as a network of competitive auctions in which prices respond quickly and completely to changes in economic conditions. Basing their decisions on these market prices, households and firms automatically deploy the economy's real resources—its labor, raw materials, factories, and equipment—fully and efficiently. Activist monetary policy has no place in this world. Policy actions designed to alter the pattern of economic activity are ineffective and unnecessary.

Competition among many small households and firms makes the Classical economy efficient. In the Classical system, overall supply and demand conditions determine the prices people pay and the wages they earn. No business or individual is big enough to manipulate market conditions to its own advantage. Any firm that tried to charge above-market prices for its product would lose all of its customers to competing producers. Any worker that held out for above-market wages would lose his or her job to competing workers.

This environment may sound harsh, but it gives firms the incentive to perform at peak efficiency. Given the wage-price structure, each firm faces just one basic decision: how much to produce. And in its quest for profits, the firm will automatically choose a production level that balances consumer preferences with resource availability.

Consider the typical firm. For each unit it produces, it gets the market price. It also incurs costs equal to the price of the requisite labor and materials. The more it produces, the more it is prone to operating inefficiencies that push up per-unit production costs. At some point, the cost of producing another unit would exceed the product's market price. Expansion beyond that point would cut into profits, so the firm expands no further. Following this strategy not only maximizes the firm's own profits, it promotes overall economic efficiency as well. The product's market price measures its worth to the consumer. Wages and other input prices measure workers' and resource suppliers' valuation of their time and materials. So, in effect, the firm is producing only the units whose benefits to the consumer justify the burden their production imposes on workers and other resources.

Of course, economic conditions are constantly changing. Consumers' preferences shift away from one product and toward another; a new production technology comes along and displaces an old one. But in the Classical view, market prices and wages adjust quickly to changes in supply and demand, providing firms with the incentives to keep the economy's resources fully and efficiently employed. With the market system allocating resources so effectively, there is no reason to use monetary policy to alter the level of economic activity. But it's just as well. Because in the Classical world, any attempt at activist policy would fail.

The Classical economists developed the theory that money has no effect on economic activity. Clearly, prices are crucial to people's economic decisions in the Classical system. And usually we think of prices being quoted in terms of money. Yet the Classical economists maintained that changing the money supply would have no impact on output or employment. How can this be?

The Classicals claimed that when the money supply changed, all prices and wages would change in equal proportion, leaving the relationships among them unchanged. Consequently, households and firms would stick by their original employment and production decisions, leaving the real economy unaffected.[1]

Suppose, for instance, that the central bank pumps up the money supply. This increases the overall demand for goods and services, pushing up market prices. But workers recognize that higher prices erode the purchasing power of their wages. So they are willing to work the same hours and expend the same effort only if they get wage increases commensurate with the increase in market prices. Firms, competing for workers, agree to pay for the raises out of their inflated sales revenues, and they maintain their original level of employment and output. All that remains of the money supply increase are higher prices and wages.

The Classical economists recognized that, as a practical matter, these adjustments to a change in the money supply would not always proceed as smoothly as their theoretical analysis might suggest. But their message comes through clearly enough: the money supply ultimately affects the level of prices, not the level of economic activity.

The New Classical economists reinvigorated the Classical argument that monetary policy is generally ineffective. The Classical perspective on money's role in the economy was among the casualties of the Great Depression. The Keynesian Revolution swept through the economics profession and gave birth to the activist monetary policies of the postwar period. But in the early 1970s, some economists resurrected the Classical viewpoint. In fact, by combining parts of the Classical tradition with the notion of "rational expectations," these New Classical economists emerged with an even stronger position: monetary policy cannot systematically affect the real economy. Instances in which monetary policy actions alter employment or output levels are occasional, random events.

The New Classical analysis of money's impact on the economy is a variation on the old adage "knowledge is power." In keeping with their Classical tradition, the New Classicals maintain that markets are competitive enough to drive the economy to full employment, and responsive enough to keep it there in the face of shifting economic conditions. To this they simply add that a key element in markets' responsiveness is market participants acting upon rational expectations about where the economy is headed. The New Classicals assume that market participants understand the underlying structure of the economy and use the available data on current economic conditions to formulate accurate forecasts about future economic performance. Presumably, participants' actions in the marketplace today reflect those rational expectations.

The New Classicals go on to argue that market participants pretty much know what to expect from the monetary authority. Competitive market prices and wages automatically reflect those expectations, thus neutralizing the impact of any anticipated policy actions on output and employment.

Admittedly, policy actions that take people by surprise can affect economic activity. But, the New Classicals point out, such "surprises" must, by definition, be occasional and without pattern. So the monetary authority cannot systematically influence the level of output or employment.

The New Classicals emphasize that even when a monetary policy action does take people by surprise, its impact is temporary. It lasts only as long as it takes for the markets to find out what the central bank has done and respond. And in the interim, people—particularly workers—are not necessarily better off.[2]

Textbook versions of the New Classical view assume that product prices respond to sudden shifts in economic conditions more quickly than wages do. For one thing, wage agreements, whether formal or informal, may cover several months, a year, or even several years—all periods much longer than it takes for product prices to change. Even where wages are set more frequently, workers usually agree to a certain wage without the benefit of complete information on the prices of the products they intend to buy. Consequently, when an unexpected monetary expansion comes along and pushes up product prices, firms find they can retain, and perhaps even expand, their work force without raising wages very much. And they make the most of the opportunity. They pay a slightly higher wage, hire more workers, produce more output, and sell it at the new, higher prices. Hence the expansionary monetary policy boosts aggregate employment and output.[3]

Of course, the workers eventually catch on. They shop. They see the higher product prices. And the next time they negotiate a wage, they demand compensation for their loss in purchasing power. Once wages rise as much as prices have, firms revert to their original hiring and production patterns. So money is, in the last analysis, neutral.

Overall, the New Classical analysis of money's impact on the economy casts activist monetary policy in a very dim light. First of all, the New Classicals see the economy exhibiting a strong tendency toward full employment that makes it unnecessary for the monetary authority to focus on the level of economic activity. But even beyond that, attempts to conduct an activist policy do more harm than good. An expansionary policy anticipated by the public simply creates instant inflation. If, as occasionally happens, the policy is not anticipated by the public, it affects output and employment essentially by tricking people into producing at a pace they would not have chosen if they were fully informed.

Given this perspective, the New Classicals' advice to policymakers is straightforward: do not try any surprise moves. Choose a simple money growth plan consistent with your inflation goals. Announce the plan far enough in advance to allow markets to react. Then just follow the plan.[4]

THE NEW KEYNESIANS' CASE FOR AN ACTIVIST POLICY

The New Keynesians don't see things quite the way the New Classicals do. The

READING 32 Activist Monetary Policy for Good or Evil?

New Keynesians see an economy in which firms face only limited competition. These imperfectly competitive firms restrict their output to keep prices high and respond only partially to shifting demand conditions. As a result, the economy shows the tendencies toward underemployment and price "stickiness" that are very much a part of the traditional Keynesian perspective. The New Keynesians believe that in this world, regardless of how people form their expectations, monetary policy can and should be used to expand the level of economic activity.

Without strict market discipline, firms are less likely to achieve maximum economic efficiency. The difference between the Classical competitive firm and the imperfectly competitive firm is simple: the competitive firm must take the market price of its product as a given, whereas the imperfect competitor has the power to set price to its own advantage. And the right price structure for the imperfect competitor is not necessarily best for the overall economy.

In the competitive market, each firm is small and its output is nothing special. So its decision about how much to supply has no appreciable impact on the market price. If Farmer Jones decided to withhold some of his wheat from the market, how far could he drive up the price of wheat? If he tried to charge extra for Farmer Jones Wheat, who would pay the premium? No one.

Imperfect competitors have larger operations. Their product may have some special characteristic—real or imagined—that differentiates it in the mind of consumers. For these firms, size or special niche gives them some power over the price of their products. If General Mills were willing to cut its supply of breakfast cereal, cereal prices would rise. And if it decides to increase the price of Wheaties, some people would be willing to pay the premium.

In short, the imperfectly competitive firm has some advantage that frees its pricing structure from the strict discipline of the market. Of course, the firm is still subject to the Law of Demand: the higher the price it sets, the fewer units it will sell. So it must choose between setting a high price and selling to a limited number of customers, or setting a low price and grabbing the lion's share of the market. But one thing is for sure: it will not set as low a price as a Classical competitive market would establish. It will always find it profitable to set a higher price and maintain it by keeping output below competitive levels.

Exercising market power may make individual firms more profitable, but it imposes costs on society as a whole. From the social standpoint, imperfect competitors' prices are too high and their production is too low. Society would be better off if these firms would cut their prices to levels more consistent with resource costs. This would expand sales, production, and employment to more socially desirable levels.

Neither the notion of imperfect competition nor its impact on social welfare are original to the New Keynesians.[5] But the analysis offers them a rationale for their belief that the economy tends to underemployment. And it offers them something more—a jumping-off point for a new theory of how

253

monetary policy can help alleviate the problem.

The New Keynesians believe monetary policy can work on imperfect competitors. Traditional theories of imperfect competition can explain underemployment, but they cannot explain why monetary policy should be effective in combating it. As long as prices and wages respond flexibly, the monetary authority is still powerless to affect firms' output and employment decisions. But the New Keynesians add a new wrinkle to the theory of imperfect competition: imperfectly competitive firms' prices are not as flexible as competitively established market prices. So real activity may respond to monetary policy actions.

In the Classical world, competitive markets adjust prices quickly and completely to every shift in economic conditions. In a world of imperfect competition, firms must set prices. When demand shifts are relatively small, these firms may not find changing prices worthwhile. It may be more profitable to maintain current prices and adjust production accordingly.

Economists have labeled the costs firms bear when they change their product prices "menu costs." That name captures the most obvious cost of repricing: printing new menus and catalogs and changing price tags and signs. But there are other costs as well. To find the new profit-maximizing price, the firm must estimate the likely nature, magnitude, and duration of the shift in customer demand. That kind of research and analysis uses up resources. In addition, frequent price changes may alienate customers and cost the firm some of its good will.

It's difficult to say how large menu costs are. It may seem that, as a practical matter, the cost of changing prices ought to be relatively small. But the New Keynesians emphasize that the benefits to changing prices can be small for imperfect competitors, too. So even small menu costs can thwart a price change.

When the demand for an imperfect competitor's product increases, the firm can respond in any number of ways. At one extreme, it can take the opportunity to raise its prices without losing sales. At the other extreme, it can hold the line on prices and take the opportunity to pick up sales volume. If the demand shift that the firm is experiencing is large, then choosing the right strategy can have a substantial impact on profits. But if the demand shift is relatively small, there is little advantage to choosing one over the other. A firm that simply maintains its original prices will not get as much as it could on each unit, but it will sell more units. So its profits will not be substantially compromised.[6] Once menu costs—even small ones—enter the equation, they can tip the scales in favor of maintaining current prices. Thus the profit-maximizing imperfect competitor may choose to accommodate a small demand shift without changing the price of its product.

This tendency for prices to be sticky in an imperfectly competitive environment affords the central bank some opportunity to influence overall output and employment. Suppose the central bank increases the money supply and thereby boosts overall demand for goods and services. Further suppose that individual firms decide that the demand increase is too small to make a price adjustment profitable. Instead, they decide to hold the line on prices and fully accommodate the increased demand for their products. In order to increase their output, they begin to hire more workers. So both output and employment pick up. Meanwhile, since product prices are not rising, workers are not demanding an inflation adjustment to their wages, so both wages and prices remain relatively constant.[7]

The New Keynesians recognize that the central bank's ability to raise output and employment in this way is circumscribed. If monetary policy actions create too large a demand shift, firms are more likely to raise prices than increase output. Furthermore, every firm faces different demand conditions and menu costs. Some will have lower thresholds for changing prices than others. So almost any policy action is likely to affect aggregate prices as well as aggregate output. In short, the New Keynesians acknowledge that a central bank cannot engineer dramatic or persistent increases in output and employment without driving up prices and wages. Nonetheless, New Keynesian analysis suggests that an activist policy can be successful, if used judiciously.

Overall, the New Keynesians see the potential for an activist monetary policy to improve the performance of an imperfectly competitive economy. Monetary policy may not be a cure-all, but it can help offset what New Keynesians see as the economy's chronic bias toward underproduction and underemployment in modern, imperfectly competitive economies.

Add to this underlying bias the fact that the economy is subject to sudden shifts in overall demand, and the New Keynesians' case for an activist monetary policy seems even stronger. For if price stickiness accentuates the impact of monetary policy on economic activity, it also accentuates the impact of other demand shifts as well. Thus a sudden decline in overall demand could drop the economy well below its potential level of performance. This suggests that monetary policymakers should be alert to these shifts and stand ready to offset them.[8]

WHO'S RIGHT?

Both the New Classicals and the New Keynesians offer explanations for monetary policy's impact on the economy. But the New Keynesian approach certainly casts activist monetary policy in a more positive light. Which explanation should we believe? One way to evaluate competing theories is to "let the data decide." But at this point, empirical tests do not provide a clear answer.

The New Classical theory has been around longer and been subjected to more empirical study. The results are not favorable to the hard-line New Classical view that only unexpected policy actions affect real activity. Statistical analyses seem to show output and employment responding to anticipated policy actions too. But, ironically enough, these kinds of results have prompted some New Classicals to support a theory that attributes even less potency to monetary policy actions: the *real business cycle* theory. According to this theory, monetary policy never causes fluctuations in economic activity. Rather, anticipated fluctuations in the economy cause the public to increase or decrease their demand for money. The central bank and financial system simply accommodate these demand fluctuations.[9]

The New Keynesian theory is relatively new, and empirical evidence is scantier. There is some supportive evidence, however. In countries where inflation is relatively low, which would suggest that expansionary monetary policies have not been pursued too aggressively, policy shifts seem to have more impact on real activity—as the New Keynesians would predict. But tests of the New Keynesian model are really in too early a stage to provide a convincing case one way or another.[10]

Empirical issues aside, there are unsettling aspects to both the New Classical and the New Keynesian models. Perhaps the most unsettling theoretical aspects have to do with the functioning of the labor market. Both groups admit they have trouble explaining why monetary policy actions that affect output have such a large effect on employment and such a small effect on wages. According to the New Classical theory, an unexpected increase in product demand induces firms to produce more because it pushes the product price up before wages have had a chance to rise in response. But firms need more workers in order to expand production. Won't that increased demand for labor itself push up wages?

The New Classicals' answer: some, but not much. True to their Classical perspective, they maintain that labor markets are competitive. They simply assume that labor supply is very sensitive to wage changes. Thus when labor demand increases, it evokes many more hours of work at only a slightly higher wage. The problem is that, as a practical matter, willingness to work does not seem to be all that sensitive to wage changes.

New Keynesians face a similar conundrum. According to them, when firms face a small increase in product demand, they hold the line on prices and expand output. Again, to expand output, firms need more workers. Granted, product prices are not increasing, so there is no inflation pressure on wages. But won't firms have to raise the wage they pay in order to induce more people to work? The New Keynesians' answer is no. True to the Keynesian tradition, they claim that there is a pool of involuntarily unemployed workers from which firms can always draw workers at the going wage. But to explain the involuntary unemployment, they must resort to some unconventional theories of the labor market.

Imperfectly competitive firms charge high prices, which restricts both output and employment. Nonetheless, the New Keynesians claim, these firms tend to pay the people they do employ relatively high wages. Different economists offer different reasons for this tendency. Proponents of the "efficiency wage" theory emphasize that by paying workers more than they would expect to earn if they had to go look elsewhere for a new job, the firm gives the worker the incentive to perform more effectively. Proponents of the "insider/outsider" theory emphasize that employees whose experience on the job is valuable to the firm can exact wage concessions from the firm. In either case, with wages high and employment opportunities limited, there is routinely a pool of willing workers unable to get jobs. Whenever firms want to expand output, they can tap this pool for workers without increasing the wage they pay.[11]

In short, both the New Classicals and the New Keynesians have a long way to go before either can proclaim their approach to be theoretically complete.

THE ACTIVIST POLICY DEBATE RENEWED

When the New Classical economics came on the scene in the early 1970s, it jolted academic economists and policymakers as well. The New Classicals were trying to explain precisely why monetary policy actions affect real activity. They concluded that money temporarily affects output and employment by tricking people into deviating from their preferred activity levels. This conclusion hardly cast activist monetary policy in the most favorable light, but there was little theoreticians could offer in rebuttal.

Now the New Keynesian school is offering an alternative explanation for money's impact on economic activity. That analysis, based on theories of imperfect competition, looks more favorably on activist monetary policy. The New Keynesians conclude that the economy tends toward underemployment and that an activist policy can help overcome the problem.

The New Keynesians can hardly claim to have overcome the New Classical paradigm. But they have reinvigorated the battle over the efficacy of an activist monetary policy.

ENDNOTES

1. To see this, suppose that initially bread costs $1 and workers earn $6 an hour, making a loaf of bread worth 10 minutes' work. If both prices and wages double, bread goes to $2 and wages go to $12, but a loaf of bread still trades for 10 minutes' work.
2. Thomas Sargent and Neil Wallace, in their article "'Rational' Expectations, the Optimal Monetary Instrument and the Optimal Money Supply Rule," *Journal of Political Economy* (April 1975) pp. 241-54, present a clear statement of the New Classical notion that expected monetary policy actions have no effect on economic activity.
3. Analyses stressing the role of wage contracts in limiting short-run wage flexibility can be found in Stanley Fischer's "Long-Term Contracts, Rational Expectations, and the Optimal Money Supply Rule," *Journal of Political Economy* (February 1977) pp. 191-205, and John Taylor's "Aggregate Dynamics and Staggered Contracts," *Journal of Political Economy* (1980) pp. 1-24. The idea that wages adjust imperfectly because workers are not completely aware of current product prices is more consistent with the original New Classical formulation by Robert Lucas in "Some International Evidence on Output-Inflation Tradeoffs," *American Economic Review* (June 1973) pp.326-34.
4. The New Classical argument for this approach to monetary policy has most recently been articulated by Bennett McCallum in *Monetary Economics: Theory and Policy* (Macmillan, 1989).
5. The term "imperfect competition" is used here as a convenient expression for "monopolistic competition" a market model that can be traced back to the work of E.H. Chamberlin in the 1930's. Texts such as Paul Samuelson's *Economics* (McGraw-Hill) provide readable discussions of this market type.

PART V   Monetary Theory

6. This idea is sometimes called the PAYM insight because it emerged from the work of economists Michael Parkin, George Akerlof, Janet Yellen, and N. Gregory Mankiw. Specific references are to Parkin's "The Output-Inflation Tradeoff When Prices Are Costly to Change," *Journal of Political Economy* (1986) pp.200-24; Akerlof and Yellen's "Can Small Deviations From Rationality Make Significant Differences to Economic Equilibria?" *American Economic Review* (September 1985) pp.708-21; and Mankiw's "Small Menu Costs and Large Business Cycles: A Macroeconomic Model of Monopoly," *Quarterly Journal of Economics* (May 1985) pp.529-37.

7. Olivier Blanchard and Nobuhiro Kiyotaki develop this argument formally in "Monopolistic Competition and the Effects of Aggregate Demand," *American Economic Review* (September 1987) pp.647-66.

8. Prospects for this kind of policy get some theoretical support in Lars Svensson's "Sticky Goods Prices, Flexible Asset Prices, Monopolistic Competition, and Monetary Policy," *Review of Economic Studies* (1986) pp.385-405.

9. Frederic Mishkin provides a more complete discussion of the evidence on the New Classical hypothesis in *A Rational Expectations Approach to Macroeconometrics* (University of Chicago Press, 1983). For a good discussion of the real business cycle view and its monetary policy implications, see "Monetary Policy with a New View of Potential GNP," by John Boschen and Leonard Mills, this *Business Review* (June/July 1990) pp.3-10.

10. This New Keynesian result is presented by Laurence Ball, N. Gregory Mankiw, and David Romer in "The New Keynesian Economics and the Output-Inflation Trade-Off," *Brookings Papers on Economic Activity* (1988:1) pp.1-65. For an up-to-date discussion of the empirical evidence on the New Keynesian economics, as well as a good evaluation of its theoretical underpinnings, see Robert Gordon, "What Is New Keynesian Economics?" *Journal of Economic Literature* (September 1990) pp.1115-71.

11. Lawrence Katz provides an excellent overview of these modern labor market theories in "Some Recent Developments in Labor Economics and Their Implications for Macroeconomics," *Journal of Money, Credit, and Banking* (August 1988, Part 2) pp.507-30.

QUESTIONS

1. Compare the positions of the New Classicals and New Keynesians regarding: (a) market competition; (b) flexibility of prices and wages; and (c) speed of price and wage adjustments.

2. According to the New Classical view, what can be accomplished with an activist monetary policy? Why? How would New Keynesians respond to the New Classical views?

3. If the New Classical view is correct, how should the Fed conduct monetary policy?